BECOMING
FREE

The struggle
for
human
development

BECOMING FREE

The struggle for human development

William L. Ewens

SR Scholarly Resources Inc.
104 Greenhill Avenue · Wilmington, Delaware 19805

Scholarly Resources Inc.
104 Greenhill Avenue
Wilmington, Delaware 19805

Library of Congress Cataloging in Publication Data

Ewens, William L., 1938–
   Becoming free.

   Bibliography: p.
   Includes index.
   1. Autonomy (Psychology)—Social aspects.   2. United
States—Social conditions.   I. Title.
BF575.A88E94   1984   155.2'32   84–13872
ISBN 0-8420-2208-2
ISBN 0-8420-2233-3 (pbk.)

For Sandra,
    whose words have stimulated me,
        whose actions and suggestions have challenged me,
      whose character I have admired, and
        whose love has always meant so much to me.

For Erin and Jason Ewens,
    whose presence has brought so much happiness and
    joy into my life.

And for Edith and Albert Ewens,
    who gave me life,
      who sacrificed so much to ensure
        my upbringing and schooling, and
          who continue to enlighten me and
        broaden my existence.

Acknowledgments

I would gratefully like to acknowledge the initial idea for this book which was developed in conversations with Barbara J. Bank who is currently the sociology chairperson at the University of Missouri. Further thanks are extended to my friends and colleagues at Michigan State University who did much to sustain me in this work, especially Richard Child Hill, Barrie Thorne, Cyrus S. Stewart, James B. McKee, John Useem, Marilyn Aronoff, Ruth Simms Hamilton, and Kevin D. Kelly. Also helpful were sociologists Hans O. Mauksch, Michael P. Johnson, and Carl J. Couch.

Special regard too must be expressed to Philip G. Johnson and Carolyn J. McVeigh who are both editors at Scholarly Resources. They helped me with their suggestions, editorial comments, and with their patience and encouragement while the book was being written.

Finally, I express my gratitude to Sandra J. Ewens who has worked so hard and has been so instrumental in bringing this work into reality. Sandy contributed to all stages of the writing process; she helped conceive the general outline and ideas expressed in the book, assisted with the proofreading, and gave me the type of advice without which this volume would not have been written. I also owe much joy and insight to my daughter, Erin, who is now twelve years old, and to my son, Jason, who is now a teen-ager.

William L. Ewens
East Lansing, Michigan

Contents

Introduction

> Under what conditions do people want to be free and capable of acting freely? Under what conditions are they willing and able to bear the burdens freedom does impose and to see them less as burdens than as gladly undertaken self-transformations? And on the negative side: Can people be made to want to become cheerful robots?
>
> —C. WRIGHT MILLS

Most of us, I think, are in the same uncomfortable situation. On the one hand, whether we believe it or not, we are basically intelligent and competent human beings. Certainly we have spent more money and time on our educations, have traveled more, have gained more knowledge and experience through television and other media, and have had more leisure time and financial resources with which to develop our own inner potentials and talents than almost any persons in any society since the beginning of human history.

The central problems of today, on the other hand, do not just revolve around material needs; most of us are relatively well fed and have obtained some level of physical security. Instead, we are more concerned about the types of persons we are becoming. Our individual competence is not always translated directly into personal responsibility or control over our own lives. Or, put another way, a basic contradiction for many of us is that, despite our own substantial capacities for self-management and decision making, almost everything we do—or have done in the past—is dictated by somebody else.

Think about it for a moment. For most of us the first quarter to one-third of our lives is spent in schools. Rather than being a voluntary exercise in self-exploration and growth, however, regular school attendance is required by law. The "educational" process itself tends to be one in which duly appointed and certified "knowledge experts" pour their abundant wisdom into our empty skulls, with our scope of action as students typically restricted to that of receiving, filing, storing, and regurgitating these valuable knowledge deposits.[1]

Once out of school, this outside control of our lives continues; unless we are lucky enough to have very rich parents, most of us now must work for somebody else in order to make a living. This means that the largest part of our waking time—perhaps fifty hours per week at work, including traveling back and forth— is spent meeting the demands and expectations of our chosen employers. "The results of our labors may sometimes correspond to our own needs," observed Brecher (1972: x), but our "work is just as likely to destroy our own social and natural environment, make our work-time still more oncrous, increase our subordination, and build the weapons that may destroy us all."

Although this domination is often more subtle in character, our personal lives outside work are not entirely our own either. As prospective consumers and as citizens, we are bombarded increasingly by countless billboard displays, television commercials, and a wide variety of other advertisements and public relations messages. Each year, for example, we may watch 25,000 television commercials and become accustomed during each hour of this viewing to an average of twenty to twenty-five salespeople beseeching us to improve our existence by following this example or by buying that product.

In this process both our dreams and our frustrations are carefully researched, packaged, and sold back to us in a commodified form. Thus, our masculinity and lack of physical prowess with women is boosted by drinking a prescribed brand of "light" beer, our marriages improved by washing our clothes with the correct laundry detergent, our life problems solved by swallowing the advertised headache remedy, and our business success guaranteed by gargling the right mouthwash or smoking the right cigar. Irrational and impulse buying become virtues, and the relevant mirrors by which we can judge our stature as persons become the cost of the cars we drive and the expensive vacations we take.

GROWING CORPORATE DOMINATION

What is really disturbing, however, is that this basic split between our increasing self-management capacities and the increasingly pervasive external controls over our lives, at the present time, is growing ever bigger. We live in a rationalized society where larger areas of our lives are being brought under the direction of various large-scale corporate and governmental bureaucracies. Moreover, in these massive formal organizations, power has shifted gradually from domination that simply emanated from the personal relationships between individual bosses and their immediate subordinates to a much more sophisticated system of impersonal domination in which power increasingly flows from the formal structure of the organization itself. These emerging structural controls are not only embedded in the machines, architecture, and the physical structure of the organization—for example, in the operation of the assembly line—but also are increasingly embedded in the social structure of the bureaucracy, as in the organization's job categories, wage scales, codified work rules, formal evaluation procedures, and definitions of responsibilities. Thus, in such structurally controlled organizations, as Edwards (1979: 139) emphasized, "the definition and work performances, and the distribution of rewards and imposition of punishments, have all come to depend upon established rules and procedures, elaborately and systematically laid out."

The sheer size and power of these new rational bureaucratic organizations are truly impressive. The annual sales of global corporations such as Exxon and General Motors, for example, are now greater than the total gross national products of countries like Switzerland, Pakistan, and South Africa; the sales of Royal Dutch Shell bigger than Iran, Venezuela, and Turkey; and the sales of Goodyear Tire larger than that of Saudi Arabia. Furthermore, the average growth rate of the most successful global corporations is presently two to three times that of most advanced industrial nations including the United States. It is estimated that global corporations already control more than $200 billion in physical assets, and even more astounding is the fact that some analysts now predict that within a decade 200 to 300 global firms will control 80 percent of all productive assets in the non-Communist world.[2] "In the process of developing a new world," concluded Barnet and Müller (1974: 15) in their definitive study of these growing multinational corporations, "the managers of managers of firms like GM, IBM, Pepsico, GE, Pfizer, Shell, Volkswagen, Exxon, and few hundred others are making daily business decisions which have more impact than those of most sovereign governments on where people live; what work, if any, they will do; what they will eat, drink, and wear; what sorts of knowledge schools and universities will encourage; and what kind of society their children will inherit."

REACTING TO OUTSIDE DOMINATION

How have we reacted to this increasing outside domination in our lives? Many of us have merely struggled to adapt our aspirations and dreams to this bureaucratic system in which we have found ourselves and from which we can visualize no escape. We therefore channel all our available energies into the frenzied pursuit for more education, a better career, an even higher paying job, or a larger home. This general individual advancement solution, however, was much more successful in previous years when the overall American economy was rapidly expanding. While the real annual rate of growth of the U.S. gross national product (adjusted for inflation) averaged 3.9 percent from 1959 to 1968, it fell to 2.4 percent from 1969 to 1976 and has been declining ever since. Also, as the number of unemployed workers has steadily increased, the real weekly earnings for nonsupervisory employees has fallen by more than 5 percent since 1972. At the same time, the price of higher education has increased during the last decade at a rate almost double that of the overall inflation rate.[3] In good times this individual advancement solution clearly provided little relief from the alienation caused by this increasing outside domination, but in these present hard times it is less effective as a strategy for improving even our own individual material circumstances.

Others of us protect ourselves from the personal pain inflicted by this impersonal and often arbitrary system by adopting a fatalistic or resigned attitude; which to some extent insulates us from emotional involvement in the outside world. Since the bureaucracy is invincible and you cannot beat the system anyway, it is better not to take chances or make waves. A more realistic goal is to privatize our existence and attempt to achieve whatever comfort and security we can within the immediate context of our own personal lives.

Another way of coping with this increasingly outside domination is to scapegoat various elected officials. The social discomfort we are feeling then becomes the fault of the president, Congress, governor, or mayor, and our task one of throwing them out and bringing in more capable political leadership. These new civic reformers cannot cope with fundamental bureaucratic contradictions either, and we thus get caught in a perpetual cycle of ever seeking and then casting aside new sets of political leaders.

Finally, even more ironically, another response to this increased bureaucratic domination is to create even more bureaucracy. If our basic institutions are causing us problems, then this pain can be remedied by creating even larger and more complex organizations—the multinational conglomerate, the statewide university system, or the consolidated federal super agency—to remedy the problems created by the now outdated and discredited bureaucracy. The predictable outcome is a still more rationalized system that is considerably more alienated and even more separated from the immediate control of the people whose lives are being dominated by it.

DECLINING IDENTIFICATION WITH AMERICAN INSTITUTIONS

One general indicator of this growing separation between persons and their society are the consistent findings of national opinion surveys, conducted during the last two decades, of a growing distrust in major U.S. institutions. Polls taken by the University of Michigan's Center for Political Studies, for example, reported that the percentage of the public expressing "a great deal of confidence" in seven major American institutions—the federal executive, Congress, Supreme Court, military, major business corporations, labor unions, and higher education—has dropped, on the average, from about 50 percent to approximately 30 percent in less than a decade. Findings from these same surveys also demonstrated a growing awareness of this outside bureaucratic domination, with the latest poll showing that almost three times as many of the random sample of adult respondents were willing to endorse the statement that "the government is pretty much run by a few big interests."[4]

One specific example of this generally pervasive decline of public confidence in American institutions is presented by

George H. Gallup and his associates who have repeatedly surveyed Americans concerning their attitudes toward public schools.
As shown in Table 1 below, between 1974 and 1982 there has
been a decline of more than one-half in the percentage of parents
who would give public schools a favorable report card rating of
"A." This data also shows a corresponding increase in the percentage of parents giving these schools an unsatisfactory "D"
rating.

In our age, the task of becoming free has come to mean the
devising of strategies and life-styles for coping with this growing
outside domination of our lives and for reducing these potential
self-management/external bureaucratic control contradictions
within ourselves. We thus live mystified, stymied by a lack of
essential power over our own lives. Any possibility for a better
existence will only come through the struggle to alter our present
ways of thinking and living. Only through critical reflection upon
our current reality and through constructive social action to
change it can we hope to become fully developed persons.

Table 1. Trend Toward Declining Support for Public Schools

Ratings Given Public Schools	National Totals								
	1974	1975	1976	1977	1978	1979	1980	1981	1982
A	18%	13%	13%	11%	9%	8%	10%	9%	8%
B	30	30	29	26	27	26	25	27	29
C	21	28	28	28	30	30	29	34	33
D	6	9	10	11	11	11	12	13	14
Fail	5	7	6	5	8	7	6	7	5
Don't know	20	13	14	19	15	18	18	10	11

Source: George H. Gallup, "The 14th Annual Gallup Poll of the Public's Attitudes
        Toward the Public Schools," in *Education 83/84*, ed. Fred Schultz (Guilford, CT:
        Dustin Publishing Group, 1983), p. 18.

PART ONE
The Social Basis of Human Freedom

1

What It Means To Be Free

Whatever is the lot of humankind, I want to taste within
my deepest self.

—GOETHE, *Faust*

Men make their own history, but they do not make it just
as they please; they do not make it under circumstances
chosen by themselves, but under circumstances directly
encountered, given and transmitted from the past. The tradition of all the dead generations weighs like a nightmare
on the brain of the living.

—KARL MARX

Freedom is something that most everyone in America says they
support, although exactly what they mean is often not clearly
stated. Even talking intelligently about freedom is difficult sometimes because in "our land of the free" the word itself is so badly
used. Frequently it is even employed to mask the increasing
outside domination of our lives, as, for instance, when Adolf
Hitler promised to free people from freedom itself.

"Freedom," as the term shall be employed in this book,
means the full development and expression of our essential capabilities and talents; it involves our general ability to make the
best of ourselves and to know, do, and enjoy in life what is
worthwhile. It means being aware of the many assumptions upon
which, consciously or unconsciously, we are currently living our
lives and also being aware of the many alternatives available to
us. Having power involves being in control, both in the sense of
having the opportunity to live our lives in ways we want to and
in the sense of being able as persons to "make history"—that is,

to take actions that will affect the demands being placed upon us by our families, schools, workplaces, and by other institutions in our society (Flacks, 1974: 56–57).

Many important questions in our lives involve the concept of freedom: What types of freedom are possible for us as individuals? How is our freedom curtailed and restricted? How do we go about removing some of these obstacles to our freedom and thus become better persons? We do not ask these questions philosophically, as matters of abstract theory, but practically, as matters of living, and concretely within the context of our daily struggles to give meaning to our existence.[1]

Rather than studying freedom directly, social scientists most often have studied persons regarded as deficient in one way or another—psychotics, criminals, or others judged as having serious emotional or behavioral problems.[2] Sociologists and psychologists also have brought their own stereotypes and scientific biases into the study of human nature. Gustav Ichheiser, for example, noted the following tendencies in the scientific study of human behavior:

> The psychology and sociology of personality and inter-personal relations have been in the past, and still are, vitiated by three sets of assumptions and tendencies. The first is a rigid ideal of scientific exactness which produces in the minds of many social scientists a bias towards selecting, or emphasizing, those facts and aspects of reality which lend themselves best to a precise, and if possible, quantitative investigation. This results in the neglect of those facts and aspects which resist or elude precise or exact analysis. The second is the set of silent assumptions rooted in the ideological or cultural background of the society to which the particular psychologist or sociologist himself belongs. These silent assumptions often induce the social scientist to ask only those questions and to select those problems suggested by the accepted ideology (cultural pattern). The third is the tendency to neglect, or even to ignore, certain very important facts and problems because those facts and problems appear to be quite obvious. (1970: 7–8)

"GUESSES" CONCERNING THE CHARACTERISTICS OF FREE PERSONS

Below are described some of the general psychic and personality traits that social scientists have frequently described as characterizing more fully developed or "free" persons.[3] An attempt has been made to observe the problems and biases cited by Ichheiser, although the following is admittedly imprecise and certainly not exhaustive of all the varied characteristics of more fully developed persons. Nevertheless, it represents some educated "guesses" about these freedom characteristics, based both on the analysis in the following chapters and on a careful reading of contemporary social science literature. Much of the ensuing discussion, therefore, bears directly or indirectly on the validity of these personal development categories in order to understand better some of the manifold ways social environments both facilitate and inhibit the general growth process. Free persons are characterized here in terms of their increasing *openness to experience, self-confidence, sincerity, integration, ability to love,* and *democratic character structure.*

Openness to Experience

Social scientists from varying theoretical persuasions have suggested that as persons grow they move from a state of unnecessary character-armoring and more or less permanent defensiveness to a condition characterized by a greater openness to experience. Where external circumstances permit, there is a lessening of rigidity, imposition of structure on experience, and disowning of feelings and experiences that are unpleasant or inconsistent with their self-conceptions.

> The individual is becoming more able to listen to himself, to experience what is going on within himself. He is more open to his feelings of fear and discouragement and pain. He is also more open to his feelings of courage, and tenderness, and awe. He is free to live his feelings subjectively, as they exist in him, and also free to be aware of these feelings. He is more able fully to live the experiences of his organism rather than shutting them out of his awareness. (Rogers, 1961: 188)

Developing or free persons are thus moving toward living in an open, friendly, and closer relationship with themselves. Maslow (1970: 153) emphasized that, because their conceptions were less influenced by subjective needs, such developing persons—or as he labeled them, "self-actualizing" persons—were also more efficient perceivers. His survey indicated that their perceptions of the future were more often correct because these forecasts were less determined by their own wishes, desires, fears, or other character-based types of optimism or pessimism.[4] Maslow further explained:

> Since for healthy people, the unknown is not frightening, they do not have to spend any time laying the ghost, whistling past the cemetery, or otherwise protecting themselves against imagined dangers. They do not neglect the unknown, or deny it, or run away from it, or try to make believe it is really known, nor do they organize, dichotomize, or rubricize it prematurely. They do not cling to the familiar, nor is their quest for the truth a catastrophic need for certainty, safety, definiteness, and order. (1970: 155)

Discussed below, then, are the general conditions that encourage or inhibit the development of this increasing openness to experience. The problem is to understand the nature of social environments that facilitate, rather than constrain, persons in developing a basic trust in themselves and becoming more open to the consequences of their actions and aware of their essential relations with the outside world.

Self-confidence

The social science literature also can be interpreted as suggesting that developing persons display a relative lack of overriding guilt, incapacitating fears of inadequacy, and severe anxiety. This directly contrasts with neurotic persons, for example, who are often crippled by their own feelings of inferiority and even with many "normal" persons in this society who must devote much of their energies to dealing with unproductive feelings of guilt and inadequacy. As Horney explained,

> A person who eventually becomes neurotic has little chance to build up initial self-confidence because of the crushing experiences he has been subjected to. Such self-confidence as he may have is further weakened in the course of his neurotic development because the very conditions indispensable for self-confidence are apt to be destroyed. . . . Neurotic trends impair self-determination because a person is then driven instead of being himself the driver. (1945: 100)

Horney (1950: 88) further emphasized that if persons are to develop a basic self-confidence they need warmth, feeling welcome, care, protection, an atmosphere of confidence, and encouragement in their activities. Under these favorable conditions, their self-confidence will tend to reflect the objective conditions in their lives.

Developing persons have learned to trust and value the process that is themselves. "If you feel comfortable in yourself," commented Perls (1969: 34), "you don't love yourself and you don't hate yourself, you just live." By contrast, many persons waste their energies in unnecessary concern for the approval and applause of others and to avoid others' disapproval and rejection. There is a great discrepancy between the selves they are and the selves they want to be, and this creates tension and anxiety and fosters defensiveness. "I feel I have become more adequate in letting myself *be* what I *am*," concluded Rogers (1961); "it becomes easier for me to accept myself as a decidedly imperfect person, who by no means functions at all times in the way in which I would like to function."

A similar thought is echoed by Maslow, who maintained that healthy persons find it possible to accept themselves and their imperfect natures without needless anxiety or worry.

> They can accept their own human nature in the stoic style, with all its shortcomings, with all its discrepancies from the ideal image without feeling real concern. It would convey the wrong impression to say that they are self-satisfied. What we must say rather is that they can take the frailties and sins, weaknesses, and evils of human nature in the same unquestioning spirit with which one accepts the characteristics of nature. One does not complain about water because it is wet, or about rocks because they are hard, or about trees because they are green. As the child looks out upon the world with wide, uncritical, undemanding, innocent eyes, simply noting and observing or demanding that it be otherwise, so does the self-actualizing person tend to look upon human nature in himself and in others. (1970: 155–56)

Self-confidence is also closely related to openness to experience. Rogers (1961: 63–64), for instance, explained how these twin attributes of free persons develop together in the process of successful therapy. Patients find the therapist listening acceptantly to their feelings, and slowly they become able to listen to themselves. They begin to receive communications from within themselves and to realize that they are angry, frightened, and even courageous. As they become more open to what is going on within themselves, they are better able to listen to feelings that have always been denied and repressed. They learn to listen to feelings that seem "so terrible, or so disorganizing, or so abnormal, or so shameful" that they have never before been allowed into consciousness. In turn, this greater openness to experience leads to greater self-acceptance and self-confidence.

It is thus argued that self-confidence tends to develop in environments characterized by comutual social relations and by the general absence of domination. It is both a necessary condition and a general product of the other attributes of free persons. "I have seen simple people become significant and creative in their own spheres," concluded Rogers (1961), "as they have developed more trust in the processes going on within themselves, and have dared to feel their own feelings, live by values which they discover within, and express themselves in their own unique ways."

Sincerity

Persons in the process of becoming free also have been characterized as acting more often on the basis of their own perceived needs and interests rather than on the basis of facades and pretended selves. They seem to place more emphasis on doing what they want and need to do in situations instead of merely trying to live up to others' expectations or earn others' approval. More fully developed persons are described by their honesty, genuineness, transparency, and authenticity, concluded Shostrom (1968: 23); such persons are "able honestly to be their feelings, whatever they may be. They are characterized by candidness, expression, and genuinely being themselves."

Neill (1960: 111) contrasted sincere and inauthentic school children in the following manner: "Children brought up under the wrong type of discipline live one lifelong lie. They never dare to be themselves. They become slaves to established futile customs and manners, and they accept their silly Sunday clothes without question. The mainspring of discipline for them is the fear of censure." By contrast, "free children are sincere. This sincerity is the result of being approved. They have no artificial standards of behavior to live up to, no taboos to restrain them.

They have no necessity to live a life that is a lie." Neill thus concluded:

> To me, respect for a schoolteacher is an artificial lie, demanding insincerity; when a person really gives respect, he does so unaware. My pupils can call me a silly ass any time they like to; they respect me because I respect their young lives, not because I am the principal of the school, not because I am on a pedestal as a dignified tin god. My pupils and I have mutual respect for each other because we approve of each other. (1960: 194)

This relative lack of inauthenticity and pretended being is also commented upon by Maslow in his description of healthy behavior:

> Self-actualizing people can all be described as relatively spontaneous in behavior and far more spontaneous than that in their inner life, thoughts, impulses, and so forth. Their behavior is marked by simplicity and naturalness, and by lack of artificiality or straining for effect. This does not necessarily mean consistently unconventional behavior. If we were to take an actual count of the number of times that the self-actualizing person behaved in an unconventional manner the tally would not be high. His unconventionality is not superficial but essential or internal. It is his impulses, thought, consciousness that are so unusually unconventional, spontaneous, and natural. (1970: 157)

If individuals behave sincerely, there is an essential "congruence" between their experience, awareness, and communication (Rogers, 1961: 50–55). Often they prefer instead to hide behind a false front, being afraid that they will be swept away in the violence of the feelings they might discover pent up in their private worlds. In the process of therapy, however, clients gradually come to express more fully both their positive feelings (tenderness, admiration, liking, love) and their negative feelings (resentment, anger, shame, jealousy) to members of their families and to others. It is as though clients in therapy discover that it is possible to discard the masks they have been wearing and become more genuinely themselves. Consider, in this regard, the process of increasing sincerity as described by one such patient undergoing therapy:

As I look at it now, I was peeling off layer after layer of defenses. I'd build them up, try them, and then discard them when you remained the same. I didn't know what was at the bottom and I was very much afraid to find out, but I *had* to keep on trying. At first I felt there was nothing within me—just a great emptiness where I needed and wanted a solid core. Then I began to feel that I was facing a solid brick wall, too high to get over and too thick to go through. One day the wall became translucent, rather than solid. After this, the wall seemed to disappear but beyond it I discovered a dam holding back violent, churning waters. I felt as if I were holding back the force of these waters and if I opened even a tiny hole I and all about me would be destroyed in the ensuing torrent of feelings represented by the water. Finally I could stand the strain no longer and I let go. All I did, actually, was to succumb to complete and utter self pity, then hate, then love. After this experience, I felt as if I had leaped a brink and was safely on the other side, though still tottering a bit on the edge. I don't know what I was searching for or where I was going, but I felt then as I have always felt whenever I really lived, that I was moving forward. (Rogers, 1961: 110–11)

The process of therapy is one of gradually learning that life can be lived on the basis of true feelings and needs rather than in terms of projections and defensive pretenses. This increasing sincerity is also closely linked with openness to experience and self-confidence. If children are allowed to express their own personal feelings and are seldom artificially rewarded or punished by authoritarian parents for the presentation of false selves, then they are seldom forced to disown their real feelings in order to be loved. They therefore grow up respecting themselves as unique individuals and learn to be more open in comprehending and expressing their true beliefs and emotions.

Integration

Lack of openness to experience, self-confidence, and sincerity all lead to inner splits and fragmentation within people's selves. In these instances there arise, in Rogers's words, extreme "incongruences" in the relationships among individuals' experiences, beliefs, and activities. This is a result, in the first instance, of individuals blocking out unwanted information and not allowing themselves full awareness, either of their own impulses or of the outside world. It is also the result of lives being lived on the basis of pretenses and deceptions instead of honest feelings and direct creative dealings with external reality. Persons in growth-inhibiting environments are often forced to guide their conduct by what they think they should be like as persons and what will please powerful others instead of what they really are. This basic split between fantasized existence and actual existence in neurotics was eloquently described by Laing:

> Since the self, in maintaining its isolation and detachment does not commit itself to a creative relationship with the other and is preoccupied with the figures of fantasies, thought, memories, etc., which cannot be directly observable by or directly expressed to others, anything (in a sense) is possible. Whatever failures or successes come the way of the false-self system, the self is able to remain uncommitted and undefined. In fantasy, the self can be anyone, anywhere, do anything, have everything. It is thus omnipotent and completely free—but only in fantasy. Once committing itself to any real project, it suffers agonies of humiliation—not necessarily for any failure, but simply because it has to subject itself to necessity and contingency. It is omnipotent and free only in fantasy. The more this fantastic omnipotence and freedom are indulged, the more weak, helpless, and fettered it becomes in actuality. The illusion of omnipotence and freedom can be sustained only within the magic circle of its own shut-upness in fantasy. And in order that this attitude be not dissipated by the slightest intrusion of reality, fantasy and reality have to be kept apart. (1960: 84)

However, as we have seen, freedom is based on attributes such as openness to experience, self-confidence, and sincerity. Persons raised in growth-facilitating environments that promote these human capacities also tend to develop more complete and integrated personalities.

> We believe that the realization of the self is accomplished not only by an act of thinking but also by the realization of man's total personality, by the active expression of his emotional and intellectual potentialities. These potentialities are present in everybody; they become real only to the extent to which they are expressed. In other words, *positive freedom consists in the spontaneous activity of the total, integrated personality.* (Fromm, 1941: 284)

Maslow also emphasized that developing individuals are becoming more fully integrated and whole people. Many of the conflicts and contradictions that exist unresolved in less healthy persons find a new unity and higher level of resolution in free persons.

> At several points . . . what had been considered in the past to be polarities or opposites or dichotomies were so *only in less healthy people*. In healthy people, these dichotomies were resolved, the polarities disappeared, and many oppositions thought to be intrinsic merged and coalesced with each other to form unities. . . . For example the age-old opposition between heart and head, reason and instinct, of cognition and conation was seen to disappear in healthy people where they become synergetic rather than antagonists, and where conflict between them disappears because they say the same thing and point to the same conclusion. In a word in these people, desires are in excellent accord with reason. (1970: 178)

As we shall see in Chapter 2, this inner splitting and fragmentation of personality results in the disowning of unacceptable thoughts and feelings and in the draining of persons' vital energies. The process tends to become a vicious cycle because the severing of these essential ties between persons and their own activities and consciousness, other persons, and the external world, in turn, leads to further inauthenticity and repression as persons attempt to maintain their identities in the absence of these vital relations. These new defenses also lead to further isolation and severance of basic ties and to the progressive alienation within persons. In Perls's (1969: 42) words, "you do not allow yourself— or you are not allowed—to be totally yourself. . . . So your ego boundary shrinks more and more. Your power, your energy, becomes smaller and smaller. Your ability to cope with the world becomes less and less—and more and more rigid, more allowed only to cope as your character prescribes it."

Ability To Love

Love, stated Horney (1967: 249), involves "the capacity to give spontaneously of oneself either to people or to a cause or to an idea, instead of retaining everything for oneself in an egocentric way." In this regard, social scientists have sometimes suggested that less free persons have reduced capacities for love because of the insecurities and latent hostilities that they carry around inside themselves. Being forced to be more closed-minded and having acquired little self-confidence, they consequently tend to communicate falsely, which often makes them feel even worse about themselves and further separates them from other persons. As Horney concluded regarding neurosis,

> The neurotic person is generally not capable of love, because of the anxiety and the many latent and open hostilities that he has usually acquired early in life. . . . These hostilities have considerably increased in the course of his development. However, he has repressed them again and again out of fear. As a consequence, either because of his fears or because of his hostility, he is unable to give of himself, to surrender. For the same reasons, he is incapable of real consideration for others. He hardly takes into account how much love, time, and help another person can give or wants to give. He therefore takes it as an injurious rejection if someone needs to be alone sometimes or has time and interest for other goals or other people. (1967: 249–50)

More fully developed persons, on the other hand, have greater capacities for forming deeper and less inhibited relationships with others. At the physical level this means greater "orgastic potency," or the ability to have natural, nonalienated sexual relationships. "Orgastic potency is the capacity to surrender to the flow of biological energy, free of any inhibitions," stated Reich (1973: 102), "the capacity to discharge completely the dammed-up sexual excitation through involuntary, pleasurable convulsions of the body." Reich further concluded that, as opposed to mere "erective potency," or the ability to have orgasms, this ability to give completely of oneself during the sex act is not as common as many people think. "Not a single neurotic is orgastically potent, and the character structures of the overwhelming majority of men and women are neurotic." Full orgasm is thus synonymous with the full ability to relate to one's partner without blockages to emotional contact caused by insecurities and unresolved problems within the person. This orgastic potency is therefore both a measure and an expression of overall mental health.

Reich believed that the most disturbed of all were men who like to boast and make a big display of their masculinity, bragging that they had possessed or conquered as many women as possible, and who could "do it" again and again in one night. Though they were erectively very potent, such men typically experienced very little pleasure at the moment of ejaculation, or in many cases they experienced the exact opposite, disgust and unpleasure. Moreover, "the precise analysis of fantasies during the sexual act revealed that the men usually had sadistic or conceited attitudes and that the women were afraid, inhibited, or imagined themselves to be men. For the ostensibly potent man, sexual intercourse means the piercing, overpowering, or conquering of the woman. He merely wants to prove his potency or to be admired for his erective endurance" (1973: 100).[5]

Lowen also distinguished between sexually "sophisticated" and sexually "mature" persons on the basis of their orgastic potency.

> The sexually mature person, as I see him, is neither sophisticated nor burdened with sexual guilt. He is not a performer; his sexual behavior is a direct expression of his feelings. He is not an ideal, but neither is he a pretender. He is not sexually fulfilled in every experience, because the vicissitudes of life do not allow for perfection. Success or failure is not a criterion by which he judges his sexual behavior. He knows that sexual satisfaction cannot be divorced from overall satisfaction in living. Yet these satisfactions are his because his maturity represents a realistic and whole-hearted commitment to live and love. (1965: 16)

More fully developed persons also have been characterized as having greater capacities for empathy and mutual dialogue with other persons. "Self-actualizing people have deeper and more profound interpersonal relations than other adults," observed Maslow (1970: 166). "They are capable of more fusion, greater love, more perfect identification, more obliteration of the ego boundaries than other people would consider possible." Most persons see the problem of love primarily as that of being loved, wrote Fromm (1956: vii), rather than in terms of one's capacity to love. However, the capacity to love is related to the general development of the person's total personality such "that satisfaction in individual love cannot be attained without the capacity to love one's neighbor, without true humility, courage, faith and discipline." In other words, the capacity to love is positively related to the general development of one's other essential human capacities and potentials.

The general conditions that promote or hinder the full development of human love will be explored in Chapters 2 and 7. Through love we confirm others by recognizing in them the persons they have been created to become. Through love we also confirm ourselves in the process and strengthen the essential social relations necessary for the growth of our own self-potentials. "Thus the relationship which I have found helpful is characterized by a sort of transparency on my part, in which my real feelings are evident; by an acceptance of this other person as a separate person with value in his own right; and by a deep empathic understanding which enables me to see his private world through his eyes," as Rogers put it (1961: 34). "When these conditions are achieved, I become a companion to [the other person], accompanying him in the frightening search for himself, which he now feels free to undertake." In this process, I move toward becoming more fully the type of person I am capable of being.

Democratic Character Structure

Chapters 2 and 7 describe the dynamics of personality, or character formation, in freedom-promoting, as opposed to freedom-inhibiting, social environments. These latter environments are characterized as authoritarian environments because in them social order is created and maintained through the use of external rewards and punishments and the subsequent creation of internalized guilts and compulsive morality within persons. It will be argued that it is these authoritarian social relations that produce persons who are closed-minded, unsure of themselves, insincere, fragmented, and unloving—in short, persons who are unfree. Moreover, the enduring effect of prolonged participation in these authoritarian environments is the creation of character structures that are inflexible and heavily armored against recurring clashes with powerful outside authorities and increasingly armored against repressed and disowned inner desires and drives. Authoritarian persons display, in Fromm's (1941) words, sadomasochistic personalities—that is, they often function in terms of either hurting others or having others hurt themselves—and have been socialized to function more effectively in hierarchical, dominant-submissive social relations.

Therefore freedom, defined in terms of full human development, is closely related with the formation of democratic character structures. Such persons, having been reared in comutual social relations, tend to be more comfortable with freedom and with the two-way dialogue and negotiated problem solving that are intrinsic features of democratic environments. As Maslow explained regarding self-actualizing persons, "all my subjects without exception may be said to be democratic people in the deepest possible sense."

> These people have all the obvious or superficial demo-
> cratic characteristics. They can be and are friendly with
> anyone of suitable character regardless of class, education,
> political belief, race, or color. As a matter of fact it often
> seems as if they are not even aware of these differences,
> which are for the average person so obvious and so impor-
> tant. They have not only this most obvious quality but their
> democratic feeling goes deeper as well. For instance they
> find it possible to learn from anybody who has something
> to teach them—no matter what other characteristics he may
> have. In such a learning relationship they do not try to
> maintain any outward dignity or to maintain status or age
> prestige or the like. It should even be said that my subjects
> share a quality that could be called humility of a certain
> type. They are all quite well aware of how little they know
> in comparison with what *could* be known and what *is* known
> by others. Because of this it is possible for them without
> pose to be honestly respectful and even humble before peo-
> ple who can teach them something that they do not know
> or who have a skill they do not possess. (1970: 167)

In Chapter 7 the formation and development of democratic character structures will be related to these above-described characteristics of more fully developed persons. Such individuals, it is argued, have been allowed to develop a degree of character flexibility and self-regulation that, in appropriate situations, allows them to become more self-confident, open to experience, sincere, integrated, and genuinely loving and empathetic in their every-day lives and routine dealings with other persons.

The psychic and character traits described in this chapter are therefore general and, at present, undoubtedly imprecise esti-mations of the possible characteristics of more fully developed persons. A next logical question concerns the processes of growth and general social conditions that promote and hinder the unfold-ing of these essential human capacities and potentials. How, then, do individuals develop these positive mental and emotional traits? What can be said about the types of homes, schools, workplaces, and other immediate social environments that pro-mote, rather than restrict, human freedom and growth?

Thus, an underlying theme of Chapters 2 and 7 is that persons are always a part of a larger set of circumstances. They develop their basic human capabilities through their essential relations with themselves—that is, ties with their own activities and consciousness—with other persons, and with the outside world. In Chapter 2 we will discuss the essential nature of social environments that sever these necessary ties and consequently alienate persons from their own self-potentials. Chapter 7, then, will focus on the contrasting environments that actually may strengthen these essential relations and promote human growth and freedom.

2

Becoming Separated from Ourselves

The individual who has become a stranger to himself has
lost the capacity for genuine self-renewal. He can no longer
return for sustenance to the springs of his own being.
—JOHN GARDNER

Social life is never a neutral process. Our upbringing either can
serve to make us more unfettered, self-governing, and capable
of the practice of freedom or it can serve to dehumanize and
domesticate us, making us ever more reliant on outside authority.
As persons, it is natural for us to seek freedom. What, then, is
the nature of social environments that distort our normal impulses and deflect us from our intrinsic vocation of becoming more
fully human?

FREEDOM AND INTERDEPENDENCE

Let us begin by recognizing that everywhere and always people
have lived in association with nature and with one another. The
separate individual is an abstraction; we all grow up in social
environments and become human through our associations with
other persons. Without these social relations we would not have
developed our specifically human capacities and skills, and without any relations with nature we would all cease to be living
human beings, assuming that these relations once existed, otherwise we would never have endured in the first place.[1]

People are thus born into an ongoing society that precedes
them in time, and for individual humans the universality of social

19

existence is a biological necessity since they cannot even survive if left alone. As LeBarre (1954: 54) observed, in the roughly evolutionary sequence of lemur-monkey-ape-human being, the offsprings become smaller, more helpless, and more immature at birth. The period of more or less total dependency upon the parents lengthens from a few hours for lemurs to a few days for monkeys, a few months for apes, and a few years for humans. Similarly, the time needed to learn to walk is lengthened as one moves up the evolutionary ladder to a period sometimes exceeding twelve to eighteen months for human beings. In the same sequence the suckling period is greatly extended, as is the time needed to achieve social independence and general sexual maturity.

Studies of Social Isolation

Social contact has been shown important among numerous species of animals. Levine (1960), for instance, reported laboratory experiments in which the physical, mental, and emotional development of rats was drastically affected by the amount of handling they received. In addition, these experiments demonstrated that the chemistry of the brain and even resistance to leukemia in rats seemed to be favorably affected by handling.

Given their greater social dependence, however, we would predict the effects of social isolation to be even more devastating at the higher rungs of the evolutionary ladder. This conclusion is amply demonstrated by the Harlows' research on rhesus monkeys, in which these investigators concluded that social isolation from birth for as little as three to six months renders these animals socially and personally inadequate. Consider, for instance, the Harlows' description of the behavior of fifty-six such animals who were housed in separate wire cages with no physical contact with others of their species:

> The laboratory-born monkeys sit in their cages and stare fixedly into space, circle their cages in a repetitive stereotyped manner and clasp their heads in their hands or arms and rock for long periods of time. They often develop compulsive habits, such as pinching precisely the same patch of skin on the chest between the same fingers hundreds of times a day; occasionally such behavior may become punitive and the animal may chew and tear at its body until it

bleeds. Often the approach of a human being becomes the stimulus to self-aggression. This behavior constitutes a complete breakdown and reversal of the normal defensive response; a monkey born in the wild will direct such threats and aggression at the approaching person, not at itself. (1962: 4)

When such isolated monkeys were later placed together in cages, they paid little attention to one another, preferring instead to sit in opposite corners with only rare interactions. The Harlows (1962: 5) further reported that no sexual behavior "has ever been observed between male and female cagemates, even between those that have lived together for as long as seven years." Isolated female monkeys, who were successfully impregnated by artificial means, also showed abnormal maternal behavior that ranged from indifference to their offspring to outright abuse. As the Harlows (1962: 9) observed, "whereas it usually requires more than one person to separate an infant from its mother, these mothers paid no attention when their infants were removed from the cages for the hand-feeding necessitated by the mothers' refusal to nurse."

Social Isolation Among Humans

Restricted communication and the absence of normal social relations are even more devastating for human development. After surveying the literature on human isolation, Maslow (1972: 35) concluded that "deprived of the society of others man becomes a monster. He cannot regress to his pre-cultural state, because such a state never existed."

Until about fifty years ago, for instance, children who were hospitalized for long periods of time within the first few years of life regularly died from a disease known as *marasmus* (from the Greek word meaning "wasting away"). This disease today is known as "hospitalism" and has been traced to a lack of physical contact and normal social relations between hospitalized infants and other persons (Montagu, 1950: 55–67). Numerous research studies—for instance, Spitz (1945) and Patton and Gardner (1963)—also have shown that institutionally reared children deprived of routine human interactions during early childhood tend to sink into an irreversible decline and are more prone to

die from various common diseases. Other cases of partially isolated children result from intentional neglect by parents and
guardians, and many of these cases, like that of Isabelle described
below, demonstrate even more dramatically the effects of social
deprivation on human development.

Isabelle was an illegitimate child, kept in seclusion for that
reason. Her mother, a deaf-mute, spent much time with Isabelle
in a dark room shut off from the rest of the family. She was
sometimes held by her mother but could only communicate by
means of gestures, and, when discovered by outsiders at age six
and one-half years, she displayed many infantile behaviors. As
observed by a psychologist (Davis, 1947: 436), "she was apparently utterly unaware of relationships of any kind. When presented with a ball for the first time, she held it in the palm of
her hand, then reached out and stroked my face with it. Such
behavior is comparable to that of a child of six months."

Specialists working with Isabelle initially believed her to
be mentally retarded, and even on nonverbal tests her performance was extremely low. Through pantomime and dramatiza-
tion, however, these specialists began to see progress. Results
were very slow at first, and it required a week of intensive effort
before she even made her first attempts at vocalization.

> She went through the usual stages of learning charac-
> teristics of the years from one to six not only in proper
> succession but far more rapidly than normal. In a little over
> two months after her first vocalization she was putting sen-
> tences together. Nine months after that she could identify
> words and sentences on the printed page, could write well,
> could add to ten, and could retell a story after hearing it.
> Seven months beyond this point she had a vocabulary of
> 1,500–2,000 words and was asking complicated questions.
> Starting from an educational level of between one and three
> years (depending on what aspect one considers), she had
> reached a normal level by the time she was eight and a half
> years old. In short, she covered in two years the stages of
> learning that ordinarily require six. (Davis, 1947: 436)

Davis further reported that the corrective therapy was apparently
successful, and, when he last observed Isabelle, "she gave him
the impression of being a very bright, cheerful, energetic little
girl."

As demonstrated by these cases of partial isolation, human
freedom therefore is a collective development.[2] The "I" cannot

exist without a "you," or, to be more accurate, outside the context of a community of other human beings. We develop many of our species powers and capabilities through our social relations with other persons, and a general condition of interdependence is an inescapable fact of human existence.

AUTHORITARIAN RELATIONS AND THE GENERAL DOMESTICATION PROCESS

If individuals develop their human capabilities through their relations with other persons, what can be said about the types of social relations that facilitate, rather than constrain, human development? Why do some homes or schools, for instance, produce spontaneous and creative children while others produce neuroses and fearful compliance? The argument thus far has been that, if persons are placed outside the normal meanings of social life, their natures are reduced to that of conditioned animals or infants. Therefore, given that people do not develop their full human potentials outside of their social environments, what can be said about the nature of the social relations that make persons more unfettered and self-governing as opposed to those that domesticate them and make them more reliant on others?

The general distinction I would make in this regard is between "authoritarian" and "democratic" social relationships. As a basic thesis, it is thus proposed that, on the one hand, social environments that constrain human development tend to be characterized by authoritarian relationships, while, on the other hand, social environments that facilitate human development tend to be characterized by democratic relationships.

Authoritarian Versus Democratic Relationships

Authoritarian relationships are relations of domination. They are characterized by *unilateral* decision making and enforcement. There is power inequality in the relationship, and joint activities are explicitly or implicitly based on the use or the threat of force. Thus, the dominating person in the relationship (the "authority") is invested with the power to make judgments and decisions that affect the dominated person's behaviors and that force him to comply with the authority figure's wishes.

Throughout history most societies have maintained social order by relying heavily on authoritarian relationships. Relations of domination also characterize major institutional areas in our society such as economic production, government, schooling, child rearing, relations between whites and nonwhites, relations between adults and children, and relations between men and women. Our personal experience therefore is shaped by authoritarian social relations as these are reflected in our dealings with parents, teachers, bosses, political authorities, police, and the numerous other power figures in our lives.

Paulo Freire (1970), for example, provided an illuminating description of the authoritarian relationships characterizing most traditional schools. Authoritarian education, claimed Freire, involves the relationship between a narrating Subject (the teacher) and patient, listening Objects (the students). Instead of dialogue and two-way communication, teachers issue communiqués and directives that the students patiently memorize and repeat. This, then, is a "banking" concept of education in which the task of teachers is to "fill" the students with the contents of their narration and the role of the students is to absorb and store this valuable knowledge. According to Freire (1970: 59), these authoritarian school relationships can be described concretely:

1) the teacher teaches and the students are taught;

2) the teacher knows everything and the students know nothing;

3) the teacher thinks and the students are thought about;

4) the teacher talks and the students listen—meekly;

5) the teacher disciplines and the students are disciplined;

6) the teacher chooses and enforces his choice, and the students comply;

7) the teacher acts and the students have the illusion of acting through the action of the teacher;

8) the teacher chooses the program content, and the students (who were not consulted) adapt to it;

9) the teacher confuses the authority of knowledge with his own professional authority, which he sets in opposition to the freedom of the students; and

10) the teacher is the subject of the learning process, while the pupils are mere objects.

The more completely students accept the passive role imposed on them and work at storing their deposits, the more they tend simply to adapt to the world as it presently exists rather than developing the critical consciousness necessary to transform it. Authoritarian "bank-clerk" teachers thus play the role of domesticators; they perpetuate the present authoritarian order and submerge students still further in the existing relations of domination.

By contrast, democratic relationships are ones characterized by mutual decision making and enforcement. Both parties in the relationship have the ability to veto joint decisions. There is power equality, and neither of the persons has the ability to make the other do things that are against that person's will. Even in highly authoritarian civilizations the daily lives of ordinary persons are characterized by numerous democratic relationships. These relations are typified by the processes of dialogue and negotiated decision making. As will be argued in Chapter 7, democratic relationships are the real nurseries of human nature by means of which we develop many of our distinctly human capacities and potentials. These relations are personified by the concept of "friendship" which is a central social category, or set of categories, in most known societies.

Freire also described the democratic relationships that could exist in schools. He proposed that teachers truly committed to freedom must abandon the educational goals of deposit-making and communiqués and replace these by the processes of problem-posing and genuine two-way communication. The basic teacher-student contradictions are thus resolved through cointentional education in which the teacher is no longer merely the one who teaches but now is the one who is also taught through mutual dialogue with students. Rather than being just docile listeners, the students become critical coinvestigators in dialogue with the teacher. Together these "teacher-students" and "student-teachers" become jointly responsible for the process by which they all grow.[3] In reality, though, existing social relations are never completely authoritarian nor completely democratic but rather exist at certain points between these extremes along a continuum and thus in each real life situation reflect some characteristics of both categories.

Dual Nature Dilemma

How, then, do authoritarian social environments restrict full human development? As illustrated for social relations by the above-isolation studies, it is assumed that people grow and develop many of their human capabilities through their essential relations with their own activities and consciousness, with other persons, and with the outside world. Authoritarian environments, in turn, produce tensions and contradictions within individuals that lead to the severance of these essential ties and therefore produce a general state of alienation or estrangement.[4] In such environments, persons are forced to become double beings in which their outward verbal expressions and public behavior often do not reflect their innermost thoughts and impulses, and this initial split between their public and private selves leads to many crucial types of inner secondary fragmentation. Below we will consider the general way authoritarian environments produce this type of dual nature dilemma in people's lives.

Creation of Public Selves

Spontaneous activity refers to behavior that directly and actively expresses one's natural impulses and needs, without conscious effort or premeditation. As implied by the Latin root *sponte*, which literally means "of one's free will," it is free activity that arises from internal needs rather than from external demands or expectations. Through spontaneous activities, persons both realize their own self-potentials and straightforwardly relate themselves to the outside world.[5]

As opposed to this natural spontaneous behavior, the emphasis in authoritarian environments is on the "external" shaping of people's activities and character through social reinforcement. "Most children brought up in authoritarian homes," observed Mussachia (1974: 50), "are subjected to a great variety of rigid strictures that basically boil down to *extreme* repression of their desires to do what they want when they want, be it play, when to go to bed, kinds of food, sexual explorations, sitting posture in chairs, going to school, or behavior in the presence of adults."

Through these external social reinforcements, persons with power in given situations—that is, "authority figures"—are therefore often able to gain control, wholly or partially, of other people's behavior.[6] At the most general level, these social reinforcements can be categorized roughly as either "rewards" or "punishments." Rewards are whatever means are possessed by these authorities to satisfy the person's needs and which therefore tend to increase the probability that the person will again perform

a given activity. Conversely, punishments are defined as whatever means are possessed by authorities to withhold either things
the person needs or actually cause the person pain or discomfort
and which therefore tend to reduce the probability that the person will again perform a given behavior.

In authoritarian homes, for example, we can imagine in the
beginning that infants often act spontaneously on the basis of
their immediately felt needs and emotions. Thus, they may cry
when hungry, smile or coo when contented, and sleep when tired,
but we can also imagine that the child's parents will view these
spontaneous activities differently. Given their power over the
child because of their superior physical strength, greater verbal
activity, more complete knowledge of society's religious and moral
traditions, and greater support from other adult authorities, they
will tend to encourage or reward some of the child's activities,
be indifferent toward or not pay attention to other activities, and
actively suppress or punish still other activities.

The basis of this social conditioning—parental power over
the child—is *force*, which is applied directly in the form of various
types of corporal punishment (for example, spankings), or indirectly in the form of threats or deprivations (for example, making
the child sit in a chair or miss a meal). Socially conditioned
approval and rewards serve the same function by also making
the child dependent on outside evaluations and by leaving the
child more vulnerable to reward-withdrawal, which is merely a
backhanded sort of punishment.[7]

Extensively studied in our increasingly "managed" society
have been some of the factors that relate to the overall effectiveness of this external social conditioning process. Apart from
the specific characteristics of the authority figures themselves
and their relations to the persons being controlled, three situa-
tional factors have been most emphasized by social scientists
studying the effectiveness of social conditioning: immediacy, contingency, and the size of the reinforcement (Skinner, 1953: 59–
90). As one might guess, an immediate social reinforcement—
usually within one second or less—singles out the specific activity
that is being reinforced from all other activities that the person
has performed. Thus, other things equal, immediate reinforcement tends to be more effective in externally shaping another
person's behavior.

External social control is also most effective when reinforcement seldom or never occurs except after the given behavior has
been performed; the authority figure must make the reward or

punishment truly contingent on the person performing the given activity. Interestingly, research under experimental conditions demonstrates that, although important, the size of the reward or punishment is often less significant than its immediacy and contingency in shaping behavior.[8]

Creation of Basic Insecurity

As a general process, therefore, social conditioning is completely artificial and arbitrary. Based on prevailing social customs or personal preferences, authority figures will choose to punish some activities while rewarding or disregarding others. For the most part, which activities are reinforced positively or negatively varies widely among societies and even within societies. The results of this authoritarian upbringing are socially conditioned persons who have been carefully taught to take seriously the standards and beliefs of outside authorities whether or not these standards or beliefs possess any intrinsic significance to the persons themselves.

This persistent external reinforcement by authorities creates a major dilemma. On the one hand, persons experience continuing natural impulses and pressures that result from the normal functioning of their bodies and minds. In addition to these natural urges, there are now the artificial social expectations and requirements that emanate from these important authority figures. Persons in authoritarian situations simultaneously inhabit two worlds—a social world and a natural world—which often demand contradictory activities on their part. For example, lacking language and the conceptual equipment necessary for preoccupation with the distant future or past, very young children are hedonistic, seeking immediate pleasure and being preoccupied with their present circumstances. Later on they will experience more sharply defined sexual urges, at first mostly autoerotic urges often related to the erogenous zones of their own bodies, and still later sexual impulses more directly related to possible interpersonal sexual activities.

Also imposed on the child are the requirements of the social world as mediated by the rewards and punishments of authority figures. Thus, from the beginning pressures are placed on the child to conform to social requirements and to behave in ways convenient for the parents. The child, for instance, is pressured to sleep all night, to wear appropriate clothing in public, to eat only at mealtimes, to speak correctly, to refrain from masturbation or sex play with other children, and, in general, to behave according to accepted adult standards of etiquette and propriety.

A result of being placed in these two often contradictory worlds during early childhood is the creation of a general or basic insecurity, which is felt as pervasive anxiety or apprehensiveness that is the outcome of not being the Subject of one's own life. Children in authoritarian environments feel isolated and helpless in the midst of a potentially threatening and hostile world. Their insecurity is a direct consequence of the social relations of domination and of being dependent for the gratification of their essential needs on the outside rewards and punishments administered by these powerful others.

As Laing (1960: 39) observed, it is possible for the secure person to encounter all the hazards of life "from a centrally firm sense of his own and other people's reality and identity." It is often difficult for a person with such a "sense of his integral selfhood and personal identity" to understand "the world of an individual whose experiences may be utterly lacking in any unquestionable self-validating certainties." This basic insecurity is a direct consequence of attempting to deal with environments controlled by powerful authorities and the "absence of assurances" that these others will not arbitrarily violate one's own personal needs and interests. Therefore, basically insecure persons cannot take their own autonomy and natural identity for granted but rather must "contrive ways of trying to be real," of "preserving their identities," and of "preventing the loss of self."

ABANDONING THE REAL SELF. Because of their basic insecurity, persons in authoritarian environments are forced to put increasingly more energy into becoming the types of persons demanded by these powerful others. Therefore, they progressively abandon their real private selves as their energies are diverted from spontaneous activities and the development of their actual abilities to the realization of their public selves. Like the creation of a Frankenstein monster, their public selves usurp their vital energies and increasingly they become driven toward the goal of actualizing the images and performances that are acceptable to the relevant authority figures.

Horney (1950: 21) emphasized that in a "competitive society," where the relations of domination are paramount, persons feel ashamed and inferior; this, in turn, is the beginning of self-alienation.

Not only is his real self prevented from a straight growth, but in addition his need to evolve artificial, strategic ways to cope with others has forced him to override his genuine feelings, wishes, and thoughts. To the extent that safety has become paramount, his innermost feelings and thoughts have receded in importance—in fact, they had to be silenced and have become indistinct. (It does not matter what he feels, if only he is safe.) His feelings and wishes thus cease to be determining factors; he is no longer, so to speak, the driver, but is driven. And the division in himself not only weakens him in general, but reinforces the alienation by adding an element of confusion; he no longer knows where he stands, or 'who' he is. (1950: 21)

People's secret private lives therefore become divorced from their official lives, as the social rewards and punishments administered by these powerful others force them to override their own genuine feelings, wishes, and thoughts. The outcome, as Perls (1969: 19) noted, is that these persons become increasingly separated from their own capacities and potentials and increasingly invested in the images that they are busily projecting to others.

PORTRAIT OF AN ACCOMPLISHED FAKE. Psychotic and neurotic persons often provide extreme examples of this separation of public and private selves. Consider, for instance, the case study of David as presented by Laing (1959: 69–77). At age eighteen, David's whole manner was artificial and contrived. His hair was too long and his shoes were too big. He attended lectures in a secondhand theater cloak that he wore over his shoulders and arms. He carried a cane, and his speech was made up largely of quotations.

David was the product of an authoritarian home and had been raised entirely by his father since his mother's death when he was ten. He learned to cope with the fear generated by his father's unrealistic expectations and arbitrary punishments by withdrawing into himself and by almost completely splitting his own inner feelings and impulses from his outward activities. Thus, as a child David often felt exposed and defenseless, but by always playing a part, he found he could in some measure overcome these weaknesses. David's ideal was never to give himself away to others, and therefore his actions became a series of contrived impersonations that allowed almost no true self-expression. As Laing commented,

His self was never directly revealed in and through his actions. It seemed to be the case that he had emerged from his infancy with his 'own self' on the one hand, and 'what his father wanted him to be,' his 'personality,' on the other; he had started from there and made it his aim and ideal to make the split between his own self (which only he knew) and what other people could see of him, as complete as possible. He was further impelled to this course by the fact that despite himself he had always felt shy, self-conscious, and vulnerable. By always playing a part he found he could in some measure overcome his shyness, self-consciousness, and vulnerability. He found reassurance in the consideration that whatever he was doing he was not being himself. (1959: 71)

The organization of David's character rested on a disjunction between his private inner "self" and his outer public "personality." Over the course of his neurotic development, he was able to disown most of his real capacities and self-potentials and shut himself off almost completely from possible harm, first from his father and then later from the rest of the outside world.

COFFEE, TEA, OR ME.   The dual nature dilemma is also present in the everyday lives of "normal" persons as they cope with authoritarian environments. Terkel (1972) described the divided selves of workers who, in their jobs, must confront these relations of domination. Consider, for instance, Terkel's interview with Terry, an airline stewardess, who commented that working as a stewardess is not as glamorous as she thought it would be. The airlines want stewardesses who have nice personalities and who are pleasant looking. Everything is supposed to be becoming to the male passengers.

> . . . our supervisors tell us what kind of make-up to wear, what kind of lipstick to wear, if our hair is not the right style for us, if we're not smiling enough. They even tell us how to act when you're on a pass. Like last night I met my husband. I was in plain clothes. I wanted to kiss him. But I'm not supposed to kiss anybody at the terminal. You're not supposed to walk off with a passenger, hand in hand. (1972: 72–82)

This training in artificial appearance and demeanor begins at stewardess school, in which an entire week is devoted to the topics of makeup and poise. The idea is to be sexy without being "too obvious about it." "That's the whole thing, being a lady but still giving out that womanly appeal, like the body movement and the lips and the eyes." For instance, the stewardesses are carefully coached about how to have male passengers light their cigarettes for them.

Terry thus works in a controlled environment. If a stewardess has a problem with blemishes or a slightly black eye, she is taken off the flight until the "appearance" counselor thinks she is ready to go back. The problem, reflects Terry, is that "they won't let you have your own personality." She admits that she usually does not have the nerve "to speak up to anybody that's pinched me or said something dirty." She is afraid of complaints or "onion letters" because when the airline receives these letters the stewardess must talk with the supervisor and is subject to being fired.

Terry's life is not one of spontaneity and self-expression but instead one of pretenses and artificially contrived behavior. Like many other salaried employees, she has been carefully conditioned to organize her work activities around outside demands and expectations rather than in terms of her own natural feelings and needs.

DESTRUCTIVE CONSEQUENCES OF DIVIDED SELVES. These case studies illustrate some of the destructive consequences of the split between real and public selves. People's real selves are the source of their spontaneous interest and activities and of their essential relations with themselves, other persons, and the outside world. In authoritarian environments they must stifle many of their basic impulses and shut themselves off from these persistent sources of outside irritation.

The results of abrasive authoritarian relations are persons with more or less shut up selves, being isolated to some degree and unable to be enriched by outside experiences. Their inner worlds become impoverished, and, without an open two-way circuit between fantasy and reality, they may also develop egocentricities and unrealistic goals and expectations, as Laing observed:

> The self, as long as it is 'uncommitted to the objective element,' is free to dream and imagine anything. Without reference to the objective element it can be all things to itself—it has unconditioned freedom, power, creativity. But its freedom and its omnipotence are exercised in a vacuum and its creativity is only the capacity to produce phantoms. The inner honesty, freedom, omnipotence, and creativity, which the 'inner' self cherishes as its ideals, are cancelled, therefore, by the coexisting tortured sense of self-duplicity,

of lack of any real freedom, of utter impotence and sterility. (1959: 89)

Such persons, in fantasy, may visualize themselves as great lovers but in actual lovemaking situations be shy, inarticulate, or impotent. They may be utterly ambitious and constantly dream of effortless success but in real life neglect the everyday preparation and discipline necessary for such accomplishments, or they may dream of being slender and glamorous but insatiately stuff themselves at meals to relieve the unresolved tensions produced by authoritarian relations.

As persons put increasingly more energy into realizing their public selves, they have correspondingly less energy available for actualizing their real selves. Much of their efforts must be invested in pretenses, false claims, and living up to outside expectations, with the predictable result of increasingly unresolved inner conflict and fragmentation in their lives. They must divide their energies between those activities necessary for success in the eyes of their parents and administrative superiors, for instance, and those endeavors that would help them develop as individual persons. A destructive outcome of authoritarian social relations, therefore, is this waste and misdirection of vital human effort.

Another result of shifting energy from people's real to public selves is that these pretended selves become the measuring rods against which persons measure their actual being. Because it is usually easier to pretend perfection than actually achieve it, their real selves suffer from the comparison. Realizing that they cannot measure up to their public performances, such persons may learn to hate and despise their real selves. Lack of consciousness of this inner rage against themselves also creates tensions that may cause such symptoms as headaches, fatigue, ulcers, depression, or a variety of other serious physical illnesses. The relations of domination thus do not provide satisfactory grounds for developing self-confidence. Large parts of people's personalities are unavailable for their constructive use, and this tends to diminish the possibilities for actual accomplishment.

In summary, then, individuals grow through their essential relations with their own behaviors and experiences, with other people, and with the outside world. Such relations are developed through spontaneous activities that accurately reflect their natural impulses and needs. The emphasis in authoritarian social environments, however, is upon the external molding of people's activities through socially proscribed punishments and rewards. This forces individuals to bridge two often contradictory worlds, one based on the logic of the functioning of their own bodies and minds and the other based on the arbitrary demands of the relevant authority figures in their lives.

The result of this dual nature dilemma is a basic feeling of helplessness or insecurity at being the object of forces outside their own control. Because of this basic insecurity, persons are motivated to abandon their real selves and to put increasing amounts of energy into the construction of acceptable appearances for the benefit of these powerful others. As in the above case studies, persons therefore learn to divide their energies between those activities required of them if they are to be successful in the evaluations of relevant authority figures and those activities that would facilitate their own personal growth as individuals. The result is a severing of essential relations and a general impoverishment of their inner being. Moreover, these pretenses waste and misdirect vital human effort and are a cause of low self-confidence and the development of self-hatred.

Separation from Activities

Through productive activity, persons are able both to develop their own personal powers and to change nature so as to make it more facilitative of greater human development. It is through an active involvement in the outside world, for instance, that children begin to experience, explore, and expand their capabilities. They often take great delight in repeating over and over again newly discovered words and actions. As Marx (1967: 177) stated, "by thus acting on the external world and changing it, he at the same time changes his own nature. He develops his slumbering powers and compels them to act in obedience to his sway."

Activity is the chief means by which we make the world a part of ourselves and ourselves a part of the world. "The world of objects as it exists at any one time," observed Ollman (1976: 99), "constitutes the real limits for the realization of man's powers." It is through the active transformation of nature that we can make these current realities more conducive to growth and self-actualization. "In creating a nature which is adequate, in producing food which he can eat, clothes he can wear and a house he can live in," explained Ollman (1976: 99), "man is forever remolding nature, and with each alteration enabling his powers to achieve new kinds and degrees of fulfillment."

Inauthenticity

The public self we create is based on inauthenticities, or "false performances," that do not accurately portray our true feelings and beliefs. "We monitor, censor our behavior and disclosures," suggested Jourard (1964: 10–11), "in order to construct in the mind of the other person a concept of ourselves which we want him to have."

> Our disclosures reflect, not our spontaneous feelings, thoughts, and wishes, but rather pretended approval. We say that we feel things we do not feel. We say that we did things we did not do. We say that we believe things we do not believe. The person sells his soul, his real self, in order to purchase popularity, his mother's affection, or a promotion in the firm.

In social life this often involves the wearing of "masks" and the presentation of "false" selves. In a job interview, for example, we present ourselves as interested, ambitious, disciplined, industrious, and outgoing even though all we are really feeling is a lump in our stomach. At a party we seem entertaining, sociable, and witty although we are actually tired, hung over, and bored out of our minds. Thus, in school, with our parents, on the athletic field, or at church we become different persons depending on our perceptions of the social requirements of different situations. Like a chameleon that seeks protection through blending with its environment, persons with authoritarian upbringings are skillfully tuned to the changing external demands upon them.

Alienated Labor

One of the original and most perceptive descriptions of this alienation from basic activities has been given by Karl Marx (1964: 106–19). For Marx, the significance of being salaried employees lies in the fact that such persons are required to relinquish control over much of their waking hours. Therefore, these laborers are not free to do what they want on the job but must follow the dictates of an employer who decides what is to be

produced and how and when. In a society based on such forced
labor, declared Marx, people are no longer the masters of their
own activities. "What, then, constitutes the alienation of labor?"
asked Marx:

> First, the fact that labor is *external* to the worker, that is,
> it does not belong to his essential being; that in his work,
> therefore, he does not affirm himself but denies himself, does
> not feel content but unhappy, does not develop freely his
> physical and mental energy but mortifies his body and ruins
> his mind. The worker therefore only feels himself outside
> his work, and in his work feels outside himself. He is at
> home when he is not working, and when he is working he
> is not at home. His labor is therefore not voluntary, but
> coerced; it is forced labor. It is therefore not the satisfaction
> of a need; it is merely a *means* to satisfy needs external to
> it. Its alien character emerges clearly in the fact that as soon
> as no physical or other compulsion exists, labor is shunned
> like the plague. External labor, labor in which man alienates
> himself, is a labor of self-sacrifice, or mortification. Lastly,
> the external character of labor for the worker appears in
> the fact that it is not his own, but someone else's, that it
> does not belong to him, that in it he belongs, not to himself,
> but to another. Just as in religion that spontaneous activity
> of the human imagination, of the human brain and the
> human heart, operates independently of the individual—
> diabolical activity—so is the worker's activity not his spon-
> taneous activity. It belongs to another; it is the loss of his
> self. (1964: 110–11)

Marx also emphasized that another way one's activities
provide opportunities for appropriation and growth is through
the products and accomplishments that are the results of these
activities. Passing an exam, building a house, or winning a tennis
tournament encapsulates our activities in the form of products
helping us better understand and judge our own capacities and
potentials. In authoritarian environments, where persons are cut
off from their own activities, however, they also become separated
from the products of these activities. To gaze at a picture painted
just to please an art teacher or earn a passing grade will probably
not tell us much about our real perceptions or understanding of
the world.

There is thus a vicious cycle involved in such coverup activities. New defensive positions separate individuals still further

from themselves and their outside worlds. Such persons become ever more conflicted and fragmented and progressively more alienated from the activities of their daily lives.

Separation from Consciousness

As we have seen, the human infant is biologically under-developed compared with infants of other animal species. Humans do have drives, but these drives are highly unspecialized and undirected. Persons lack the necessary biological means to provide order and stability for their conduct. Given the increased size and complexity of the human brain, however, much of this stability that is lacking on the basis of instinctual endowment is, nevertheless, provided through learning and conscious choice. This is the basis, then, for awareness, imagination, and all those faculties such as speech, art, and ethics that uniquely charac-terize human existence.

Persons must therefore confirm and manifest themselves through knowing as well as acting. They must develop a self-consciousness and awareness of themselves as individuals active in pursuing their own ends. As was noted, the physical basis for human consciousness is provided by the large brain and central nervous system that are the products of species evolution. Thus, for the newborn human about one-seventh of its total body weight is brain and nervous system. As the evolution of the human brain has proceeded, it also has taken over progressively more of the spinal functions, bringing former reflex actions under the control of consciousness and will. Instinctual activities, therefore, give way in humans to the more flexible choices based on intelligence and learning.

Since persons grow and develop their abilities through an active involvement in the outside world, separation from one's activities is at the core of the human domestication process. Through estrangement from their behaviors, individuals have reduced opportunities, both to appropriate experience and to shape the outside environment to meet their needs. With the development of language and consciousness persons further extend their human capacities and potential ties with the world. In addition to separation from activities, they are now vulnerable to being estranged from their own feelings and conscious capac-ities as well. Described below are some of the ways persons in authoritarian environments become separated from their own consciousness.

Developing a Guilty Conscience

The original bases of adult authority, as described previously, lie in such things as childrens' fear of punishment and the possible withdrawal of parental love, but these *external social controls* are often inefficient and time-consuming. In particular, the consistent application of outside reinforcement requires constant surveillance by authority figures, since such external conditioning requires that they be physically present to observe and punish children's transgressions. Therefore, as children develop language and memory, authority figures may choose to control their conduct increasingly through *internalized social controls*. As Freud explained,

> The chronological sequence, then, would be as follows. First comes renunciation of instinct owing to fear of aggression by the external authority. (This is, of course, what fear of the loss of love amounts to, for love is a protection against this punitive aggression.) After this comes the erection of an *internal* authority, and renunciation of instinct owing to fear of it—owing to fear of conscience. In this second situation bad intentions are equated with bad actions, and hence come a sense of guilt and a need for punishment. (1961: 75).

This mechanism of internalized social control, therefore, is *guilt*, a pervasive and disruptive feeling of having failed to meet some high expectation or standard set by outside authorities. Effective socialization in such environments implies that over time the fear of punishment increasingly becomes moral inhibition, and the conflict between authority figures and individuals becomes an internal struggle within persons themselves.[9] This process by which the external voice of authority begins to be internalized is aptly illustrated by Allport:

> A three-year-old boy awoke at six in the morning and started his noisy play. The father, sleepy-eyed, went to the boy's room and sternly commanded him. 'Get back into bed and don't you dare get up until seven o'clock.' The boy obeyed. For a few minutes all was quiet, but soon there were strange sounds that led the father again to look into the room. The boy was in bed as ordered, but putting an

arm over the edge, he jerked it back in, saying, 'Get back
in there.' Next a leg protruded, only to be roughly retracted
with the warning. 'You heard what I told you.' Finally, the
boy rolled to the very edge of the bed and then roughly
rolled back, sternly warning himself, 'Not until seven o'clock!'
(1955: 70)

Therefore, after acquiring language and memory, children
learn to anticipate many of the external rewards and punishments that authorities are likely to administer. Such children
may reason if they wear this dress or do their homework this
will please their parents and earn their approval, but if they steal
a quarter they may be caught and spanked. Over time children
thus develop a *conscience* based on this guilt and the internalization
of the expectations and standards of authority figures. People's
consciences become internal monitoring mechanisms that decide
on the moral quality of their actions and motives. In authoritarian societies, conscience and guilt can become a primary
method of social control. In addition to the objective consequences that flow from their actions, persons also learn to anticipate social approval and standards and internally administer
praise and condemnation for their own activities and thoughts.

"A threatened external unhappiness—loss of love and punishment on the part of the external authority—has been
exchanged," wrote Freud (1961: 75), "for a permanent internal
unhappiness, for the tension of the sense of guilt." He further
observed that society "obtains mastery over the individual's dangerous desire for aggression by weakening and disarming it and
by setting up an agency within him to watch over it, like a
garrison in a conquered city." Thus, behavior in authoritarian
settings is no longer spontaneous; persons have become morally
conditioned, that is, domesticated, human beings. The more "vir-
tuous" such persons become, the more guilty and distrustful they
feel, "so that ultimately it is precisely those people who have
carried saintliness furtherest who reproach themselves with the
worst sinfulness" (Freud, 1961: 70–72).

Repression

When the contradictions are *between* the person and external
authorities, the coping mechanisms—for example, inauthenticity—are frequently direct and relatively uncomplicated, but the
matter becomes more complex in the case of internalized social

controls. Now the conflicts are *within* the person, being between two parts of the individual's own personality: 1) the person's conscious awareness of certain actions or thoughts, and 2) the person's internalized social standards that are now reinforced by conscience and guilt. How are individuals to deal with wishes and desires, for instance, that are in sharp opposition to their own consciences and incapable of being reconciled with them?

Freud described the process of repression as a basic method of resolving these internalized struggles. Through repression the person actively excludes or dissociates this unwelcome knowledge from consciousness. Peace and inner harmony are temporarily restored by suppressing awareness of wishes and actions that violate people's internalized moral standards. Freud described the basic nature and functions of repression:

> In all those experiences, it had happened that a wish had been aroused, which was in sharp opposition to the other desires of the individual, and was not capable of being reconciled with the ethical, aesthetic and personal pretensions of the patient's personality. There had been a short conflict, and the end of this inner struggle was the repression of the idea which presented itself to consciousness as the bearer of this irreconcilable wish. This was, then, repressed from consciousness and forgotten. The incompatibility of the idea in question with the 'ego' of the patient was the motive of the repression, the ethical and other pretensions of the individual were the repressing forces. The presence of the incompatible wish, or the duration of the conflict, had given rise to a high degree of mental pain; this pain was avoided by the repression. This latter process is evidently in such a case a device for the protection of the personality. (1957: 12)

However, disowning parts of the self through repression limits human development in many of the ways already described regarding inauthenticity. The process is never completed and demands a constant expenditure of energy. The repressed thoughts and feelings exercise a continuous straining toward consciousness so that the balance has to be kept by means of a steady counterpressure. Insecurity and anxiety also are created since persons must display constant vigilance lest some hint or sign of the repressed knowledge comes to the surface. The end product is a deeper estrangement between people's outward dealings with the world and their innermost thoughts and feelings.

Often there is the additional problem of the development of "neurotic" symptoms that signal the further loss of control of the individual's conscious activities. Freud observed that the impulse

> . . . develops in a more unchecked and luxuriant fashion if it is withdrawn by repression from conscious influence. It ramifies like a fungus, so to speak, in the dark and takes on extreme forms of expression, which when translated and revealed to the neurotic are bound not merely to seem alien to him, but to terrify him by the way in which they reflect an extraordinary and dangerous strength of instinct. This illusory strength of instinct is the result of an uninhibited development of it in fantasy and of the damming-up consequent on lack of real satisfaction. (1957: 90)

Neurotic symptoms, therefore, become "substitute satisfactions" for individuals who have been alienated from the direct and open fulfillment of their essential needs. These alternative gratifications are themselves often bizarre and can cause additional problems and contradictions within persons.

Reich presented a case study, illustrating the general nature of repression and some of its consequences. A married, working-class housewife complained that she could not stay in a room alone because she had an overwhelming fear of burglars and imagined that they were going to attack her with knives. Reich described the woman's background:

> Before she was married, this woman met a man who pursued her with propositions which she would have liked to accept had she not been morally inhibited. She was able to put off the solution of this conflict by comforting herself with thoughts of eventual marriage. That man gave her up and she married another, without, however, being able to forget the first. The memory of this first man disturbed her incessantly. Meeting him again on some occasion, she again fell into an acute conflict between her desire for him and the demands for conjugal fidelity. Under these conditions the conflict became intolerable and insoluble, the desire for the other man being as strong as her moral sense. She now began to avoid him and, finally, seemed to forget him. It was, however, not real forgetting but a repression. She thought she was cured and consciously never gave him another thought. (1972: 31–33)

The conflict between the woman's moral standards and her repressed wish to commit adultery eventually led to the burdensome symptom of a constant, obsessive fear of being knifed by a burglar. Analysis showed that the burglar imagined in the fantasy resembled her first lover, without the woman realizing it. Thus, desire was transformed into fear, and the woman was able temporarily to live with herself through the development of these neurotic symptoms.

Authoritarian Character Structure

Reich (1972: 171) defined character as "modes of reaction characteristic of one's specific personality." These characteristic modes of reaction are manifested in the person's demeanor: his walk, facial expression, stance, manner of speech, and other modes of behavior. The person's character structure, added Reich, "is molded from elements of the outer world, from prohibitions, instinctual inhibitions, and the most varied forms of identifications."

Are there any commonalities in the character structures, or typical modes of reaction, of persons who have been subjected to prolonged participation in authoritarian social environments? Given the high level of abstraction of our present discussion and the fact that concrete environments characterized by authoritarian relations vary widely, we would naturally expect great variation among persons in such environments. Nevertheless, on the basis of this present analysis, there do appear to be common problems faced by persons participating in authoritarian settings.

Character formation in authoritarian environments is characterized by frequent collisions between the natural impulses of children and the frustrations imposed on them by a repressive upbringing. Characteristic reactions and modes of behavior thus arise as attempts by children to defend themselves in conflict situations with parents and other outside authorities. Through inauthenticity, repression, and other such defenses, Reich (1972: 155) proposed there is a "hardening" of the self as persons "armor" themselves against this outside domination. They therefore close themselves off and restrict the open communications between themselves and the outside world. They protect themselves from outside hurt by erecting strong and more or less permanent barriers between their real and public selves.

While protection against the outside world is the main reason for the original formation of authoritarian character armor, this is not its main function for persons who have developed internalized social controls. As persons are forced to protect themselves through repression of dangerous cognitive and emotional experiences, it is these internal dangers against which the character mechanisms guard. After individuals have come to rely on compulsive morality to control their unruly impulses, increasingly their character traits have the function of protecting their personal images of themselves as socially decent and worthy persons. In this case, the character structure locks the unacceptable impulses and redirects the person's energies, acting both as a repressing agent and controlling the resulting anxiety (Ollman, 1973: 41).

The result of prolonged domination is a further severing of essential relations with themselves, other persons, and the outside world. The person's repressions and inauthenticities are organized into characteristic patterns that further insulate the person and reduce both the impact of disturbing outside stimuli and dangerous inner drives. As Ollman noted,

> Character structure also deadens people sufficiently for them to do the boring, mechanical work which is the lot of most people in capitalist society. The same dulling insulates people from outside stimuli, reducing the impact on them of further education and of life itself. Finally, the increased sexual blockage which results from damming up the libido is responsible for various reaction formations, chief of which is an ascetic ideology, which in turn increases the blockage. (1973: 42)

INNER FRAGMENTATION. Reich (1970: xi) proposed that the character structures of persons socially conditioned to behave in terms of outside authority can be characterized by three distinct layers. Because of this situation of reinforcing external and internal threat, persons isolate themselves from these recurring hurts by developing an intermediate defensive layer of character that even more permanently separates their public behaviors and conscious attitudes, on the one hand, from their inner core of real feelings and personal needs, on the other. Below we will describe briefly each of these three layers of authoritarian character, as schematically presented in Figure 1.

1) SURFACE LAYER. Persons in authoritarian environments must pretend much of the time and constantly monitor and control their thoughts and actions in ways congruent with their public

Figure 1. Character Structure of Persons Socially Conditioned To Behave in Terms of Outside Authority

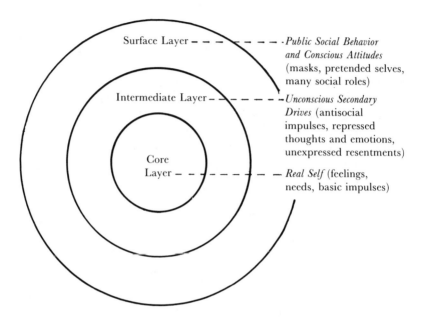

Surface Layer – – – ⟍ – – – – -*Public Social Behavior and Conscious Attitudes* (masks, pretended selves, many social roles)

Intermediate Layer – – – – – – -*Unconscious Secondary Drives* (antisocial impulses, repressed thoughts and emotions, unexpressed resentments)

Core Layer – – – – – – – — *Real Self* (feelings, needs, basic impulses)

Authoritarian Character Structure
(in condition of more or less permanent internalized threat)

pretensions. They also must learn to function in environments characterized by guilt, disowned parts of self, and unexpressed resentments toward authorities. "On the surface layer of his or her personality," observed Reich (1970: xi), "the average person is reserved, polite, compassionate, responsible, conscientious." This exterior becomes progressively disconnected, however, from the authentic, inner self of persons as this basic split develops between their real and public selves.

2) INTERMEDIATE LAYER. This intermediate character layer is the result of repression. It consists of cruel, sadistic, unacceptable impulses that are the residues of the dual nature dilemma. This layer of personality was characterized by Freud as the "unconscious" and by Reich as "secondary drives." Thus, behind the outward veneer of the socially conditioned domesticated person are the repressed impulses that, according to Freud, have

grown like a fungus in the dark and consequently possess the force of a dammed-up reservoir of water.

> There would be no social tragedy of the human animal if this surface layer of the personality were in direct contact with the deep natural core. This, unfortunately, is not the case. The surface layer of social cooperation is not in contact with the deep biologic core of one's selfhood; it is borne by a *second*, an intermediate character layer, which consists exclusively of cruel, sadistic, lascivious, rapacious, and envious impulses. It represents the Freudian 'unconscious' or 'what is repressed.' (Reich, 1970: xi)

While internalized social controls often lead to self-hatred and self-destructiveness, it can be added that this intermediate layer of character is also the source of much of the destructiveness and hostility that persons feel toward others and the outside world. In authoritarian environments, Fromm (1941: 202) emphasized, "I can escape the feeling of my own powerlessness in comparison with the world outside of myself by destroying it." Thus, the destruction of the world is "the last, almost desperate attempt to save myself from being crushed by it."[10]

Dominated persons are often in situations where they are powerless to realize their own capacities and potentials. They are in social environments in which their inner security and spontaneity is sharply curtailed by the actions and threats of outside powerful others. In these situations, Fromm concluded:

> The more the drive toward life is thwarted, the stronger is the drive toward destruction; the more life is realized, the less is the strength of destructiveness. *Destructiveness is the outcome of unlived life.* Those individual and social conditions that make for suppression of life produce the passion from which the particular hostile tendencies—either against others or against oneself—are nourished. (1941: 207)

3) CORE LAYER. If one penetrates this intermediate layer of repressed, antisocial impulses deeper into the biological substratum of persons, one discovers, suggested Reich, a third layer of character which can be called the biological core. This inner character layer is composed of people's authentic feelings, needs, and impulses.

> In this core, under favorable social conditions, man is an essentially honest, industrious, cooperative, loving, and,

if motivated, rationally hating animal. Yet it is not at all possible to bring about a loosening of the character structure of present-day man by penetrating to this deepest and so promising layer without first eliminating the nongenuine, spuriously social surface. Drop the mask of cultivation, and it is not natural sociability that prevails at first, but only the perverse, sadistic character layer.

It is this unfortunate structuralization that is responsible for the fact that every natural, social, or libidinous impulse that wants to spring into action from the biologic core has to pass through the layer of secondary perverse drives and is thereby distorted. This distortion transforms the original social nature of the natural impulses and makes it perverse, thus inhibiting every genuine expression of life. (Reich, 1970: xi–xii)

Therefore, persons in authoritarian environments learn to armor themselves as a defense, first from external social domination and then later, after the development of a socially imposed conscience, as a protection from their own unacceptable thoughts and emotions.

Psychiatrist Frantz Fanon (1967) described how this pervasive split between the surface and core layers of personality develops among black persons in the African Antilles. Blacks growing up in this society are confronted with a basic dilemma: turn white or disappear. The official language spoken is French, and teachers keep a close watch over the black children to make sure they do not use their native Creole. Blacks are frequently insulted by whites and kept in constant subjection. When addressing black persons, for instance, whites behave like adults with children, observed Fanon; they start smirking, patronizing, and whispering. In the colonialized Antillean culture, black also symbolizes evil, sin, ugliness, and darkness. Black children are sung French love songs by their mothers, in which there is no mention of black persons. Later they begin reading white books and gradually begin to take into themselves the prejudices, myths, and folklore that have come to them from Europe.

Black school children thus learn to identify themselves with the white explorer, the bringer of civilization, the white person who carries truth to the savages. They recognize that the Negro is the symbol of sin and consequently develop a deep sense of inferiority and try not to think of themselves as black persons. They want to escape being themselves, and the deep insecurity and inferiority feelings falsify both their internal and external relations. As Fanon (1967: 60) stated, "in the man of color there is constant effort to run away from his own individuality, to annihilate his own presence." Having been made to feel inferior, the Antillean black "proceeds from humiliating insecurity through strongly voiced self-accusation to despair."

Ambivalence Toward Freedom

As we have seen, the relations of domination produce divided and contradictory persons. Having been socialized to rely upon outside controls and having never been given responsibility for their own lives, domesticated persons naturally lack confidence in their own capabilities. While longing for freedom, they nevertheless grow to fear freedom and to doubt their own capacity to govern themselves. "If we take 'freedom' to mean first and foremost the responsibility for each individual to shape personal, occupational, and social existence in a rational way," stated Reich (1970: 320), "then it can be said that there is no greater fear than the fear of the creation of general freedom."

Therefore, while recognizing that their socialization for dependency restricts and limits their possibilities for growth, socially reinforced persons also have been taught to doubt their own abilities. Authoritarian socialization has made them both themselves and the authority figures whose images they have incorporated. As Freire emphasized, "the oppressed suffer from the duality which has established itself in their innermost being. They discover that without freedom they cannot exist authentically. Yet, although they desire authentic existence, they fear it" (1970: 32).

The separation, then, from consciousness has now become complete. As a final irony, individuals have become so dependent upon external authority that they are no longer preoccupied with the task of achieving freedom. Rather, they have come to rely upon outside controls as a basis for their conduct and to look upon domestication as the natural mode of human existence.

Separation from Other Persons

Authoritarian environments create many conflicts and problems within persons which also lead to interpersonal separation. One of these basic inner contradictions relates to the necessary development of ambivalent love-hate attitudes toward authority figures. A fundamental fact in authoritarian homes, for instance, is that children are utterly and completely dependent on the wishes and commands of their parents who, at the same time, have appropriated the authority to suppress and frustrate many of their children's wishes and basic growth impulses. Thus, interrelated with children's natural feelings of love and affection for their parents are also anger and resentment resulting from these arbitrary socially imposed restrictions.

Depending on individual circumstances, these personal conflicts produced by authoritarian relations may be reflected in people's lives in various ways. Below are considered three basic conflict reduction mechanisms that both result from, and further reinforce, this severance of essential social relations: *identification with authority, compulsive rebelliousness,* and *resignation.*

Identification with Authority

This basic ambivalence toward authority produced by dominance relations can be extremely uncomfortable, leading persons to repress either their dependency feelings (and become generally and compulsively rebellious), or repress their hostile feelings (and compulsively identify with the outside authority). By identification, Reich explained (1970: 46), is meant "the process whereby a person begins to feel at one with another person, adopts that person's characteristics and attitudes, and in his fantasy puts himself in the other person's place. This process entails an actual change in the identifying person, inasmuch as the latter 'internalizes' characteristics of his model."

The child, therefore, comes to see that the way to secure his parents' love and approval is to strive to become like them. By striving to be like his father, for instance, the boy wins his father's approval and also comes closer to the possibility of eventually possessing the power, privilege, and independence that the father now has. As Reich further explained,

> Identification comes about in such a way that, say, the person who brings up a child and who is simultaneously loved and hated by the child is 'absorbed' by it: the child 'identifies' with the teacher, i.e., makes the teacher's attitudes or precepts its own. . . . This is based on the following contradiction or conflict: 'I love X; because he is my teacher, he forbids me to do many things, and for that reason I hate

him; I would like to destroy or eliminate him, but I also love him and for that reason I want him to stay.' From this contradictory situation, which cannot continue as such if the conflicting urges reach a certain intensity, there is the following way out: 'I absorb him, I identify myself with him, I destroy him (i.e., my relationship with him) in the outside world, but I keep him within myself in an altered form: I have destroyed him and yet he stays.' (1972: 35–36)

In the short run, persons are able to reduce their natural ambivalence toward their parents and other authority figures through identification. This involves a stifling of their anger and the natural expression of their rebelliousness, however, and as a result of this incorporation of authority, much of this anger must be turned inward against the "bad" parts of themselves. People's consciences and internalized standards impel them to live up to the artificial demands and expectations of parental authority and convert feelings of anger and rebellion into feelings of guilt about those parts of themselves that fail to meet these internalized social standards.

A considerable amount of aggressiveness must be developed in the child against the authority which prevents him from having his first, but nonetheless his most important, satisfactions, whatever the kind of instinctual deprivation that is demanded of him may be; but he is obliged to renounce the satisfaction of this revengeful aggressiveness. He finds his way out of this economically difficult situation with the help of familiar mechanisms. By means of identification he takes the unattackable authority into himself. The authority now turns into his superego and enters into possession of all the aggressiveness which a child would have liked to exercise against it. (Freud, 1961: 76)

In authoritarian environments, it is these relations of domination that provide individuals with their models of "personhood." Instead of striving for freedom, they themselves often want to dominate others. They are submerged in the reality of domination, and their consciousness is only an awareness of existence as lived within the context of power relations. "It is a rare peasant," observed Freire (1970: 30), "who, once 'promoted' to overseer, does not become more of a tyrant toward his former comrades than the owner himself." Therefore, it is not to achieve freedom that such peasants desire agrarian reform but in order to become bosses over other workers.

Extensively studied after the Second World War were the authoritarian personality tendencies of persons who were attracted to Hitler and similar right-wing political movements.[11] This "Fascist mentality," Reich (1970, originally published 1934) had earlier proposed, was really the mentality of the "little man, who is enslaved and craves authority and is at the same time rebellious." Such persons are the "drill sergeants of our highly industrialized civilization." Basic to this Fascist mentality, Fromm (1941: 163) later suggested, was a desperate attempt to "escape from freedom" through giving up "the independence of one's individual self" and fusing "one's self with somebody or something outside of oneself in order to acquire the strength which the individual self is lacking." These pro-Fascist tendencies were defensive predispositions to identify with authority and to conform uncritically with standards and commands supported by these authority figures.

As later researched, such pro-Fascist tendencies also were found to be the outcome of childhood situations, in which children had learned to repress most of their hostility against their immediate authorities—their parents—which formed the basis for the later prevailing tendency to identify with authority in general. The following portrait of such persons emerged from this extensive research tradition, as summarized by Greenstein:

> The foregoing authoritarian traits hang together in a fashion which puts little strain on our common sense: dominance of subordinates; deference toward superiors; sensitivity to power relationships; need to perceive the world in a highly structured fashion; excessive use of stereotypes; and adherence to whatever values are conventional in one's setting. (1973: 64–65)

Authoritarians are thus persons with strong but ambivalent dispositions toward figures of authority. Denial of the negative side of these feelings is central to such persons' functioning. Moreover, they are able to conceal their rage toward authority only by extensive repression of critical, or otherwise unacceptable, impulses toward authority and a bending over backward in excessive praise of it. This identification with authority is therefore generally disruptive of essential relations between persons, and the resulting hostility tends to be rechanneled toward those perceived as weak and powerless.

Compulsive Rebelliousness

Instead of identifying with and repressing hostilities toward authorities, persons socialized in authoritarian environments may repress the other side of their basic social ambivalence: their feelings of dependency and reliance upon authority. This may result in a generalized antiauthoritarian rebelliousness that in many ways appears to be the antithesis of the authoritarian syndrome described above. Bay (1958: 206) defined this compulsive rebelliousness "as a defensive predisposition to oppose uncritically standards and commands supported by authorities." Such a disposition arises as a result of children repressing their "dependency needs" toward their parents and results in the severing of essential relationships with themselves and other persons.

Freud (1966) originally proposed that rebellious boys were frequently unable to identify fully with their fathers and therefore unable to resolve their infantile hostilities toward authority. Horney (1945: 63–72) also suggested that the tendency to "move against" people can become a basic orientation for persons growing up in hostile social environments. This aggressive attitude seems to be an outgrowth of competitive, power-oriented social relations and results in persons who strongly repress the "softer tendencies" in themselves and who distrust and are uncooperative with outside authorities.

In environments characterized by outside domination, this anger and rebelliousness may be intensely felt but not fully expressed. A characteristic of many socially conditioned persons, for instance, is their "passive aggressiveness"; their anger toward authority may be manifested in such actions as being late for appointments or by sulken stares, but it is seldom expressed openly. Rather than being directly stated, this anger smolders inside them in the form of resentments. As expression of an impasse, such resentments can be particularly destructive with regard to human growth. Perls explained this problem:

> Anything unexpressed which wants to be expressed can make you feel uncomfortable. And one of the most common unexpressed experiences is the resentment. This is the unfinished situation *par excellence*. If you are resentful, you're stuck; you neither can move forward and have it out, express your anger, change the world so that you'll get satisfaction nor can you let go and forget whatever disturbs you. (1969: 48)

Perhaps the most important resentments in most persons' lives are those they hold against the original authority figures in their lives—their parents. "Until you are willing to let go of your parents," concluded Perls (1969: 42), "you continue to conceive of yourself as a child. To let go of parents and forgive them is the hardest thing for most people to do."

Like identification with authority, then, this generalized rebelliousness is a compulsive character trait that is disruptive of essential interpersonal relations. The scars of a repressive, authoritarian upbringing are such that these persons tend to lack the empathy and understanding necessary for successful collective endeavors and, consequently, for their own personal growth.

Resignation

Besides identification with authority and compulsive rebelliousness, a third conflict reduction mechanism in authoritarian environments is that of resignation. Instead of allowing themselves to be caught up in this "no-win" situation of either repressing their hostility or dependency feelings toward authority, some persons learn to cope with this outside domination by detaching themselves and withdrawing their energies from these essential social relations. Horney explained this defensive solution:

> In short there was an environment which made explicit and implicit demands for him to fit in this way or that way and threatened to engulf him without sufficient regard for his individuality, not to speak of encouraging his personal growth. So the child is torn for a longer or shorter time between futile attempts to get affection and interest and resenting the bonds put around him. He solves this early conflict by withdrawing from others. By putting an emotional distance between himself and others, he sets his conflict out of operation. He no longer wants others' affection nor does he want to fight them. Hence he is no longer torn by contradictory feelings toward them and manages to get along with them on a fairly even keel. Moreover, by withdrawing into a world of his own, he saves his individuality from being altogether cramped and engulfed. (1950: 275)

Putting emotional distance between themselves and their significant others, however, usually impairs essential social relations. As Horney (1950: 264–65) observed, such persons may enjoy only distant or transitory relationships and must constantly repress tendencies to become more emotionally involved. They must not become so attached to others as to need their company, their assistance, or sometimes even sexual relations with them. Such persons become onlookers at life and learn to expect little from others. Even in emergencies it may not occur to them to ask for help. Although a necessary tactic to escape outside domination, this avoidance of close emotional attachments with other persons is ultimately destructive of freedom and the development of people's full human potentialities.

Alienation and Social Dependency

Once persons learn to cope with authority figures by employing techniques such as identification, compulsive rebelliousness, or resignation, these behavior patterns tend to recur over and over again as they habitually repeat successful prior patterns in their dealings with new sets of authority figures in their lives. A tragedy of domination is its generalizing effect. The problems with new authorities tend merely to be "new editions of the old conflict" in the context of which persons "would like to behave in the same ways as they did in the past" (Freud, 1966: 454). This phenomenon was labeled "transference" by Freud, who observed that in therapy persons often expressed many positive and negative attitudes originally developed in their relationships with dominating parents. As he remarked regarding the relationship between male therapists and female patients,

> Transference can appear as a passionate demand for love or in more moderate forms; in place of a wish to be loved, a wish can emerge between a girl and an old man to be received as a favorite daughter; the libidinal desire can be toned down into a proposal for an inseparable, but ideally nonsensual, friendship. Some women succeed in sublimating the transference and in moulding it till it achieves a kind of viability; others must express it in its crude, original, and for the most part, impossible form. (Freud, 1966: 442)

Therefore, for persons who have adapted to the relations of domination by identifying with authority, for instance, the original motive may have been to achieve their father's affection and to gain, at least vicariously, some of his independence and power. Having successfully reduced these tensions in their lives on this initial occasion, however, these persons are increasingly more likely to identify with other authorities in the future when they again experience the contradictions engendered by authoritarian relations. In turn, then, these relations of domination slowly affect the whole of their existence, gradually severing ever larger portions of their essential ties with the outside world.

Having socialized persons for dependency and reliance upon outside authority in their lives, there is a particularly harmful and insidious set of self-justifying expectations that often are employed in authoritarian societies such as ours. Being predicated on the assumption that individuals must be molded and controlled from the outside, the institutions and social relations deny these persons the resources, experiences, and training that would be necessary to make them truly independent, self-regulating persons. As a product of their upbringings and general experiences of life, such dominated persons often have little confidence in themselves. This fact is then turned against them by the institutional guardians as a justification for the manager-controlled homes, schools, and workplaces that have caused these human deformities in the first place. Thus, this process of progressive alienation becomes a vicious cycle, feeding upon and simultaneously reinforcing itself.

The various types of alienation discussed in this chapter combine and reinforce one another. Becoming separated from their activities, persons experience reduced feedback on their capabilities and potential achievements. Separation from consciousness causes further isolation and insecurity and can produce complicating compulsions and phobias that appear as neurotic symptoms. These types of alienation are further reinforced by separation from other persons whose relations sustain individuals' language and conscious capacities and from the communal context within which most of their potential human achievements can take place.

The cumulative effect of these partial alienations, as vividly portrayed in the cases of advanced mental illness, is a more or less complete and enduring separation from reality. There is a progressive separation of real and public selves as this process relates increasingly to larger areas of the individual's existence.

> We have long observed that every neurosis has the result, and therefore probably the purpose, of forcing the patient out of real life, of alienating him from actuality. . . . The neurotic turns away from reality because he finds it unbearable—either the whole or parts of it. The most extreme type of this alienation from reality is shown in certain cases of

hallucinatory psychosis which aim at denying the existence of the particular event that occasioned the outbreak of insanity. But actually every neurotic does the same with some fragment of reality. (Freud, 1957: 38)

Just as each of these types of partial alienation can be traced back to their roots in authoritarian social environments, thus also can this more total alienation from reality be seen as a product of these relations of domination, at least in instances where this occurs among persons with "normal" biological inheritances. Depending upon the severity, consistency, and date of onset of the authoritarian suppression and its developmental history, persons will display the scars of their domination through reduced human capabilities and potentials for relating to the outside world.

Hierarchy, therefore, produces alienation. In direct opposition with the characteristics of free persons described in Chapter 1, such authoritarian environments serve to create individuals who are less open to experience, who are insincere, fragmented, and plagued by self-doubts, and who are often uncaring and possess generally authoritarian character structures.

How, then, can this domination be transcended? What are some of the characteristics of the homes, schools, and workplaces that strengthen and support the essential relations between persons and other people, the outside world, and themselves? How, in other words, can social conditions be created that facilitate the development of human freedom? Reinforced by the general alienation perspective described in this chapter, it is this reverse question regarding the nature of growth-producing social environments that will be discussed in subsequent chapters.

PART TWO
Freedom and American Society

3
Women, Men, and the Modern Origins of Domination

Throughout history people have knocked their heads against the riddle of the nature of feminity. . . . Nor will *you* have escaped worrying over the problem—those of you who are men; to those of you who are women this will not apply— you are yourselves the problem.

—SIGMUND FREUD

Three things have been difficult to tame: oceans, fools, and women. We may soon be able to tame the ocean; fools and women will take a little longer.

—SPIRO T. AGNEW, former
U.S. vice-president

Freedom, as we have seen, is not essentially a personal matter. Both our individual troubles, on the one hand, and our potential accomplishments and skills, on the other, are affected innumerable and varied ways by the overall nature of our social and physical environments. At this point, we are confronted with a difficult perceptual problem. Because the reality and general contours of these underlying institutional and social forces often remain unconscious and hidden from view, our understanding of ourselves is limited to our immediate experiences and the private orbits in which we live. Our vision, therefore, is often confined "to close-up scenes of job, family, and neighborhood," and we fail to grasp the essential connections, as Mills (1959: 4) declared, between our own private problems and the underlying social forces that are responsible for them.

59

In a large city when only one person is unemployed, observed Mills (1959: 9), that may be a case of individual problems relating to the character, skills, and immediate opportunities open to that single person. However, when in a nation of 100 million salaried workers 10 million experience forced joblessness, that is a public issue, and "we may not hope to find its solution within the range of opportunities open to any one person." In this latter situation, then, understanding the problem and its possible solutions requires us to consider how society itself is structured.[1] We must therefore possess the general ability, in other words, to translate our personal troubles into public issues. More generally, Mills continued,

> In so far as an economy is so arranged that slumps occur, the problem of unemployment becomes incapable of personal solution. In so far as war is inherent in the nation-state system, and in the uneven industrialization of the world, the ordinary individual in his restricted milieu will be powerless—with or without psychiatric aid—to solve the troubles this system or lack of system imposes upon him. In so far as the family as an institution turns women into darling little slaves and men into their chief providers and unweaned dependents, the problem of a satisfactory marriage remains incapable of purely private solution. (1959: 10)

If hierarchy and authoritarian social relations are so antithetical to personal freedom, we must ask why these autocratic relations developed in American society in the first place and why they persist. Why, in other words, does the United States continue to be characterized by boss-dominated workplaces, teacher-dominated schools, administrator-dominated government agencies, and parent-dominated homes? What are some of the major obstacles to change, and what are the forces that prevent us from obtaining a more democratic society and more personal freedom and humanistic life-styles for ourselves? Finally, how might these authoritarian structures be transcended and replaced by a society in which persons themselves are in greater control of their own lives?

Thus, in Part Two we will consider the issues relating to the historical origins and development of social domination as it is anchored in major U.S. institutions, beginning in this chapter with the development of patriarchy and traditional gender relations between women and men and, in subsequent chapters,

proceeding to discuss work, schooling, and other principal institutional areas in American life. The problem is to understand
better some of the forces that serve to maintain and promote this
hierarchy and authoritarianism and that prevent us from obtaining the democratic and self-affirming life-styles that might otherwise characterize our lives.[2]

DEVELOPMENT OF EARLY RURAL PATRIARCHY

In modern society, institutions such as family living, business,
government, and formal education have become extremely specialized and more or less distinct and separate areas of life. In
the earlier America of the seventeenth through nineteenth centuries, these various areas of living were centered around one
primary institution—the family. Then, as now, it was the family
that was the "operating base" of daily living and the institution
that brought up new generations and taught them how to cope
with everyday life. In this earlier period the family also performed
many other basic institutional functions such as the care of the
sick and aged, formal education and career preparation of children, and economic production and the manufacturing of the
basic material necessities of life.

Early American life was largely self-sufficient, with most
men working as field laborers, storekeepers, or craftspersons, and
women performing the essential activities—processing food, caring for children, keeping house, gardening—and various home
industries such as weaving and clothesmaking. The family was
also the basic unit of social authority, with society organized into
separate households each ruled by the father (or grandfather)
who legally and socially represented the women and children.

Hierarchy in society was anchored in a patriarchal system
in which men, by virtue of their positions as heads of households,
thereby controlled both the production of the family members
and the processes of socialization and reproduction that took
place within the family context. Patriarchy was thus a system of
male dominance and female and child dependence, in which the
men's position as family heads was also supported by their ownership of property, ability to earn money, and extensive legal
rights over women and children. Within this authoritarian system, for instance, women were virtually forced into marriage and
failure to marry usually meant a lonely life. Furthermore, once
married "it was nearly impossible for a woman to choose not to

have children," observed Easton (1978: 16), "not only because birth control information was relatively unavailable, but also because everyone, including the woman herself, expected that once she married she would have children." Women who remained childless were therefore pitied and likely to regard themselves as failures.[3]

The traditional marriage service itself publicly declared women's general obedience to their husbands, their multiple domestic duties, and their lowly station in life. Although these dominance relations probably seemed perfectly natural to most couples contemplating marriage, some early "marriage contracts" eloquently displayed aspirations for more egalitarian and democratic family relations. In 1855, for instance, Lucy Stone and Henry Blackwell joined hands at their wedding and read aloud a statement that expressed their nontraditional conceptions of marriage. In part it declared:

> While we acknowledge our mutual affection by publicly assuming the relationship of husband and wife . . . we deem it a duty to declare that this act on our part implies no sanction of, nor promise of voluntary obedience to such of the present laws of marriage as refuse to recognize the wife as an independent rational being, while they confer upon the husband an injurious and unnatural superiority.

From the seventeenth to the nineteenth century, "civil death" aptly described women's status in social and political matters. There were several scattered instances during the prerevolutionary war period in which women voted in local elections, but suffrage for American women did not come about until the comparatively recent date of 1920. Moreover, the inferior status of women was further reinforced by religion.

> Next to common law, the most potent force in maintaining woman's subordinate position was religion. The colonists might be dissenters of one kind or another against the Church of England, but they were at one with it in believing that woman's place was determined by limitations of mind and body, a punishment for the original sin of Eve. However, in order to fit her for her proper role of motherhood, the Almighty had taken especial pains to endow her with such virtues as modesty, meekness, compassion, affability, and piety. (Flexner, 1974: 8)

Patriarchy also reinforced and perpetuated authoritarian relations between parents and children. Besides their responsibilities for the care of their wives, men were generally obliged to discipline and control their children as well as to oversee the daily execution of this parental discipline by their wives. In the popular 1709 pamphlet on childrearing, for instance, John Banks exclaimed that fathers who "neglect making use of the rod" will weep when they realize that their children have become "wild and wicked."[4]

The persistence of this general theme of parental control over children, based upon patriarchal power relations, is reflected in another of the most popular early child-care guides. James Nelson, in his book *An Essay on the Government of Children* (1735), argued that although individual children vary they nevertheless, "while young, may be compared with machines which are or should be set in motion or stopped at the will of others." For fathers, therefore, good upbringings "implied such a government of our children as tends to regulate their conduct by making their actions what they ought to be." Nelson further reasoned that

> The basis of government is authority. . . . Cities, armies, and kingdoms are all sustained by it and so too must private families be. By authority I do not mean that stern brow, that trembling awful distance . . . that favors more the tyrant than the parent. No, I mean a rational yet absolute exercise of the degree of power necessary for the regulating of the actions and dispositions of children till they become wise enough to govern themselves. (Quoted in Beekman, 1977: 60)

As was true regarding dominance over women, fathers' control of their children in this rural and small-town society was reinforced by the encompassing network of law, church pronouncements, and the general informal system of social traditions in the local community. In addition, it was from their parents that children learned most of their occupational skills and adult ways of living.

Analyzing the control of seventeenth-century fathers over their sons in rural Andover, Massachusetts, for instance, Philip Greven emphasized the long period of childhood dependency. He found that entrance into adulthood was commonly measured by the age of marriage, and for the sons in this community the average age was more than twenty-five years, with nearly one-quarter of the sons not marrying until after age thirty. Greven explained this tradition of late marriage by showing that the fathers were often very reluctant to allow their sons to go off on their own because the offsprings provided so much valuable labor on the fathers' farms.

Not only were the sons fully dependent upon their fathers as long as they remained at home but also, if the sons wanted to leave, they still needed parental assistance and money in order to purchase land elsewhere. Moreover, parental authority continued after marriage, since Greven found that a majority of the fathers "continued to own the land which they settled their sons upon from the time the older men received it . . . to the day of their deaths" (1978: 27). For the sons, therefore, independence from their fathers was not possible during the latters' lifetimes.

This somewhat stable and well-developed system of patriarchal control was thus instrumental in maintaining and perpetuating hierarchy in the largely rural and village preindustrial America. The authority of fathers as the heads of households was the relatively direct, personal, and effective dominance mechanism that confronted individuals throughout their lifetimes. Moreover, in these relatively stable rural and small-town communities, the influence of the fathers was reinforced by a whole cultural complex including a large body of local laws, customs, and religious prescriptions. This hierarchy also was reinforced by the fact that the production system in society was in general harmony with the socialization and reproduction process by which society perpetuated these authoritarian relations over time.

INDUSTRIALIZATION AND THE CHANGING CHARACTER OF THE FAMILY

Industrialism became the dominant mode of production in American society during the early nineteenth century, with the widespread development of factories and the increasing employment of wage laborers.[5] The proportion of industrial production doubled every decade between 1820 and 1860, for example, and productive property was increasingly replaced by wages as the economic basis of the family. Also during this early formative period in American capitalism, manufacturing was typically conducted in very small family-owned production units, averaging only about twelve employees as late as the 1850s (Ryan, 1979: 153).

Given the widespread poverty of the time, many women and children were desperate for employment and were available to employers looking for cheap labor. Following the pattern of the earlier English factories, many employers in such industries as weaving and textiles initially hired this cheaper child and female labor almost exclusively. The manufacturing labor force of 1 million U.S. workers in 1850, for instance, included an estimated 225,512 women, and the number of female factory workers increased steadily during the succeeding decades to 270,987 in 1860 and 323,370 in 1870 (Flexner, 1974: 78, 131).

The Struggle Over the "Family Wage"

Patriarchy and the traditional hierarchical division of labor within the home was increasingly threatened as women and children joined men in the factories. That these formerly subordinate persons could now earn wages separately from men undermined their dependence upon traditional family relations, and, once these families were brought together in factories, women and children were no longer directly supervised and controlled by the fathers but by foremen and managers. As Zaretsky (1976: 47–48) observed, "industrial capitalism required a rationalized, coordinated, and synchronized labor process undisturbed by community sentiment, family responsibilities, personal relations, or feelings."

Given the preceding centuries of general dependency and reliance upon patriarchal authority, women had several comparative disadvantages upon entering the wage labor force (Hartmann, 1979: 215). Having previously been excluded from many of the male-dominated guilds and skilled craft societies, women were often less well trained and had fewer occupational skills than did men. They also had been accustomed to lower wages than men in the limited wage labor tradition prevailing in preindustrial America, and this discriminatory tradition was perpetuated by employers who were driven by the logic of capitalism to hire labor as cheaply as possible.

Perhaps the greatest handicap for women competing for scarce jobs, however, was a result of the superior organization of men. As the recognized heads of households, males had traditionally voted in elections, held political offices, dominated the professions and dealt with many social and political matters affecting the community. Most early labor organizations were also male controlled, and these male workers increasingly resisted the wholesale entrance of children and women into the labor force and often sought to exclude them from union membership. In the 1840s, for instance, male-dominated labor organizations began calling for limits of eight hours of work per day for children nine to thirteen years of age and excluded the employment of younger children. "That male workers viewed the employment of women as a threat to their jobs is not surprising, given an economic system where competition among workers was characteristic," declared Hartmann (1979). Why their response was to attempt to exclude women rather than to organize them is explained, not by capitalism but by patriarchal relations between men and women; men wanted to ensure that women would continue to perform the appropriate tasks at home.

The policy of early American trade unions, therefore, generally became one of female exclusion, or of only limited female participation based upon "protective" legislation for women workers. An 1846 labor pamphlet, the *Ten-Hour Advocate*, proclaimed:

> It is needless for us to say, that all attempts to improve the morals and physical condition of female factory workers will be abortive, unless their hours are materially reduced. Indeed we may go so far as to say that females would be much better occupied in performing the domestic duties of the household, than following the never-tiring motion of machinery. We therefore hope the day is not distant when the husband will be able to provide for his wife and family, without sending the former to endure the drudgery of a cotton-mill. (Bridges and Hartmann, 1977: 19–20)

In a similar vein, although women always had been typesetters since the colonial period, the National Typographical Union in 1854 resolved not to "encourage by its act the employment of female compositors." In 1878, twenty years after the Cigarmakers International Union had stopped excluding women, the Cigarmakers' president, Adolf Strausser, proclaimed: "We have combated from its incipiency the movement of the introduction of female labor in any capacity whatever, be it bunch maker, roler, or what not." One year later Strausser further stated: "We cannot drive the females out of the trade, but we can restrict their daily quota of labor through factory laws. No girl under eighteen should be employed more than eight hours per day; all overwork should be prohibited" (Farley, 1978: 53–54).

One labor struggle that dominated the latter nineteenth century in the United States was the demand for a "family wage" by which the father-husband could receive a salary sufficient to support his entire family.[6] The establishment of the family wage system altered and stabilized patriarchal relations, making this traditional form of sexual hierarchy viable in a newly industrializing capitalist society. Moreover, this early resolution of problems between capitalism—with its need for cheap labor power—and patriarchy—with its need for continued domination of women—established the general pattern of gender relations, with men as breadwinners and providers and their spouses as stay-at-home mothers and general purpose supporters.

Separation of Women and Men

It was thus during this period that the belief in separate "spheres" for women and men began to dominate the ideology of the family. The image of woman increasingly became that of the mother-wife who was freed from labor outside the home and therefore could devote herself wholly to her husband and children.

In her study of the early stages of American industrialization, Ryan (1979) showed that it was not until the 1830s that female and male temperament became the object of widespread interest. It was also not until this period that male and female characters came to be expressed in the familiar dichotomies: rational/emotional, aggressive/passive, courageous/timid, and strong/delicate (Ryan, 1979: 153). After this time women were increasingly expected to define themselves in terms of housework, child care, and emotional support for their husbands. They were expected to be warm, supportive, emotional, and to complement the action-oriented personalities of men who, given these family wage arrangements, were assigned the breadwinning responsibilities for their families. The upbringing of women was therefore more restricted, with little girls often being expected to inhibit their natural impulses and display more passive "ladylike" and "feminine" qualities. The dominant image of women became that of the mother who was expected to devote her full attention to her family.

Men, on the other hand, were supposed to be the breadwinners and increasingly to define themselves in terms of their jobs, or "careers". It was the husband-father who was ultimately responsible for the financial and material well-being of the family, and thus he was expected to be "unemotional," especially with regard to displaying fear and vulnerability. The important characteristics of males were those of strength, dominance, and the ability to take charge of situations.

Heightened Childhood Dependency

The increasing separation of family and work life inevitably led to the increasing separation of women and men who were assigned separate spheres of influence and different personal attributes. The family wage system also excluded children from wage labor which heightened childhood dependency. Because in a wage labor society people's value tends to flow from their wages, children in this new economic order became viewed increasingly as "dependent" rather than family contributors. Keniston explained:

> The economic 'value' of children to families has changed. . . . If weighed in crass economic terms, children were once a boon to the family economy; now they become an enormous economic liability. The total costs of housing, feeding, and clothing one child as well as educating him or her through high school add up to more than $35,000 [in 1977] by very conservative estimates for a family living at a very modest level. . . . Moreover, as schooling has lengthened, the financial drain of having children is prolonged to an average of twenty years. Nor can children today be counted on for an economic return in the form of informal old-age assistance.[7] (1977: 14–15)

In the nineteenth century, children were first assigned a separate identity, and childhood was seen as a special time of life characterized by innocence and a lack of adult responsibilities (Aries, 1962). Instead of being just young adults or little people, children were seen as a special category of dependent human beings who needed much specialized care and "mothering."

Ryan (1979: 159–60), for example, demonstrated that as late as the 1830s childrearing was believed to be the obligation of both parents. Men were advised in the available child-care literature of their patriarchal responsibility to oversee the education and moral training of their offsprings and to supervise the vocational instruction and occupational placement of their sons. With the rise of the new "cult of motherhood" in the nineteenth century, however, women were given general responsibilities for their children's moral and social development as well as their physical well-being. Motherhood came to be seen as the woman's "one duty and function, that alone for which she was created," and this increased responsibility for the total development of children further heightened their general subordination and dependency upon their parents.

PATRIARCHY IN CRISIS

Patriarchy as a system of hierarchical control survived by adapting and accommodating itself to the emerging American urban-industrial realities. This accommodation was not without its price, as the system of dominating patriarchy was weakened by this taking away of the traditional functions of economic production from the direct supervision and control of the fathers. In the latter nineteenth century, the family was also less prominent in other important areas such as the formal education of children; the care of the aged, the sick, and the mentally ill; the imparting of basic religious attitudes and values; and the relief of the poor. With regard to health care, for example, a century ago most treatment of the sick was primarily a family function, whereas today the family plays a greatly diminished role in this area, with parents being responsible for following the doctor's orders (Keniston, 1977: 16–17).

This overall decline in marriage/family functions precipitated a general crisis in this institution by the end of the nineteenth century. Four developments gave rise to this crisis, according to Lasch (1977: 8–12): the increasing divorce rate, the falling birthrate among "the better sort of people," the changing position of women, and the so-called "revolution in morals." Between 1870 and 1920, for instance, the number of divorces grew fifteenfold, and by 1924 one out of every seven marriages ended in divorce. Champions of the "new morality" at the time also proclaimed the joys of the body, defended birth control and divorce, raised doubts about monogamy, and condemned community interference with sexual life.

Early Struggles for Women's Rights

The traditional restrictions of women's activities, by the mid-nineteenth century, were in increasing contradiction with the norm of equal opportunity that was held to govern public life, and this obvious contradiction led many women to demand the social and political rights that had always been granted to American men (Easton, 1978: 17–18). In the context of a society rapidly moving away from traditionalism, the patriarchal restrictions on women's activities appeared increasingly anachronistic. A capitalistic system that promised equality of opportunity to all was vulnerable to protest from groups such as blacks and women who had been excluded from these opportunities.

Ironically, many early advocates of equality for women came from the antislavery struggles that began after the Nat Turner slave revolt in 1831. It was in this abolitionist movement that many women first became conscious of their own oppressed position in society and learned to organize, hold public meetings, and conduct petition campaigns. "As abolitionists," explained Flexner (1974: 41), women "first won the right to speak in public, and began to evolve a philosophy of their place in society and of their basic rights." Moreover, these two movements to free slaves and liberate women generally reinforced and strengthened one another for the next quarter century.[8]

Injustice and sexism existed in the United States, but what was needed was leadership and a program. This was provided by the 1848 Seneca Falls Convention in New York, from which the beginning of the Women's Rights Movement in this country is commonly dated. Early leaders of this movement included Elizabeth Cady Stanton, an outstanding thinker and writer, and Susan B. Anthony, whose leadership was based primarily on her abilities as an organizer and strategist. Of immediate concern to women's rights advocates were such pressing matters as control by women of property and earnings, guardianship, divorce, opportunities for education and employment, lack of legal status (women still could not sue or bear witness), the whole concept of female inferiority perpetuated by established religion, and, two decades later, the right to vote (Flexner, 1974: 82).

Most nineteenth-century feminists did not attack the patriarchal family directly, however, but rather concerned themselves with these various secondary types of social and legal discrimination against women. This seems to have been a consequence of the fact that most women during this period had no real option to marriage. Because of their lack of education and job skills and the commonly accepted practices of discrimination against women in employment, most could not support themselves through their own labor. Furthermore, the absence of reliable contraception made celibacy or extramarital pregnancy the sexual consequences for women who abandoned the male-dominated marriage/family institution.

> The overwhelming majority of working women were much less skilled, earned much less money, and, more importantly, were herded into a very few all-women industries— garment and textile manufacturing, and domestic work. Such women lacked the very thing that was the nineteenth-century worker's source of dignity, pride, and sense of self-worth, and which suffragists hoped would provide the basis for working women's feminism, a skill. Put another way, the feminist vision of independence and equality with men had little meaning for women whose wages did not even reach the subsistence level and who had no male coworkers with whom they could demand equality. (DuBois, 1979: 143)

Therefore, by attacking many of the inequalities that existed in the patriarchal family, women's rights advocates during this period were often more prone to defend the institution of marriage than to condemn it. When Stanton began criticizing unconsenting sexual relations within marriage as "legalized prostitution" and seemed to be very close to attacking the institution of marriage itself, she found women less enthusiastic and her audiences began to fall off. "A too-public focus on the 'compulsory adulteries of the marriage bed,' and a call to women to leave it," observed DuBois (1979: 148), "alienated the women who, at the private parlor talks on marriage and maternity, had responded so enthusiastically."

Origins of the Modern Women's Movement

Having already confined itself to the fight for equality in public life, the feminist movement in the late nineteenth and early twentieth centuries became focused on the campaign for women's suffrage. When women's right to vote was finally won in 1920, the feminist movement began to lose much of its former mission and strength, not to reemerge as a vital force in American life until the mid-1960s. In this four-decade dormant period,

however, it became increasingly apparent that the right to vote
meant formal equality in public life, although it was not in itself
sufficient to guarantee full equality for women. Therefore, "the
new feminists reversed the priorities of their predecessors," concluded Easton (1978: 20). "While they recognized the importance
of continuing to fight for equality in the public arena, their central
concern was the question of women's subordination within the
family."

One source of the new feminism of the 1960s was a class
of educated, professional women who had arisen in increasing
numbers to management and professional positions in areas such
as government, the trade unions, and education. These women
had experienced first-hand humiliating discrimination on the job
in spite of their high positions and various degrees of guilt and
confusion for not fitting into their expected domestic feminine
roles. Because of the existing patterns of female job segregation
and sexual harassment, many of these women still found themselves in the position of quasi-housewives. As Friedan (1977:
102) explained regarding women in high government posts, "the
highest job to which women were being promoted had titles like
'Assistant to the Assistant Secretary of State' in charge of flower-
arranging. A new job would be created—to arrange fashion shows
or pick out paintings for embassies—outside the regular line of
promotion to decision-making jobs."

Another important root of the 1960s feminism was the civil
rights and antiwar movements. During this period many young
women found themselves again being drawn into public life as
part of the protests arising from "outrage at a society that pro-
fessed democratic and humanitarian principles while practicing
racism and military aggression" (Easton, 1978: 20). While these
social movements gave women a chance to be a meaningful part
of history, to develop organizing skills, and "to work with powerful role models—the strong, older black women who were the
backbone of many voter registration drives," these organizations
nevertheless maintained patterns of male dominance which kept
women from policymaking roles, perpetuating their dependency
as coffeemakers and typists (MacLean, 1980: 234). In short, these
movements "had opened for them a new sense of their own
potentials," while "simultaneously thrusting them into mental
domestic roles," concluded Evans (1979); modern "feminism was
born in that contradiction—the threatened loss of new possibility."

In the meantime, old patriarchal values had begun to crumble, so that the new feminism that emerged from both of these
sources did not merely focus upon the equal participation of

women in public life but also began to focus on the central problem of male domination of women in the family.

> These women were able to criticize the family in a way that their feminist forebearers could not because in the social milieu of the new feminists patriarchy was rapidly breaking down. Many of them were unmarried and quite able to support themselves; if they married, it was likely to be more than necessity, and they were likely to retain the ability to leave marriage if necessary. More importantly, those young women moved in a world in which the old patriarchal values were beginning to falter. A man whose education was in no way superior to his wife's, and whose work was, by his own standards, no more valuable than hers, might lack the old male self-confidence in proclaiming his superiority. A cultural vacuum had been created, and it was possible for the new feminism to walk into it and create a new set of values. (Easton, 1978: 25)

As a system of authoritarian social relations, patriarchy thus constrains freedom and human development in all the ways previously described and therefore has become increasingly vulnerable to enlightened social criticism in the modern period. These relations of domination both reflect and simultaneously create the inauthenticity, repression, and resentments that are essential features of alienated existence and, as described above, also further reduce the possibilities of growth-producing disclosure, honest feedback, modeling, and social support that are possible within the family context.

Problems Associated with the Breakdown of Patriarchy

It should be remembered that by patriarchy we do not simply mean male supremacy but rather a specific organization of family and society in which men, because they were heads of families, thereby "controlled not only the reproductive labor, but also the production by all family members" (Gordon and Hunter, 1977: 12). This system of domination prevailed in preindustrial Europe and the United States, and it was only with industrialization and the removal of both production and formal education from the home that undercut patriarchy's material base. Without property or skills to pass on to sons and deprived of much of their authority to shape the world views of their offsprings, proletarianized fathers lost much of their traditional power. This weakened state, in turn, left patriarchy vulnerable to attacks by advocates of women's rights and others who were able to describe and explain, with increasing effectiveness, the destructive effects of these hierarchical, male-dominated relations. "In the twentieth century, the virtually absolute economic and legal power that men once held over their families has been ended," exclaimed Easton (1978: 13). "As men lose their formal rights it becomes easier to attack the ideals of female inferiority and the division of labor between the sexes that were shaped by patriarchy."

The establishment of democratic family and gender relations, however, would mean the creation of an androgynous, genderless society, "in which one's sexual anatomy is irrelevant to who one is, what one does, and with whom one makes love" (Rubin, 1975: 204). Simply undermining the material basis and institutional supports for patriarchy is not, in itself, sufficient to undermine male domination generally or to bring about a genderless society. Rather, it means that if men are to continue to dominate at home, in the factory, or in their personal relations with both women and children, they must, consciously or unconsciously, rely upon either more subtle or less legitimate means of control. Below we will consider some of the basic ways that male domination continues to thrive and adapt in this modern postpatriarchal period in which traditional paternal values and ideological justifications are fading.

MODERN GENDER AS A PROBLEM

What about modern women and men? Having looked at the manner in which gender stereotypes and roles developed during the nineteenth century, what can we now conclude concerning the lives of contemporary persons? What can we say about modern problems facing women and men? One problem in particular is that, whereas in 1900 work outside the home was almost totally dominated by men, who made up about 82 percent of the work force, by 1980 males were among only 58 percent of all those employed, with women now constituting 42 percent of the total labor force. Thus, in 1980, 45 percent of women with at least one child under six years old worked for wages, as did 59.1 percent of those with children whose ages ranged from six to sixteen. As opposed to the popular stereotype, most contemporary female wage-earners are employed apparently because of economic necessity rather than for pleasure or self-fulfillment, as indicated by the fact that, in 1980, 44 percent of all working women were either single, widowed, divorced, or separated. Moreover, by this time nearly one out of every seven families in the United States was headed by a single female parent.

What is even more surprising, however, is the generally widening income gap between employed women and men. In 1939, for instance, the median earnings of full-time and year-round working women was 72 percent of men's incomes. By 1960 the earning power of women had dropped to 61 percent of those of males, and by 1980 it had declined to about 59 percent, where it has apparently remained. The hardest hit category has been women with only an elementary-school education; in 1980 they averaged just 54.3 percent of the salaries of men. Women with a high-school degree did slightly better, making 57.6 percent of men's earnings, with college-educated women averaging 59.2 percent. Among those with some graduate training, the average was 65.3 percent of their male comrades.[9]

Pink-collar Occupations

Women have been making tremendous gains in traditional male-dominated occupations during the last decade, or have they? The fact is that, in the rapidly expanding female labor force, the overwhelming proportion of new women workers, as a whole, has been employed in traditional female occupations. Various studies have shown that the rate of occupational segregation by sex is greater today, or maybe even somewhat greater, than at the turn of the century.[10] According to Blau and Hendricks (1979), more than one-half of all working women in 1978 were in only 21 of the 250 detailed occupations listed by the U.S. Bureau of the Census. Moreover, just 5 of those 21 occupations—secretary, household worker, bookkeeper, elementary-school teacher, and waitress—accounted for more than one-fourth of all working women. This continued job segregation was further emphasized by the fact that a majority of all female wage-earners at that time were in occupations in which 70 percent or more of their coworkers were also women. Thus, despite real employment gains by women in some areas, men continue to monopolize most of the best jobs in this society, and most women remain in the lower status and lesser paid female occupations.

Furthermore, in contrast to the 29 percent of the male labor force which is unionized, only about 12 percent of women workers now enjoy union protection. Partly because of the general decline in the strength of the labor movement since World War Two, there has been an overall drop in the proportion of women workers who are unionized, from 15 percent in 1952 to the current 12 percent (Milkman, 1980). Established unions have generally failed to make large-scale attempts to organize clerical and service workers, departing from the traditions of the earlier unionists who successfully organized in the female-dominated textile and garment industries. Sexism also continues to flourish in the unions, with the American Federation of Labor for many years protecting male members' access to scarce jobs by supporting legislation excluding women from such jobs as meter readers, elevator operators, and streetcar conductors as well as from night work and highly paid overtime (Cluster and Rutter, 1980: 52).

Sexual Harassment

In addition to job segregation, women are kept in a position of economic inferiority by overt or more subtle pressures in the job situation itself, many of which have now come to be labeled as "sexual harassment." Most broadly defined, sexual harassment is "unsolicited nonreciprocal male behavior that asserts a woman's sex role over her function as worker" (Farley, 1978: 33). It can include any or all of the following: verbal sexual suggestions or jokes; constant leering or ogling; brushing against a woman's body "accidentally"; a friendly pat, squeeze, or pinch; a quick kiss; the indecent proposition backed by the threat of loss of job; and forced sexual relations.[11]

The sexual harassment of women in all its many forms involves an act of aggression or assertion of dominance by men that contributes to keeping women subordinate at work. As MacKinnon (1979: 1) observed, "women employed in the paid labor force, typically hired 'as women,' dependent upon their income and lacking job alternatives, are particularly vulnerable to intimate violation in the form of sexual abuse at work." What is lost in this situation is an understanding of the real female human being as a hard working person and an important contributor to the work force.

A growing number of studies document the widespread incidence of sexual harassment in U.S. workplaces.[12] *Redbook* magazine in 1976, for example, conducted a survey, to which more than 9,000 women responded. Of those women partici- pating in the study, over 92 percent reported sexual harassment as a problem, with a majority describing it as serious. Nine out of ten respondents reported they had personally experienced one or more forms of unwanted sexual attentions on the job. Some of the difficulties in dealing with sexual harassment are also shown by a study of women working at the United Nations Secretariat where women stated that when this harassment was ignored it eventually worsened in about 75 percent of the cases, and about one-fourth of the women who ignored it were even- tually hit with on-the-job penalties.

A common response of women facing sexual harassment is to quit their jobs, if not immediately then eventually as the pressures become worse. "It is not uncommon to find women who have left two, three, and even five or more jobs over their working career because of sexual harassment," reported Farley.

> To make a decision women must weigh in the balance economic necessity, prospects for other jobs, a good rec- ommendation rather than a poor one, the chances of being fired, the attitudes of husband, friends, lover, or parents, interest in the job and rate of pay, the number of times the abuse had been experienced and countless other factors. Usually after weighing each of these variables, a woman will decide to quit. This decision is basically compatible with her sex-role conditioning, since it permits escape with- out a scene and, no less important, promises the best chance of obtaining future work. (Farley, 1978: 43–44)

The hidden injuries of sexual harassment involve both the tangible costs of women changing jobs and the more subtle psy- chological effects of facing the consequences of their own pow- erlessness. "The degradation, humiliation, frustration, and severe self-criticism that accompanies this coerced situation is a torture equaled in severity to job loss," explained Waldron (1969: 1). "Regardless of which avenue the woman travels, whether refusal/ confrontation or coerced compliance, she is faced with loss of self-respect." Therefore, often reinforcing the maintenance of job segregation and also contributing independently to male domi- nation at work is this general mechanism of sexual harassment.

> The sexual harassment of women at work arose out of a man's need to maintain his control of female labor. This tactic of nonreciprocal aggression is a major element in the

maintenance of job segregation by sex. It ensures that female
wages stay low, weakens women's employment position by
undermining female seniority, and keeps women too divided
so they are incapable of organizing to change their situation.
(Farley, 1978: 261)

Mechanisms such as job segregation and sexual harassment
thus have served to perpetuate male domination in an age when
the traditional institutional supports for patriarchy are declining.
The devices allow men to control women's labor even though
males are no longer granted this privilege merely by being designated the formal heads of households. These tactics also promote
division and undermine the potential solidarity between men and
women in dealing with the common problems and concerns that
affect us all. The hierarchical society adapts to new conditions,
but the relations of domination themselves are preserved and the
consequences of alienation and divided selves are perpetuated.

Barriers to Shared Parenting

The increasing numbers of women working outside the home
for pay have also changed the basic structure of the American
family. Whereas a quarter century ago 56 of 100 families were
supported by the husband's income alone, in 1980 the U.S. Labor
Department indicated that about 60 percent of American hus-
band-wife households have at least two wage-earners. Current
projections are that by 1990 perhaps only about one in four
married women will be full-time housewives and mothers (Smith
et al., 1980). Combining household and paid labor, Walker and
Woods (1976) found that the working women they studied labored
an average of seventy-six hours per week, including the thirty-
three hours spent on housework. By contrast, men averaged a
little over ten hours per week and showed no significant variation
relative to either their hours of paid labor or the amount of
outside work by their wives. "While many fathers have come
forward to 'help out' with kids and housework, doing more work
in the family than in our parents' time," explained Ehrensaft
(1980: 42), "the full sharing of parenting between women and
men remains a rare phenomenon."
    The establishment of democratic family-gender relations in
society, however, would require the equal sharing of childrearing
and household tasks. Such arrangements would allow women

relief from their current double duties as wage-earners and as primary mothers-housewives, while simultaneously allowing men more access to their own children and to the experience and joys of childrearing. Children also would gain from these shared parenting arrangements since now they would have closer contact with both women and men.

> We women who have shared parenting with men know the tremendous support and comfort (and luxury) of not being the only one there for our children. We see the opportunities to develop the many facets of ourselves not as easily afforded to our mothers or to other women who have carried the primary load of parenting. We watch our children benefit from the full access to two rather than one primary nurturing figure, affording them intimacy with both women and men, a richer, more complex emotional milieu, role models that challenge gender stereotypes. We see men able to develop more fully the nurturant parts of themselves as fathers, an opportunity often historically denied to men. And we develop close, open, and more equal relationships between men and women as we grapple with the daily ups and downs of parenting together. (Ehrensaft, 1980: 47)

Why, despite this increased participation by women in the labor force, have the labor force, the traditional hierarchical relations, and unequal division of labor within the family been so impervious to change? Why, in other words, have women as well as men often resisted the equal sharing of parenting responsibilities? Certainly the lack of overall institutional supports in the larger society has hindered the formation of shared parenting arrangements. Despite the recent growth in the number of daycare centers in the United States, for instance, it is estimated that currently such centers would accommodate only about 4 percent of all three to six year olds of working mothers (Custer and Rutter, 1980: 56). Inadequate maternity policies at the workplace and lack of part-time jobs and jobs with flexible hours also undoubtedly hinder this movement toward more democratic family-gender relations.

Perhaps more important, however, is the fact that most U.S. working women are stuck in stereotyped female jobs, as described above. While men have traditionally dominated the public sphere of work, the woman's domain has been in the home and the family. "Particularly in the rearing of children, it is often her primary (or only) sphere of power," stated Ehrensaft.

> For all the oppressive and debilitating effects of the insti-
> tution of motherhood, woman *does* not get social credit for
> being a 'good' mother. She also accrues for herself some
> sense of control and authority in the growth and develop-
> ment of her children. As a mother she is afforded the oppor-
> tunity for genuine human interaction in contrast to the
> alienation and depersonalization of the workplace. (Ehren-
> saft, 1980: 47–48)

Shared parenting therefore demands that the mother give
up power in her domain, the domestic sphere, often with little
compensation in increased power from the occupational sphere.
Given the prevailing pattern of job segregation and sexual harassment, she is likely to have less earning power, less job opportunity, less creative work, and less occupational recognition than
her husband. She is also likely to experience many guilt feelings
for not living up to her own internalized expectations of being a
good traditional wife and mother. Men, too, may resist shared
household and parenting responsibilities since taking on the additional hassles of child care puts them at a competitive occupational disadvantage with men who have only minimal parenting
responsibilities; they now have committed themselves to a sphere
that brings little social recognition and presents many additional
problems and frustrations.

Often sharing the physical tasks between mothers and fathers is less difficult than sharing the deeper psychological responsibilities for parenting. Whereas men may help out with the
dishes or looking after the kids, it is the mother who really shoulders the major mental load associated with childrearing. Typical
in many homes, therefore, are mothers who carry around in their
heads knowledge of shoes to be repaired, dental checkups to be
scheduled, and clothes to be mended. Thus, hierarchy is perpetuated by habit, resistance to change, and this deeply internalized "mother guilt" that is residue of the previous centuries
of patriarchal domination.

POWER AND GENDER RELATIONS

Gender-based power relations persist in areas such as work and
family living despite the overall weakening of traditional patriarchal authority. Deprived of legal institutional supports, men have
had to adapt to these changing conditions, often finding more
subtle or less legitimate methods of control. Below are described

some of the ways in which this male domination is now being expressed in the general relations between women and men in American society.[13]

EMOTIONAL WITHDRAWAL.   Since contemporary women and men often have fewer social support networks outside the family, they are therefore more likely to turn to their spouses for intimacy. As traditional sources of male power in the family begin to slip away, men may be more prone to use emotional withdrawal as a power tactic. In turn, because of the greater vulnerability that deep emotional involvement implies, women also may withhold intimacy and emotional expression from men. Looking at the problem from a female viewpoint, for instance, Easton observed:

> A central theme in contemporary feminist literature is that of the difficulties that women confront in trying to establish satisfying relations with men. Men are likely to be unable or unwilling to express deep emotions, to maintain the level of intimacy that women want in personal relations. Men are described as pulling away from such intimacy, either because they cannot tolerate it or because withdrawal itself can become a weapon in their struggles with women. In *The Dialectics of Sex* Firestone quotes the remarks of patients in clinical studies: women who complain of men who are emotionally distant or who withhold commitment, men who seem at pains to show how cool and cynical they are, how emotionally uninvolved. Firestone concludes that women need love and that men can't love; she writes, 'love, perhaps, even more than childbearing, is the pivot of women's oppression today.' (1978: 29)

Given the lack of systematic protections for women in the current situation, they often learn to be reserved and guarded in their dealings with men. The overall situation can thus become one that is seldom satisfying for persons of either gender.

IDENTITY PROBLEMS.   Despite the general alienation that is engendered in a stable patriarchal system, both men and women in such traditional society know who they are and what roles they are expected to play. However, the present situation is one in which persons from both sexes are forced to construct new identities for themselves in the absence of an overall stable system of gender relations.

Women often have difficulties in finding a bridge between traditional domestic femininity and their new roles in work and the community. As we have seen, most women, even if they are part of the paid labor force, are still expected to take primary responsibilities for childrearing and housework. These employed women are thus often under pressure to behave according to two sets of standards. "Femininity still means compliance, submission to men, and childlike helplessness, while women's work requires the competence and often the aggressive self-assertion that have been associated with masculinity," explained Easton (1978: 31). "The transition from housewife to working woman involves finding a new way of looking at oneself and one's place in the world, often in the face of male resistance to what men understand as encroachment on their territory."

Many men also face conflicting pressures to behave according to two sets of standards. At work they are still required to give and take orders and perform in terms of hierarchical social relations, but, to the extent that democratic relations are now beginning to prevail at home, they must reconstruct their identities and actions in terms of sharing, mutual decision making, and negotiation. Like women, such men can find themselves playing by one type of rules in their work lives and by a second set of rules in their marriage relationships. This also involves looking at oneself differently in the two situations and reconciling conflicting role demands and pressures. The criteria of success are also different in both these situations, forcing persons to further evaluate the purpose and meaning of their lives.

INCREASED VIOLENCE TOWARD WOMEN. As the old mechanisms of male control over women break down, the blatant efforts of some men to retain that control, through rape and other forms of violence, intensify. Recent statistics indicate, for instance, that rape has increased much faster than any other type of violent crime. Over the past five years reported rapes have risen by 62 percent, while the incidence of murder, robbery, aggravated assault, and other violent crimes has increased by only slightly more than one-half that amount.[14] Studies of advertising, television programming, and pornography also indicate a rapid growth in the portrayal of violence toward women.

> In the United States in the 1970s, as women begin to take the freedom to carry themselves with new confidence, to behave in ways that many men consider outside the bounds of femininity, male anger can become volatile. Stretching the boundaries of acceptable female behavior is often described as inviting attack from men; but women who live alone, or walk alone at night, are doing no more than what

would be taken for granted by a man. With the breakdown
of patriarchy women who are without the old male protections become more vulnerable, and men, as they lose familiar avenues of control, may respond with violence. (Easton,
1978: 32)

HOSTILITY AND CONTROL. Magazines like *Playboy* and
Hustler have a combined readership of 10 million persons, which
is more than *Time* and *Newsweek* magazines put together.[15] Male
"entertainment" magazines currently make up six of the ten top
selling magazines, and pornography has mushroomed into a $7-
billion industry, more than the record and movie industries combined. As Wessendorf (1983: 5) proposed, "pornography social-
izes a view of women as unreal sex objects; women, in turn,
internalize these images because there are no alternative images
for women in the common cultural media. This socialization
process methodically reduces the ability of all humans to express
real love and care in relationships."

We all need love and affection, however. "Love is a basic
biological need; but we are not getting it, we don't know how to
give it, we're afraid to touch each other, and many experience
a constant gnawing frustration because this need isn't fulfilled,"
concluded Wessendorf (1983: 5). "This frustrated state asserts
itself in the increased antagonism and subsequent violence
between the sexes." It is not surprising that during the 1970s
and throughout the last decade women have turned to classes
in self-defense to develop fighting skills to protect themselves
against such frequently committed violent crimes as rape and
battering. "It's been a way for women to reclaim a sense of
physical integrity and the ability to control our space, our bodies,
and, by extension, our lives" (Nelson, 1983: 6).

Renewed Efforts To Restore Male Domination

Until there is real equality between the sexes at work, in
the family, and generally in the relations between men and women,
patriarchy cannot be forgotten and demands for female and child
equality cannot be put aside. Until male domination is transcended, there will be continuing tendencies for it to emerge in
new and more adaptable forms. Families become further implicated in the wage labor system as they eat more meals at res-
taurants, farm out their children to day-care centers, and hire

specialists to perform more of their household repairs. In addition, conservative and right-wing political movements take advantage of the frustrations generated in this transition period and offer both women and men the pseudocomfort of returning to the more stable authoritarian gender relations of the past.

The family has begun to crumble and Anita Bryant blames homosexuality, Congressman Henry Hyde professes abortions are weakening our home lives, Phyllis Schlafly points to the Equal Rights Amendment, and Marabel Morgan claims that female independence has ruined the "total woman." Their pitch usually combines a little modern-day psychology with some old-time religion. Morgan's total woman, for instance, can "cater to her man's special quirks, whether it be in salads, sex or sports" (Cluster and Rutter, 1980: 59).

One of the possible key sources of coherence in these right-wing proposals is a reactionary response to continued dissolution of patriarchal power relations. Morgan, for example, is very explicit in urging women to submit more completely to the control of their husbands: "It is only through God's power that we can love and accept others, including our husbands." She explained that "it is only when a woman surrenders her life to her husband, reveres and worships him, and is willing to serve him, that she becomes really beautiful to him."[16]

The solutions that these movements pose are both anti-female and generally inadequate, however, as Easton concluded:

> Seducing one's husband will not alleviate the growing pressures on marriage, suppressing homosexuality will not hold families together, and preventing abortions will not improve the status of mothers. The movements attract women not because they point to any viable solutions, but because they bring into the open problems associated with the breakdown of traditional family structure and roles. They provide arenas in which women can voice real concerns. (1978: 34)

It is only in transcending these relations of male domination, rather than reestablishing them, that these basic social problems will be relieved. The only enduring solution must be the establishment of a democratic and androgynous society in which, as Ruben so eloquently stated, persons' life-styles and chances are unaffected by their sexual anatomy.

Maintaining Hierarchy in a Fatherless Society[17]

Domestic abuse, the plight of runaway children, divorce, the increasing proportion of first births to women who have no legal marriage partners, child beating, and other issues and problems associated with family life are currently receiving widespread attention. However, parents at the present time are not so much abdicating their responsibilities, emphasized Keniston (1977), as being dethroned "by forces they cannot influence, much less control." Instead of blaming the victims of the process—the parents and children themselves—we must attempt to understand the broader social forces shaping both of their lives.

Parents are coming to rely increasingly on outside experts and technology for help and support in raising their children. They have therefore increasingly assumed an executive, as opposed to a direct controlling, function in their children's upbringing. It is the responsibility of the parents to provide good health care, consult with teachers, or monitor television watching. Unfortunately, parents play a rather weakened role in these endeavors because of their enormous handicaps in dealing with these outside authorities.

> Today's parents have little authority over those others with whom they share the task of raising their children. On the contrary, most parents deal with those others from a position of inferiority and helplessness. Teachers, doctors, social workers, or television producers possess more status than most parents. Armed with special credentials and a jargon most parents cannot understand, the experts are usually entrenched in their profession and have far more power in their institutions than do the parents who are their clients. . . . Professionals who really listen to parents or who are really able to model their behavior in response to what parents tell them are still few and far between. (Keniston, 1977: 18)

There is also a widespread conviction that parents must be "educated for parenthood," and such advice and training is given by a growing number of newspaper columns, college courses, adult training programs and seminars, and books containing expert "wisdom" and advice to parents. Unfortunately, these experts on family living often disagree with one another and often give conflicting recommendations. The overall impact of this increasing reliance on outside experts is to undermine the family's natural capacities for self-reliance.

> By persuading parents to rely on outside experts and technology, the family's capacity to provide for itself was undermined. Having monopolized the knowledge necessary to socialize the young, the agencies of socialized reproduction then parceled it out piecemeal in the form of 'parent education.' Having first declared parents incompetent to raise their offspring without professional help, social pathologists 'gave back' the knowledge they had appropriated— gave it back in a mystifying fashion that rendered parents more helpless than ever, more abject in their dependence on expert opinion. (Lasch, 1977)

As Mitscherlich (1969) emphasized a decade ago, we are now moving into an authoritarian "society without the father," where hierarchy is less directly reliant on patriarchy and more dependent on sophisticated bureaucratic controls that have been evolving during the last century. True, male dominance persists and is widespread as perpetuated by such mechanisms as job segregation, sexual harassment, and violence toward women. However, this new authoritarianism in American society currently involves other types of controls over people's work and personal lives, and these are the subjects to which we must now turn.

BEYOND PATRIARCHY

People may call it "pair bonding" rather than marriage, as Bernard (1972: 302) has emphasized, but marriage has a future, or many futures; some form of commitment must be present among human beings. The standard type of family with father as breadwinner, mother as stay-at-home housekeeper, and two children has become a minority life-style that includes less than one-tenth of all families. The future will thus be one of alternatives with no family form as predominant as it was 100 years ago.

Relationships in the future will include open-ended ones in which both partners retain their maximum options as independent individuals. Millions of words have documented the naturalness and unnaturalness of monogamy. There is nothing in human nature that favors one kind of marriage over another.

Traditional marriage will be among the many options available, but it will not retain its exclusiveness under the law. "It is not the specific forms the options will take that is important but rather the fact that there will be options," explained Bernard (1972: 303), "that no one kind of marriage will be required of everyone, that there will be the recognition of the envious differences among human beings which modern life demands and produces."

Traditional marriage will not retain its monopoly under law, and the future role will be one of marital options. The problem of perfect marriage is impossible to solve because people's needs are so variable and contradictory. We need at different times new experiences, sexual excitement, and security. It is impossible to have a marital institution that is anything but a compromise, so we make our choices and the institution reflects the biases of the movement. In this regard, there is a particular danger in that, by overthrowing patriarchy, we will move too far in the direction of independence and too far away from the pole of security.

4
Working for the Boss: The Harnessing of Contemporary Labor Power

Without work all life goes rotten. But when work is soulless, life stifles and dies.

—ALBERT CAMUS[1]

The man whose life is spent in performing a few simple operations . . . has no occasion to exert his understanding or to exercise his invention in finding out expedients for removing difficulties . . . and generally becomes as stupid and ignorant as it is possible for a human creature to become.

—ADAM SMITH
The Wealth of Nations

The last thing a good manager would think of doing would be to make his policies of shop management the subject of a referendum.

—JOHN CADER, president
Remington Typewriter Company, 1912

Work is a primary activity in the lives of most American adults. It sustains physical life by providing food, clothing, and shelter; laying a basis for personal evaluation and self-esteem; furnishing economic self-sufficiency, social status, and family stability; and, at the same time, supplying goods and services needed by other persons. Work also involves purposive action, guided by intelligence, that serves both to develop people's abilities and potentials and simultaneously to change the natural environment so as to improve its usefulness. Thus, by knitting a sweater or writing a book people extend their own natural capabilities while making the world a more suitable place for the fulfillment of human needs.

In addition, work is important because for most employed persons it consumes a greater amount of time than anything else they do during their waking hours. Without a job many people would only survive for a few weeks or months; however, working in America has increasingly come to mean working for someone else. Of the approximately 100 million workers, about 94 million, when they can locate a job, work for an outside employer. This situation involves giving up personal autonomy and direct control of one's own work activities, allowing them to be dictated by the needs and interests of one's boss. Freedom of employment, in the modern context, is therefore usually confined to a selection among different employers.

> It all adds up to the fact that the various complaints about work are rooted in having to give up the time of your life to the control of someone else. It's a bit like selling yourself into slavery, only it's done a little at a time. Of course, unlike a slave, you can always quit. But then you will just have to go to work for another employer. So, in effect, a worker is a slave to employers as a group—you get to pick your master. Conditions may be better or worse, but as long as people live in a society where those who do the work are a group distinct from those who control it, this basic situation will remain the same. (Brecher and Costello, 1976: 18–19)

Why, then, do workplaces in the United States and other industrialized countries around the world remain hierarchical, boss dominated, and ruled from the top down? If work is so crucial for freedom and human development, why is it controlled by managers and employers and not by the workers themselves? In this chapter we will consider some of the issues related to the development and persistence of authoritarian relations in the workplace. Central to this argument is the claim that modern technology did not create today's hierarchical labor system, but rather at each crucial historical stage, technology merely defined the overall realm of possibilities with regard to work structures.

Since hierarchical work relations create basic alienation and divided selves between managers and workers, it is further argued that these authoritarian work relations actually tend to be less efficient rather than, as popularly believed, more efficient with regard to the organization of work.[2]

In Chapter 3 we saw that, once developed, patriarchy created both external and internal obstacles to the establishment of democratic family and personal relations. Externally, this hierarchical system divided society into two distinct classes—the dominators and the dominated—and men as the dominant group, through such mechanisms as labor unions, the courts, and other types of formal and informal organizations, had a vested interest in perpetuating these authoritarian social relations. The culture of domination perpetuated by patriarchy, however, also created many internal or psychological obstacles in women and children who otherwise might have been more assertive in taking control of their own lives. Like dependent peoples everywhere, these domesticated persons often displayed a lack of self-confidence and an essential ambivalence or "fear of freedom" when faced with opportunities for exercising more self-direction.

The existence and persistence of hierarchy in the workplace may be best explained in the context of a capitalist system, in which authoritarian work relations thrive because they are profitable. Through greater control over the labor process, employers, as the dominant group, have found that they can increase their financial returns for reasons, as we later shall see, often having little to do with either efficiency or technological determination. Over the generations the culture of domination that accompanied these hierarchical relations has served to further undermine the self-confidence, determination, and ability of workers directly to control their own work activities.

In our modern industrial society, work has been increasingly subdivided into routine and petty operations that fail to sustain the interest or engage the critical capacities of modern workers. Moreover, these simplified work procedures often demand increasingly less skill and training among workers, even as the bureaucratic work organizations themselves have become larger and more complex. As was the case above regarding patriarchy, to understand the meaning and structure of modern work, it is necessary first to consider the development of American work relations and then to discuss some of the current workplace realities and concerns regarding the present quality of working life in this country.

THE DESTRUCTION OF CRAFT

We are often told that managerial authority and responsibility are necessary to coordinate modern factory production. Historically, however, these hierarchical controls did not come about because workers either were unable or unwilling to direct their own labors but rather to prevent them from doing so. In early nineteenth-century factories, for instance, the actual work process was often in the hands of workers instead of owners. Skilled craftspersons, who had spent years as apprentices learning their respective trades, possessed a natural monopoly over labor knowledge and techniques. "In each craft, the worker was presumed to be the master of a body of traditional knowledge, and methods and procedures were left to his or her discretion," observed Braverman (1974: 109). "In each such worker reposed the accumulated knowledge of materials and processes by which production was accomplished in the craft."

Whereas the owners might possess general merchant skills and accounting knowledge, they often knew relatively little about production. It was only after a half century of intense labor struggles that employers were finally able to gain control over the work process itself. The early chapters of U.S. labor history were thus chronicles of the owners' attempts to supplant this early worker-controlled craft mode of production.

Preindustrial Work Patterns

To understand the basis of this nineteenth-century struggle over the nature of work, it is useful to begin by considering some of the characteristics of preindustrial work patterns. Only very recently has it been perceived as "natural" for individuals to work a set number of hours each week for an outside employer. For the first 1 million or so years of human existence, people lived in hunting and gathering societies in which work was directed almost exclusively toward subsistence. Recent field studies indicate that large amounts of leisure time are normal even in present-day hunting and gathering societies. Indeed, one quantitative study reported that, "despite their harsh environment," persons in such societies only "devote from twelve to nineteen hours a week to getting food" (Study quoted by Clawson, 1980: 36–37).

Work in preindustrial societies was not governed by the clock and often did not have the same kind of compulsive quality it does today. Therefore, it was not without great resistance that such self-employed workers were forced to adopt the regular hours and uniform habits of factory production. Riots and destruction of factories were common occurrences in eighteenth-century England, for example, and working-class opposition to factory work was often a strong force keeping new factories from being built. In this regard, Clawson (1980: 52) estimated that perhaps one-third of the English factory labor force during this period was composed of prisoners, paupers, and other types of forced laborers. Indeed, many such factories, especially in the growing textile industry, were located in buildings associated with prisons, workhouses, and orphanages in order to obtain the necessary work force. Consequently, for two centuries in England and later in the United States, dependence on wages was almost universally rejected by those regarding themselves as free persons.

Outside and Inside Contracting

The overwhelming majority of Americans in the early 1800s worked for themselves; about two-thirds were farmers working their own land, and most others were self-employed proprietors and artisans.[3] Although great inequalities in wealth and life circumstances existed, freedom and independence during this period, as had earlier been the case in England, were usually equated with individual ownership of the various means of production and personal control of one's own labor activities. In 1833 an economist, Edward Wakefield, portrayed this prevailing economic individualism:

> Free Americans, who cultivate the soil, follow many other occupations. Some portion of the furniture and tools they use is commonly made by themselves. They frequently build their own houses, and carry to market, at whatever distance the produce of their own industry. They are spinners and weavers; they make soap and candles, as well as, in many cases, shoes and clothes for their own use. In America cultivation of land is often the secondary pursuit of a blacksmith, a miller, or a shop-keeper. (Quoted in Brecher and Costello, 1976: 23)

Because of the ingrained resistance in England and the United States to wage labor, early industrial production in both countries often took the form of various outside contracting or "putting out" systems in which wealthy merchants and traders would supply local craftspeople with the materials needed to produce such commodities as clothing, shoes, or various metal wares, and the workers, in turn, would manufacture such goods in their own homes, employing their traditional production techniques. These goods would then be sold back to the employer for a "piece rate" or "subcontract rate" determined by the amount and quality of the goods actually produced.

Periodic recessions during the early and middle part of the nineteenth century promoted these new putting out arrangements since during these hard times craftspersons often did not have the money needed to buy the raw materials and supplies used in production. Other self-employed persons were forced by economic necessity into a variety of inside contracting arrangements as well. As opposed to working in their own homes, the management of existing industrial firms provided floor space and machinery, supplied raw materials and working capital, and arranged for sale of the finished products (Buttrick, 1952: 205). Like the putting out system, however, these inside contractors had complete charge of production in their own area, hiring and firing their employees and supervising the work process themselves. The price that the inside contractor received for the finished goods was determined by negotiations with the company.

From its beginnings in 1855, for example, production at the Winchester Repeating Arms Company was in the hands of inside contractors. At first only one or two contractors were employed, but with the expanding market for guns and ammunition during the Civil War, the number of inside contractors increased. By 1876 "the production of guns at Winchester was divided among a dozen large departments each headed by a contractor with another half dozen minor operations performed by separate contractors working alone or with one or two helpers" (Buttrick, 1952: 208).

The Early Factory System

Both the outside and inside contracting systems thus represented early transitional forms of industrial production in which employers, reacting to worker resistance, had not yet assumed full control over the labor process. As Braverman (1974: 63) emphasized, these early subcontracting arrangements "were plagued by problems of irregularity of production, loss of materials in transit and through embezzlement, slow manufacturing, and lack of uniformity and uncertainty of the quality of the product."

The history of work relations at Winchester between 1876 and the beginning of the First World War, for instance, was largely a history of management's efforts to take control of the inside contracting system without damaging production. In addition to the types of problems mentioned by Braverman, other weaknesses of these contracting arrangements, from a management perspective, were: 1) contractors possessed monopoly powers in greater or lesser degree depending on their private knowledge of production methods and the loyalty of their employees, 2) incomes of various contractors often did not match their positions in the company's social hierarchy, and 3) the method of paying contractors was inadequate because they knew their piece rates would be cut whenever their incomes appeared excessive (Buttrick, 1952: 210).

As workers became more accustomed to these contracting arrangements, many employers found they could make higher profits by direct supervision of shop activities. This type of supervision allowed them to dictate the length of the working day, ensure intense and uninterrupted work, and enforce the rules against competing and interfering activities such as talking, smoking, and leaving the workplace. As Clawson (1980: 48) stressed, "the rise of factories meant that workers had to spend about twice as many hours a week actually working, but they still earned no more than a subsistence wage."[4] In the beginning, then, factories benefited their owners at the expense of workers, even with no difference in machinery or technology.

The Functional Autonomy of Craftspersons

As emphasized above, until the late nineteenth century employers in most industries did not direct the actual work process. Craftspeople still possessed the knowledge and skills necessary for production and also controlled the transmission of these skills through the apprenticeship system. Moreover, their "control was perpetuated and made effective by their refusal to let work be sub-divided into smaller components that did not require 'all-round craftsmen,' " observed the Work Relations Group (1978: 5). "By regulating the use of helpers and laborers, they were able to limit the labor market, maintain skill requirements, and keep up pay scales."

The craft workers generally supervised the unskilled majority of the work force and, without detailed knowledge of the work process, employers were usually unable to tell them what to do. The skilled workers also set "stints" that determined the amount of work to be done and established their own rules about the methods and equipment with which it was to be done. Montgomery (1979: 11) observed that "they often hired and fired their own helpers and paid the latter some fixed portion of their own earnings."

Enforcing a Mutualistic Ethical Code

Montgomery (1979: 12–14) also observed that the "functional autonomy" of the nineteenth-century craftsperson was protected by their mutualistic ethical code that consisted of three general principles. First, on most jobs they fixed an output quota which all workers were obliged to follow. Deviants from such quotas were often labeled with epithets like "hogger-in," "leader," "rooter," "chaser," "rusher," "runner," "swift," "boss's pet," and a host of other less polite names.

Second, the craftspersons' ethical code required a "manly" bearing toward the boss. According to this code, dignity and respectability demanded that workers refuse to cower before the foreman's glares and even quit their jobs if their employer's demands were considered unjustified. Finally, the code required cooperation and solidarity with one's fellow workers: no "undermining" or "conniving" or other behaviors that might threaten other workers' jobs or force them to work faster than allowed by the fixed output quotas.

Montgomery concluded that a simple technological explanation for the control exercised by nineteenth-century craftspersons was not adequate. Technical skills and knowledge of production techniques were embedded in a mutualistic ethical code that was passed on to new workers as part of their apprenticeship training, and together this knowledge and ethical instruction was the basis of much of the skilled workers' power and autonomy with regard to management. An example of the control that craft workers exercised over production during this period is provided by the work of coal miners, as described by the Work Relations Group:

> Each miner worked permanently in his 'room'; hired and paid his helper; did his own maintenance; decided how to perform the work; and set his own pace and hours of work. He was, in effect, an individual contractor, paid by the number of tons he produced. Supervisors represented only 1.5 percent of the underground workforce. A miner typically saw the foreman once a day. In union mines, an elected pit committee oversaw the flow of pit props, coal cars, and the like. (1978: 5)

To break this control by skilled workers, employers tried various techniques such as introducing less skilled workers into various jobs, replacing apprenticeship with a helper system controlled by the employers, and promoting competition among various craftspersons who had become inside contractors. The skilled workers, in turn, responded by enactment of detailed formal union work rules that attempted to codify the functional autonomy established by earlier craft work culture. A committee in each shop enforced the union work rules and wage scales (Work Relations Group, 1978: 5–6).

Breaking the Power of Skilled Workers

Craft control was possible in the nineteenth century because most businesses were extremely small by today's standards. In 1849, for example, the world's biggest farm implement company, the McCormick Company, employed only 123 workers in its Chicago harvester works, and the nation's second largest brewery, later called the Pabst Brewing Company, employed less than 100 workers (Edwards, 1979: 25).

The rise of the large industrial corporations in the period immediately surrounding the turn of the twentieth century, however, shifted the balance of power against the skilled workers and substantially weakened the craft unions. During this wave of business consolidations and mergers, thousands of small companies were reorganized into a few hundred huge ones, dominating the major national markets. In the steel industry, for example, where competition had been particularly intense in the 1880s and 1890s, the financier, J. P. Morgan, created the U.S.

Steel Corporation from a conglomeration of 165 existing steel companies. This new industrial colossus, in turn, controlled about 60 percent of the entire steel market and, not surprisingly, the long-term decline in steel prices was halted. Such merged companies were also organized prior to World War One, as Edwards (1979: 44) explained, "by the producers of products as diverse as biscuits (National Biscuit), bananas (United Fruit), chewing gum (Wrigley's), paper (International Paper), meat (Swift and Armour), bicycles (American Bicycle), photographic supplies (Eastman Kodak), typewriters (Union) and sewing machines (Singer)."

To accommodate this growth in business size and complexity, a new organizational form was developed—the corporation—in which companies were legally given the status of artificial persons and thus could assume debts, own other companies, make contracts, and conduct business. The growth of these large corporations since about 1920 has effectively divided the U.S. economy into two distinct types of business enterprises. On the one hand, there exists a few hundred large "core" corporations with many thousands of employees and with extensive market and political powers, while on the economy's "periphery" there exists the remaining 12 million or so small- and medium-sized companies that have continued to survive in this corporate-dominated economic system (Edwards, 1979: 72).

These large core corporations, in turn, exercised much more potential power over the skilled workers than did their smaller nineteenth-century predecessors. "Their huge financial resources, ability to withstand long strikes, shift work from one plant to another, employ machinery which reduced their dependence on craft skills, and mobilize the forces of the state against workers," emphasized the Work Relations Group (1978: 6), "created a new power balance the craft workers were unable to shift more than temporarily and occasionally." The skilled workers and groups that remained in these large corporations were usually too fragmented and diverse for them to exercise the degree of worker influence that had characterized the earlier period of craft production.

Struggle for Control of Steel

The conflicts between skilled workers and owners in the steel industry during the latter nineteenth century have been carefully studied by researchers like Brody (1960) and Stone

(1974). These struggles for control over steel production were similar in many ways to the battles waged in other basic industries as they moved from an earlier stage of craft production to a later stage of management-controlled production. "In some cases, such as the textile industry, the power of the earlier skilled workers was destroyed at the same time that factories and machine production developed; in others, workers' power was broken only long after mechanization occurred," concluded Brecher and Costello (1976: 30). "Other industries, and even many white-collar occupations, have gone through much the same transformation."

In the 1880s many steel mills operated according to an inside contract system, under which skilled workers would hire their own helpers to do the heavy parts of the work and pay these assistants out of their own paychecks. The skilled workers, in turn, were paid a certain sum—called a "tonnage rate"—for each ton of steel they produced. This tonnage rate was governed by an agreed upon price that fluctuated with the market price of steel, above a specified minimum rate below which wages could not fall. This sliding scale was thus a profit-sharing arrangement based on the principle that the workers should participate both in the risks and the fruits of production.

This cooperative arrangement further meant that employers had little direct control over the work process. They could not use the wage as an incentive to ensure a desired level of output. The price was determined by the market, and the methods of production and pace of work were decided by the workers themselves. The workers controlled the plants and decided how the work was to be done. Employers could not speed up the workers nor introduce new machinery that eliminated or redefined jobs; they could merely contract with the workers for certain jobs to be performed.

The skilled steel workers were also organized into one of the strongest unions of their day, the Amalgamated Association of Iron, Steel and Tin Workers. Through their union, they were able to formalize their control over virtually every aspect of the steel production process. This cooperative relationship, however, between the skilled workers and the steel masters became strained during the 1880s as labor costs began rising as a percentage of total revenues and thus reduced profits. Andrew Carnegie, president of America's largest steel company at the time, therefore decided to break the union and to establish unilateral control of production. Just before the contract with the Amalgamated was to expire in 1892, Carnegie transferred managing authority of his Homestead mill in Pennsylvania to Henry Clay Frick, who was already notorious for his brutal treatment of strikers in the Connellsville coke regions.

Frick, in turn, elaborated his plans with military precision. He ordered a three-mile-long fence topped with barbed wire to be built around the entire Homestead Works. The fence would hold off strikers, while Pinkerton detectives hired by Frick would escort strikebreakers into the plant by boat and barge from the Monongahela River side of the plant. Twenty foremen were sent to major cities to find 260 skilled workers, which was the minimum number needed to begin operations, and an arrangement was made with Robert A. Pinkerton to supply 300 detectives (Lens, 1973: 72). In addition, holes for rifles were put in along the fence, platforms constructed for sentinels, and barracks built inside the fence to house the strikebreakers.

Inspired by Frick's performance, other steel companies also began vigorous campaigns to oust the union, with generally positive results. Lodge after lodge was lost in the succeeding years until by 1910 the steel industry was entirely nonunion. This victory by the steel masters allowed them to destroy the prevailing craft labor system and to introduce a new management-dominated division of labor within the plants. "They could then begin to create a new system," explained Stone (1974: 67), "one that would reflect and help to perpetuate their ascendancy."[5]

Implications for the Structure of Work

The employers' struggle to destroy the craft production system demonstrates why the structure of work must be seen as a social and not simply a technical matter. "It was a story, not just a struggle between more or less efficient techniques for producing use-values," explained the Work Relations Group (1978: 7), "but rather a power struggle between two social groups, employers and skilled workers, over how much the organization of production would reflect the interests of each."

> In most instances, breaking the power over production of the skilled workers cleared the way for management reorganization of all aspects of work. Henceforth management possessed the formal authority to decide how work would be performed; divide jobs and hire any workers it chose to

fill them; determine output levels; introduce whatever techniques and equipment it chose; and force workers to compete with each other for jobs and income.

Workers often displayed considerable bravery and ingenuity in their struggles against this increasing management domination, as demonstrated by the series of strikes and disruptions initiated by local bands of Irish miners, popularly known as the Molly Maguires, who challenged the control of the coal operators in the eastern Pennsylvania coal fields during the 1870s. Working people also battled with the first large corporate monopolies created in the United States—the national railroads—and fought in the bloody "Long Strike of 1875" and the first American nationwide strike, popularly known as the Railroad War of 1877. Besides the disastrous 1892 Homestead strike (described above) and the 1894 Pullman strike, both of which involved lengthy plant shutdowns and scores of workers killed, there were even bloodier labor wars in the western states which involved armed struggles between gold and silver miners and the mine owners in towns such as Leadville (1896) and Cripple Creek (1894 and again in 1903–04).

Perhaps nothing symbolized the intensity of these early labor struggles more fully, however, than the "Ludlow Massacre" which occurred on Easter night in 1914. Coal miners striking against John D. Rockefeller's Colorado Fuel and Iron Company in Ludlow, Colorado, were awakened to find company men and national guardsmen drenching their tents in oil.

> They had moved into these improvised homes when agents of the oil tycoon had evicted them from company-owned dwellings. Regularly harassed by soldiers' bullets they had taken the precaution of digging a cave, where they placed thirteen children and one pregnant woman. All fourteen were burned to death that night, and six other adults were shot to death, as the tent community went up in flames. (Lens, 1973: 148)

As a result of constant labor struggles and disruption, workers in the nineteenth century were organized into hundreds of local unions and trade associations to protect their traditional work prerogatives and rights. Moreover, nine garment workers in 1869 secretly formed what was to become the first national labor federation, the Knights of Labor, and this organization itself was gradually superseded by the more conservative American Federation of Labor (AFL), formed in 1886. The AFL, however, generally confined itself to the struggles of the relatively small minority of skilled workers and, with a few pragmatic exceptions such as the militant and already organized coal miners, refused to organize semiskilled machine operators and unskilled workers.

Moreover, the union leadership that emerged during this early period generally conceded the right of management to run the plants. Samuel Gompers, a Dutch-Jewish cigarmaker and first president of the AFL, for example, promoted a philosophy of "simple" unionism that underscored the limited objectives of this established sector of the American organized labor movement.[6] "We have no ultimate ends," explained Gompers; "we are fighting only for immediate objects, objects that can be realized in a few years. We are opposed to theorists. . . . We are practical men" (Lens, 1973: 57–58).

By not consciously formulating a set of political demands concerning the rights of labor to control the work process, however, organized labor left itself open to an employer offensive based on management's claims to a legitimate right to give orders. As we will see in the next section, once management learned how to do the work, workers had "no developed culture or consciousness to deal with a situation in which they were given precise and detailed orders, rather than simply general directives" (Clawson, 1980: 160).

Finally, it is important not to exaggerate or romanticize the power of workers in this nineteenth-century craft production system. The control of the work process by craftspersons always remained fixed within the boundaries of the overall capitalist production system oriented toward profits and generally controlled by the owners. Moreover, while craft organization provided skilled workers with more varied and interesting work, it also sustained substantial inequalities among workers and mostly benefited a minority of more highly paid white male native-born employees. In this regard, the craft workers' organizations and unions were often aimed against immigrants, blacks, women, and other unskilled workers, the latter of whom were often exploited as underpaid and overworked helpers. The employers' campaign against this craft system, however, was a necessary stage in their overall struggle to organize the production system for their own ends.

THE THRUST FOR MANAGERIAL CONTROL

As we have seen, nineteenth-century workers often entered salaried employment only when the prevailing social conditions left them few alternatives; for example, when they did not possess sufficient capital to maintain their own businesses or crafts. Employers, by contrast, typically entered into the employment agreement because they possessed a certain amount of capital which they sought to enlarge, and to do so they had to convert part of it into wages. Thus, the labor process was set in motion which, while in general a process for creating useful products and services, has now under capitalism also become specifically a process for the expansion of capital and the creation of profits (Braverman, 1974: 53).

Under the wage system, the capitalist purchases the rights to a worker's labor for a given period of time, but this capacity for work is only useful to the employer if the work is actually accomplished. "If labor power remains merely a potentiality or capacity," explained Edwards (1979; 12), "no goods get produced and the capitalist has no products to sell for profit." The labor process has now become the responsibility of the employers who must henceforth strive to extract actual work from this potential labor power they legally own.

Having been forced to sell their labor power, workers become increasingly alienated from the work process itself. Their labor has become a commodity; its uses are no longer organized according to the needs and desires of the workers who sell it but rather according to the needs of its purchasers, the employers seeking to expand the value of their capital. There were few problems of worker alienation or labor discipline among the self-employed craftspersons of the eighteenth century, but traditional craft pride and intrinsic work satisfaction play an ever weaker role as workers now have a less direct stake in the products of their own labor activities. Thus, from the workers' viewpoint this fact represents itself as a progressive separation or alienation from the labor process, whereas from the capitalists' viewpoint it represents a growing problem of worker management.

> When you're using someone else for your own purposes, whether it's to build your future, or to build your tomb, you must control him. Under all exploitative systems, a strict control from the outside replaces the energy from within

as a way of keeping people working. The humiliating and debilitating way we work is a product not of our technology but of our economic system. (Garson, 1975: 211–12)

The Growing Labor Crisis

Unlike the other raw materials and commodities employed in the production process, labor power is embodied in living workers who still retain their abilities to reason, organize, act, and pursue their own personal objectives and ends. Having conquered the prevailing craft system and having established formal control over the work process, the growing corporations of the late nineteenth century had to create a new system for organizing production. However, within these giant firms there were increasing contradictions between their expanding needs for labor control and coordination and their diminishing ability to maintain such control. These growing contradictions presented themselves to owners and managers as twin problems. On the one hand, given the recent destruction of the craft production system, employers had to find more effective external or management-controlled techniques for motivating workers to labor in accordance with their directions, and, on the other hand, employers must prevent workers from uniting against them.

"As firms grew from a few hundred or perhaps even several thousand workers at one or a few plants to tens or even hundreds of thousands of workers spread out in perhaps dozens of locations," observed Edwards (1979: 53), "the problem of control grew more serious." Production in these large companies acquired an increasingly social character requiring greater management coordination and top-down control. This crisis was graphically illustrated by the rapid growth of trade unions which had quadrupled in size from 447,000 members to 2,072,000 members between 1899 and 1904 (Lens, 1973: 135). There was also a growing willingness on the part of workers to undertake massive strikes to obtain or preserve union recognition such as the coal strike of 1897, the steel and machinists' strikes of 1901, and the meat-packers' strike of 1904 (Montgomery, 1979: 113). More generally, the number of worker strikes increased dramatically during this period from approximately 1,000 per year in the mid-1890s, to about 1,800 per year in 1900, to a total of almost 4,000 annually in 1904 (Lens, 1973: 135). Besides this increased trade union organizing and strikes, worker dissatisfaction was also expressed politically by increasing support for the American populist and Socialist parties as well as in the workplaces by such forms of rebellion as increasing labor sabotage, absenteeism, and nonattention to work (see descriptions in Kolko, 1963: 57–78; and Weinstein, 1968: 117–38).

Corporate owners and managers responded to this emerging labor crisis by developing more direct and systematic controls over the production process in their firms. They increased the number of foremen and shop supervisors, upgraded the formal education and professional training requirements for their managers, developed academically trained engineering staffs who were given increasing responsibilities for planning and maintaining production, improved their bookkeeping and cost accounting methods, centralized their ordering and distribution systems, and experimented with a variety of piecework and incentive wage payment plans.[7] As Montgomery (1979: 113) observed, "after 1900 a veritable mania for efficiency, organization, and standardization swept through American business and literary circles."

Many employers also responded to these deteriorating work relations by instituting various types of corporate welfare programs that promised tangible benefits to those workers who refrained from union activities and remained loyal to the firm. More than a decade before the Ludlow Massacre, for example, John D. Rockefeller, Jr., pioneered in the development of personnel management by establishing a "sociological department" at the Colorado Fuel and Iron Company which looked into every aspect of workers' lives from diet and drinking habits to public school curriculum. Its director, R. W. Corwin, explained that the company's employees were "drawn from the lowest classes of foreign immigrants . . . whose primitive ideas of living and ignorance of hygienic laws render the department's work along the line of improved housing facilities and instruction in domestic economy of the upmost importance" (Quoted in Montgomery, 1979: 40).

Workers were often resentful of these intrusions into their personal lives and skeptical about the welfare programs, considering them bribes for acquiescing to the existing paternalistic company relations. As a consequence of this general lack of effectiveness and the mounting costs of these programs, most companies abandoned them during the 1920s and 1930s.

For employers, clearly needed were programs that directly confronted the central contradictions within these giant corporations for growing labor coordination and control in a period of declining craft pride and increasing worker alienation. The emergence, during the first two decades of the twentieth century, of the management efficiency movement provided many of the basic tools these employers needed to achieve this increased labor control.

Emergence of the "Efficiency" Expert

Hearings were held in the fall of 1910 before the Interstate Commerce Commission concerning an application by northeastern railroads for an increase in their freight rates.[8] Since this request would increase their shipping costs, merchants of the area sent a team of lawyers to the hearings to oppose this new rate hike. These lawyers argued that the railroads were being operated inefficiently, and, at a crucial point in the hearings, they introduced as witnesses a number of engineers and industrial managers who testified that through the introduction of "Taylorism" the railroads could make a larger profit without raising rates. Although their claims were greatly exaggerated, some of these witnesses reported that by employing these new techniques they had actually reduced costs while raising wages from 25 to 100 percent. Harrison Emerison, an efficiency expert who had put some of these management practices into effect for the Santa Fe railroad, for example, estimated that through this system the railroads could actually save up to $1 million per day.

These Washington hearings had the effect of bringing into prominence the son of a wealthy Philadelphia merchant and lawyer, Frederick Winslow Taylor, who developed and became the chief propagandist for a management approach popularly known as "Taylorism," the "Taylor system," or, as he preferred it to be called, "scientific management."[9] Taylor's personality was described by Braverman:[10]

> In his psychic makeup, Taylor was an exaggerated example of the obsessive-compulsive personality; from his youth he had counted his steps, measured the time of his various activities, and analyzed his motions in a search for 'efficiency.' Even when he had risen to importance and fame,

he was still something of a figure of fun, and his appearance on the shop floor produced smiles. The picture of his personality . . . justifies calling him, at the very least, a neurotic crank. The traits fitted him perfectly for his role as the prophet of modern capitalist management, since that which is neurotic in the individual is, in capitalism, normal and socially desirable for the functioning of society. (1974: 92)

"All employees should bear in mind that each shop exists, first, last and all the time, for the purpose of paying dividends to its owners," explained Taylor (1903: 143); thus, management must develop strategies to obtain "the best day's work that a man could properly do, year in and year out, and still thrive under" (1911: 55). In this regard, Taylor believed that most factories produced only about one-third to one-half of their maximum output because of faulty management and laziness, or "soldiering," among the workers. Two types of soldiering were distinguished: "natural" soldiering, resulting from the innate laziness of workers, and the far more serious problem of "systematic" soldiering which involved consciously planned underworking. "Instead of using every effort to turn out the largest possible amount of work, in a majority of cases [the worker] deliberately plans to do as little as he safely can," concluded Taylor. "For every individual . . . who is overworked, there are a hundred who intentionally underwork—greatly underwork—every day of their lives" (1911: 13, 18).

The Principles of Taylorism

Having thus located the source of labor problems in this systematic soldiering, Taylor proceeded to develop a four-step program of "scientific management" to counteract these tendencies toward deliberate underworking.

1) GATHERING PRODUCTIVE KNOWLEDGE. The great defect in management practices of his time, declared Taylor, "is that their starting point, their very foundation, rests on ignorance and deceit" (1903: 45). Thus, while working as a foreman at Midvale Steel, he had come to realize that his greatest weakness was that "the combined knowledge and skill of the workmen who were under him was certainly ten times as great as his own" (1911: 53). In truth, then, the shop was run by the workers rather than the bosses, and it was these workers who together planned just

how fast each job should be done and who set the pace for each machine throughout the shop.

Taylor admitted that the problem was not that workers lacked adequate knowledge to produce quality goods but rather that their production knowledge gave them too much power over management. He proposed, as a method of appropriating this craft knowledge, that management should conduct detailed and exhaustive time-motion studies of all the tasks that every worker performed. "Under scientific management there is nothing too small to become the subject of [management] investigation," explained Taylor. "Every single motion of every man in the shop sooner or later becomes the subject of accurate, careful study to see whether that motion is the best and quickest that can be used, and as you see, this is a new mental attitude assumed by the employer which differs radically from the old" (1947: 111).

2) SEPARATION OF PLANNING AND EXECUTION. Once management had gathered detailed and accurate knowledge about the work process, Taylor further proposed that all brainwork and planning should be "deliberately taken out of the workman's hands and handed over to those on the management's side" (1947: 44). Having managers plan all the work would lead to greater increases in the number of these nonproductive employees since, under Taylorism, they now were to perform all the brainwork that previously had been spread throughout the work force. This would result in employing as many as one-third of the labor force which would now be used to direct and plan the productive labors of the other two-thirds of the workers.

Although there was no hiding the fact that basic to the Taylor system was a hitherto unheard of expansion of the size of this administrative bureaucracy, Taylor (1903: 122) nevertheless insisted that "no manager need feel alarmed when he sees the number of non-producers increasing in proportion to producers" since this system would ultimately result in lowering production costs. These new economies under Taylorism would result from the fact that, with its increased control over labor, management could now greatly speed up production. In Taylor's words, "the essence of [scientific] management lies in the fact that the control of the speed problem rests entirely with the management" (1903: 44). The increased management costs under the Taylor system would also be offset by hiring cheaper unskilled workers who would repeatedly perform specialized and less complex tasks, mindlessly obeying detailed administrative orders.

3) DETAILED MANAGEMENT CONTROL OF THE LABOR PROCESS. To gain the greatest possible efficiency, Taylor maintained,

a management that already had taken the first two steps of gathering knowledge about production and establishing a planning department should now undertake the complete control of the work process itself. Previously, employers had been guilty of only specifying general tasks for workers and, as illustrated above in the coal mining and steel industries, generally not having interfered with the skilled workers' methods of performing their labors. Taylor's genius, however, "was to overturn this practice and replace it with its opposite," observed Braverman (1974: 90); "management, he insisted, could be only a limited and frustrated undertaking so long as it left to the worker any decision about the work."

Workers must learn how to give up their own particular ways of doing things, claimed Taylor, and "grow accustomed to receiving and obeying directions covering details, large and small, which in the past have been left to [their] individual judgment" (1903: 133–34). All workers would therefore have their daily tasks clearly defined and laid out for them, and these management instructions would specify exactly what the workers are to do, how they are to do it, and how much time they are to spend on each task. Taylor further explained his philosophy of detailed worker control:

> There is no question that the average individual accomplishes the most when . . . someone else assigns him a definite task, namely, a given amount of work which he must do within a given time; and the more elementary the mind and character of the individual the more necessary does it become that each task shall extend over a short period of time only. No school teacher would think of telling children in a general way to study a certain book or subject. It is practically universal to assign each day a definite lesson beginning on one specified page and line and ending on another; and the best progress is made when the conditions are such that a definite study hour or period can be assigned in which the lesson must be learned. Most of us remain, through a great part of our lives, in this respect, grown-up children, and do our best only under pressure of a task of comparatively short duration. (1903: 69)

At first, as Taylor admitted, workers might see these detailed managerial controls as "red tape and impertinent interference." Eventually, though, "after becoming accustomed to direction in minor matters, they must gradually learn to obey instructions as to the pace at which they are to work, and grasp the idea, first, that the planning department knows accurately how long each operation should take; and second, that sooner or later they will have to work at the required speed if they expect to prosper" (1903: 133–34).

4) WAGE INCENTIVES. Taylor realized that there would necessarily be labor resistance to his planned reorganization of work. Commenting on the possible failure of workers to adjust to his new system, he predicted: "A certain percentage of them, with the best of intentions, will fail . . . and find that they have no place in the new organization, while still others, and among them some of the best workers who are, however, either stupid or stubborn, can never be made to see that the new system is as good as the old; and these, too, must drop out" (1903: 132).

In the case of such maladaptive behaviors as worker insubordination or impudence, Taylor then proposed that each workplace should have a "shop disciplinarian" who would see that a complete record "of each man's virtues and defects be kept." Taylor also adapted many of the notions about wage incentives prevalent in the management thinking of his time to his own system of management controls. For instance, he believed that "the mistake which is usually made in dealing with union men lies in giving an order which affects a number of workmen at the same time and in laying stress upon the increase in the output which is demanded instead of emphasizing one by one the details which the workman is to carry out in order to attain the desired result" (1903: 192).

Taylor's most widely popularized illustration for gaining worker compliance with his new management system was his method involving the loading of pig iron at Bethlehem Steel. This manual job consisted of lifting a load (called a "pig") of iron that weighed 92 pounds, carrying it about 40 feet and up an inclined plank into a railway car, and then placing the iron on the floor of the car. Although workers were currently loading an average of only 12½ tons per day, Taylor determined, through a detailed study of the loading process, that a superior worker could actually handle 47 to 48 tons of pig iron each day. The problem then was to get the workers to accept this "speed-up" of the work process without provoking an organized strike or other types of labor rebellion. At this new rate, each worker would be required to handle about 1,156 pigs instead of the 304 they were presently accustomed to carrying in a regular ten-hour day.

The next task was to select a superior worker and motivate him to work at this new faster pace.

We therefore carefully watched and studied these 75 men
for three or four days, at the end of which time we had
picked out four men who appeared to be physically able to
handle pig iron at the rate of 47 tons per day. A careful
study was then made of each of these men. We looked up
their history as far back as practicable and thorough in-
quiries were made as to the character, habits, and the ambitions of each of them. (Taylor, 1911: 43)

After completing this exhaustive study, one of these men, Schmidt,
was finally selected to perform according to these new management expectations. The procedure by which Taylor motivated
Schmidt to comply with these speed-up demands is described in
part:

He was a little Pennsylvania Dutchman who had been
observed to trot back home for a mile or so after his work
in the evening about as fresh as he was when he came
trotting down to work in the morning. We found that upon
wages of $1.15 a day he had succeeded in buying a small
plot of ground, and that he was engaged in putting up the
walls of a little house for himself in the morning before
starting to work and at night after leaving. He also had the
reputation of being exceedingly 'close,' this is, of placing a
very high value on a dollar.
The task before us, then, narrowed itself down to getting
Schmidt to handle 47 tons of pig-iron per day and making
him glad to do it. This was done as follows. Schmidt was
called out from among the gang of pig-iron handlers and
talked to somewhat in this way:
Schmidt, are you a high-priced man?
Vell, I don't know vat you mean?
Well, if you are a high-priced man, you will load that
pig-iron on that car tomorrow for $1.85 . . . you will do
exactly as this man tells you tomorrow, from morning till
night. When he tells you to pick up a pig and walk, you
pick it up and you walk, and when he tells you to sit down
and rest, you sit down. You do that right straight through
the day. And what's more, no back talk. . . . Now you come
on to work here tomorrow and I'll know before night whether
you are really a high-priced man or not.
Schmidt started to work, and all day long, and at regular
intervals, was told by the man who stood over him with a
watch, 'Now pick up a pig and walk. Now sit down and
rest. Now walk—now rest,' etc. He worked when he was
told to work, and rested when he was told to rest, and at
half past five in the afternoon had his 47½ tons loaded on

the car. And he practically never failed to work at this pace and do the task that was set him during the three years that the writer was at Bethlehem. (1911: 43–47)

Each of the pig-iron handlers was then given an opportunity of improving himself as Schmidt had done and, if he failed, was "either persuaded or intimidated into giving it up" (1911: 50–51). Unfortunately, Taylor found that only about one man in eight was able to handle the new work requirement of 47½ tons of steel each day and the other workers had to be let go. "Now one of the very first requirements for a man who is fit to handle pig-iron as a regular occupation," concluded Taylor, "is that he shall be so stupid and so phlegmatic that he more nearly resembles in his mental make-up an ox than any other type" (1911: 65).

Effects of Taylorism

Taylorism was too rigorous a system to total management to be immediately adopted in its entirety by most capitalist firms, and perhaps no more than thirty factories had been thoroughly reorganized by Taylor and his colleagues before 1917 (Montgomery, 1979: 113).[11] However, the essential elements of Taylor's proposals became the bedrock of work design in almost every American industry by the mid-1920s. Such features as planning departments, academically educated industrial engineering staffs, time-motion studies, systematic management analyses of each distinct production operation, detailed instruction and supervision of workers in the performance of each discrete task, and simplification, specialization, and standardization of work assignments became basic features of virtually all large- and medium-sized American companies.

These new management control techniques ran directly contrary to the attempts by the AFL craft unions to preserve the autonomy of skilled workers by promoting detailed work rules and output standards. This conflict between employers and the unions reached its greatest intensity during periods of abundant employment after 1909, when Taylorism spread rapidly through the metalworking and related industries (Montgomery, 1979: 134). There was a nationwide wave of strike activity from 1915 to 1917, for instance, but the unwillingness of the existing craft unions to organize unskilled workers on an industry-wide basis made them generally ineffective against this new management offensive. By 1923, therefore, the AFL had lost almost one-quarter of its membership. Even in the early 1930s when, as a result of the Great Depression, America was ablaze with social protest, the AFL still stressed cooperation with the new Taylorized corporations and generally continued its outmoded strategy of organizing along craft lines.

Reacting to this general stagnation of ineffectiveness of the AFL, John L. Lewis and other dissident union leaders in 1935 formed the rival Congress of Industrial Organizations (CIO) which, with its new tactic of sitdown strikes within the plants, won impressive victories over the corporations among Akron, Ohio, rubber workers in 1936 and Flint, Michigan, auto workers in 1937. This was followed with a new nationwide wave of unionizing along industry-wide lines, spurred ahead later in 1937 by the organization of U.S. Steel and most of the remaining large American steel companies. Illustrating this remarkable turn of events was the fact that in 1933 only about 8 percent of the workers in the United States were organized, whereas by the end of the decade, about 22 percent of the eligible work force had become union members (Lens, 1973: 326).

By this time, however, even the evangelical zeal and good intentions of the CIO were no match for the already accomplished fact of scientifically managed companies. A new generation of workers now faced a labor process that had been successfully divided between separate bodies of workers, some of whom, on the management side, concentrated on design, planning, calculation, and record keeping; the remainder were expected to perform the simple and routinized tasks that were assigned to them. Craft knowledge and craft skill had been effectively dissociated from the running of the factories, concluded Braverman (1974: 113); "henceforth it is to depend not at all upon the abilities of workers, but entirely upon the practices of management." As demonstrated below, this meant that in American society, even as the organization and products of labor were becoming more complex and sophisticated, its performance by human workers was becoming more petty, more boring, and more deskilled.

Routinization of Computer Work[12]

One way of understanding the impact of Taylorism and the general thrust toward management control in the modern workplace is to examine new craft occupations that have arisen in

American society and study the ensuing struggles by employers to routinize and deskill these jobs. Such a case study involves computer programming, which began as an occupation in the 1950s and which has employed increasing numbers of American workers.

The term "programmer" was originally an all-inclusive term applied to those responsible for the entire range of activities required to instruct a computer. In early computer installations, therefore, almost all work from problem analysis through actual computer operation was performed by the programmers. "I remember that in the fifties and early sixties I was a 'jack of all trades,' " reflected one such worker. "As a programmer I got to deal with the whole process. I would think through a problem, talk to the clients, write my own code, and operate the machine. I loved it—particularly the chance to see something through from beginning to end" (Quoted in Greenbaum, 1979: 64).

Enjoying the effects of a seller's market for their scarce labor power, many of these early programmers were also freewheeling, independent craftspersons whose strange work habits, haphazard time schedules, and casual dress often caused "culture shock" among the other more traditional corporate employees and managers. "In those days we really had control," stated one early programmer. "Management never understood what we were doing and we really didn't care. It was fun and what we were doing made us feel important—we felt like we were accomplishing something" (Greenbaum, 1979: 64–65).

By the early 1960s, however, management journals and marketing literature were beginning to call for standardization of job descriptions and routinization of data processing tasks. Particularly important was the fact that the salaries of computer workers had jumped 50 percent from 1958 to 1962, and there was high employee turnover, created by workers jumping to more highly paid jobs in other companies. As one influential industrial consultant, Dick Brandon, complained:

> The normal employer-employee relationship, which in part depends on the fear of termination or disciplinary action, does not exist. . . . It is not at all uncommon for a programmer to threaten resignation, while simultaneously generating the type of undocumented programs that increase management's dependence on him. Thus he is in a position of strength from which he can (and in the aggregate, often does) use mild blackmail to achieve greater status, money

or dominance over management. (Quoted in Greenbaum, 1979: 63)

An independent, craft-oriented computer labor force was clearly a threat to management, and, directly paralleling Taylor's earlier endeavors, shop floor supervisors began gathering systematic information on the specific tasks being performed by programmers. Consider, for instance, the following description of the manner by which one new supervisor in the early 1960s "turned his shop around":

> I knew that as long as the guys kept information about what they did from management that they could get away with being 'essential.' I started by observing the shop floor and writing up descriptions of what each guy did. Of course I had to get their confidence to do this. I offered them 'time off' as a reward and they loved it. If they got their job done in six hours instead of the full eight of the shift I let them go home early but still get paid for the shift. For those guys who really needed overtime, I saw to it that there was some to spread around. (Greenbaum, 1979: 72)

As with Taylorism, this improved work environment was only temporary. Being in possession of this systematic job information, the enterprising supervisor was able to "codify and define all the jobs." Within four months the work could be so accelerated that now instead of the original twelve employees "the shift would operate with five guys and no overtime" (Greenbaum, 1979: 71).

During the 1960s management also embarked on a program of job division and fragmentation, as "conceptual" tasks like programming were separated from "execution" chores such as operations. By the end of the decade, programming had been fragmented into four major subdivisions: systems analysis, programming, coding, and operations. Thus, systems analysts would interact directly with the users, define problems, and engage in the more creative aspects of "head" labor, while programmers would translate these general instructions into machine language, and the coders would perform many of the remaining clerical tasks. Machine operators, on the other hand, as Greenbaum (1979: 68) explained, would be left to "perform the most routine and repetitive actions, which, when fully rationalized, become 'hand' or manual labor."

Moreover, job fragmentation continued during the 1970s as within each of these four major categories developed an increasing number of subdivisions. Programmers thus became further specialized according to the type of industry for which they could write programs, such as insurance, banking, or manufacturing, and within these groupings they were usually classified by the type of computer language they used to code the programs (Greenbaum, 1979: 21–22).

The development of high-level programming languages (for example, *fortran* and *cobol*) and the development of "canned," or prewritten, general programs also allowed workers with less skill to program increasingly sophisticated and powerful computers. As Kraft (1979: 10) explained, "it became possible to operate computers with employees who were cheaper and less difficult to train, or replace, than old-style programmers."

The use of "structured programming" and "modularization" further helped employers transform data processing work from a craft activity to one more nearly resembling industrial production. Structured programming limits the range of choices available to programmers in designing and writing a program, as certain sequences are specified, limited, or prohibited altogether. Rules are also formulated concerning the use of subroutines, or discrete modular components, within these larger programs. Once these latter program fragments have been split off from the larger program, low-level programmers trained to follow a rigid set of management-prescribed guidelines can be assigned to write them even without knowledge of how these modules fit into the larger program. "If hardware makers could not yet have machines that wrote programs," observed Kraft (1979: 10), "the making of programs could be engineered to require that human programmers act in a standard, routine, and machine-like way."

These developments have freed managers from much of their dependence on highly skilled computer workers in designing and writing programs and have allowed them to construct an increasingly rigid work hierarchy within the computer room.

> Canned programs, structured programming techniques, and modularization of programs are designed to make the supervision of software workers easier and more like the supervision of other workers. By carefully designing and structuring the work so that the workers are forced to regulate their actions according to the demands of the work

process, the organization of the work and of the workplace
are turned against them. For all practical purposes, regulation and supervision become automatic. (Kraft, 1979: 12)

Managers thus define problems and give them to high-level analysts whose job it is to design the software system. The various
components are then given to separate and independent project
groups, each of whom in turn is hierarchically arranged, including managers, experienced specialists, and entry-level workers.
Even in complex systems these various program fragments can
be made "so routine, narrow, and restricted that they [are] essentially coding exercises, making no sense to the people doing the
work" (Kraft, 1979: 11–12).

Far from consisting of new highly satisfying jobs that sym-
bolize human work and dignity in a postindustrial society, as it
is sometimes portrayed as being, computer work instead has
become routinized and deskilled and a further monument to the
pervasive need for hierarchy and management control in our
present bureaucratic age.

> Yet, within only twenty years, job fragmentation and
> deskilling have degraded the jobs of computer workers, much
> as computer work has affected legions of clerical and pro-
> duction workers. This process, in which jobs have been
> divided, standardized, and simplified, has been neither acci-
> dental nor the action of an implacable force emanating from
> the technology itself. It is rather the logical outgrowth of
> management ideologies that attempt to impose both eco-
> nomic and social control over the workplace and the work-
> ers. (Greenbaum, 1979: 159)

A "scientifically" managed labor system such as Taylor
envisioned provides the conditions best adapted to hierarchical
organization and to profitable production in an employer-
dominated system. This thrust toward management control is
not dictated by the drive to increase the satisfaction of human
needs, but rather it is powered by the needs of the capital accumulation process. In fact, "each advance in productivity shrinks
the number of truly productive workers, enlarges the number of
workers who are available to be utilized in the struggles between
corporations over the distribution of the surplus, expands the
use of labor in wasteful employment or no employment at all,
and gives to all society the form of an inverted pyramid resting

upon an ever narrower base of useful labor," concluded Braverman (1974: 207). Within the prevailing capitalist economic order, people's needs have indeed become merely "externalities" since these nonmaterial and intangible things are not directly recorded on the companies' financial balance sheets.

MODERN WORKPLACE REALITIES

In capitalist production, employers purchase labor power, and with that purchase goes a contractual right, backed by law, to direct and control the labor process. Labor coordination occurs in capitalist production as it must inevitably occur in all organized human efforts, but in capitalism it necessarily takes the specific form of hierarchical coordination, in which the employers on the top must be able to control the workers on the bottom. These hierarchical or top-down management controls have evolved during the last century from relatively "simple" controls based on the direct, external reinforcements of individual foremen and managers to more complex and sophisticated forms of "structural" labor controls that emanate from the entire physical and social structure of the modern workplace and, especially in this present era of giant multinational corporations, from the extensive system of worldwide resources possessed by these modern global companies.

In the mid-nineteenth century, for instance, most U.S. businesses employed fewer than one hundred employees and were ruled directly by an employer, who in the larger firms might be assisted by a small group of foremen and managers. "These bosses exercised power personally," explained Edwards (1979: 10), "intervening in the labor process often to exhort workers, bully and threaten them, reward good performance, hire and fire on the spot, favor loyal workers, and generally act as despots, benevolent or otherwise." In this early competitive capitalist period, those firms that survived were often ones in which these employers and foremen were able to evolve personal management styles and systems of direct discipline that effectively motivated and controlled their workers.

Taylorism and other proposals by the "efficiency" experts, as we have seen, were a response to the emerging size of the new giant corporations and to the consequent decline in these organizations of the effectiveness of the prevailing systems of personal or simple labor controls. What Taylor and his employer-oriented colleagues proposed was a more sophisticated system of labor controls, resting on such things as management's possession of production knowledge, their appropriation of planning procedures, and their detailed control of each step of the labor process. Henceforth, worker control would be divorced from the immediate personalities of the individual foremen and owners and would increasingly rest on the entire structure of the workplace itself, which would include both the physical structure of the plant (machinery, architecture, and technology) and the social structure of the firm (rules, systems of job definitions and categories, and management evaluation procedures). Once evolved, employers found these new systems of structural controls more institutional and therefore less directly visible or attackable by workers. They also provided a means by which owners could control the proliferating layers of middle managers that had become such an essential part of the extended hierarchies of these emerging corporations.

After three-quarters of a century of evolution from Taylor's early notions of scientific management to more contemporary forms of management science, modern workplace realities today are dominated by the existence of pervasive and interlocking systems of structural controls embedded in companies' immediate physical and social structures and, in the case of modern multinational corporations, reinforced by an extensive global network of company resources and production alternatives. These more sophisticated management control systems also have led to increasingly sophisticated forms of worker organization and resistance.

In the following sections we will consider three major aspects of this battle for the control of labor: the evolution of machinery and the increasing technical control over work, internationalization of capital, and the further bureaucratization of work. Each of these three structural tendencies has developed since the time of Taylor, and each is important in attempting to understand the underlying realities of the modern workplace.

Mechanization and the Technical Control Over Work

As we have seen, Taylorism brought about a fundamental organizational revolution within companies that effectively split the planning and execution of work and destroyed the prevailing nineteenth-century system of craft production. The organization of work was dramatically changed; now each worker would do only one detailed operation over and over again within the overall context of industrial enterprises that were controlled and coordinated by management. During this period, moreover, this organizational revolution was reinforced by a technical revolution in which employers sought out and financed the development of machinery that would support and provide a material base for these new hierarchical workplace social relations.

Machinery as such can be employed in the service of many different objectives, for instance, making work more pleasant, interesting, safer, and more stimulating for workers. In an economic system based on profit maximization, however, work becomes a commodity, and workers themselves are viewed as tools to be used in the capital accumulation process. Since workers are only tools, it would be irrational within such a system to base serious business decisions on such worker development criteria. "If one production process produces a given commodity at 99 cents per piece, but requires workers who are mindless robots," declared Clawson (1980: 193), "it is still unquestionably superior [in capitalism] to another process that produces the same commodity at $1.00 each, and uses workers who can give free play to their creative abilities." Also, since "machinery never goes on strike," the decision to introduce new technology in many cases has been the result of labor disputes and the difficulties employers have had in controlling skilled workers.[13]

Another social control advantage inherent in machinery results from the fact that the pacing and running of the machine need no longer be vested in its immediate operator. These decisions can be made according to centralized criteria, controlled by management, and far removed from the actual site of production. Technical control, then, is realized when production in a plant or large segments of it is based on machinery that directs and controls the labor process. "When that happens," observed Edwards (1979: 113), "the pacing and direction of work transcend the individual workplace and are thus beyond the power of even the immediate boss; control becomes truly structural."[14]

Origins of the Assembly Line

Machine discipline of labor was first realized on a mass scale with the introduction of the endless mechanical conveyor system at the Ford Highland Park plant in 1914. It is important to realize that this early assembly line was not an independent invention that sprung full-blown from the inventive genius of Henry Ford. Rather, this innovation was a result of a long search by employers to improve mechanical means for controlling production and, as such, was the culmination of a series of technical advances that had the effect of further deskilling workers and fragmenting the labor process.

As early as the 1840s, for instance, northeastern textile manufacturers had introduced continuous flow production techniques that permitted the employer, rather than workers, to control the pace of work. Cyrus McCormick also used such methods in the production of reapers as early as 1847, and, by the turn of the twentieth century, large meat-packing firms such as Swift and Armour had come to rely on continuous flow "dissembly" lines in the slaughtering and processing of livestock. Under this new system the supervisors were no longer directly responsible for controlling the pace of individual workers; instead the line now determined the speed at which the work must be performed, and the foremen had merely to ensure that the workers followed the established pace.

It was the Ford assembly line, however, that brought this technical direction of work to its fullest realization. Founded in 1903, the Ford Motor Company originally had a total work force of only eight people, including Ford himself: three skilled mechanics and one shop assistant, patternmaker, draftsman, and blacksmith.[15] All these employees were highly skilled workers because the imperfect and unstandardized parts that they worked with had to be milled, bored, and ground before they could be satisfactorily assembled. The men worked as a team, planning production, solving design problems, and constructing the entire car as a unit.

As production grew the Ford managers began to divide the labor process and more directly control the pace of work. Unskilled workers were hired as parts carriers and stock handlers to assist the skilled mechanics, and work within and between the assembly gangs was also progressively divided. The "all-around" mechanics themselves were replaced gradually by specialized workers, as Gartman (1979: 196) explained: "One group of two to five men handled the attachment of the motor to the frame; other groups specialized in axles, springs, transmissions, etc. The gangs moved from one stationary chassis to the next as they completed their particular jobs."

The first moving assembly line was developed in the fly-wheel magneto (the early Model-T car generator) assembly process. A single worker at a bench performed the magneto assembly in about twenty minutes. A moving line was introduced in which the magneto assemblies were carried on an endless conveyor chain past fixed stations where various specialized workers performed twenty-nine separate operations. After the work force was improved by experience and substitution of new workers, assembly time was reduced to five minutes of one laborer's time, a 75 percent savings; management promptly cut the number of workers in this section of the shop from twenty-nine to fourteen (Gartman, 1979: 201). The endless conveyor chain was applied to the final assembly process of Ford automobiles in January 1914. "Within three months, the assembly time for the Model T had been reduced to one-tenth the time formerly needed," explained Braverman (1974: 147), "and by 1925 an organization had been created which produced almost as many cars in a single day as had been produced, early in the history of the Model T, in an entire year."

Why this dramatic savings in labor time? There were obviously some technical advantages to this new moving conveyor system. Gartman (1979: 201) estimated, for instance, that up to 17 percent of the savings came from the elimination of the time-consuming task of bringing parts to the car. He concluded that the reduction of labor time, due to increased specialization, was not an important efficiency factor since the work tasks had already been divided among detail workers by Ford managers long before the assembly line had been introduced.

Even after taking into account all the technical advantages of the new assembly line process, "the only possible explanation of this reduction of labor time is that capital sped up the assembly process," concluded Gartman (1979: 202). Now it was the managers and not the workers who controlled the pace of work; they could double and triple the rate at which assembly operations would be performed and thus subject workers to a greatly accelerated work process

Supervision of workers was also simpler because now they were tied to one spot and had no excuse to wander around. Moreover, the assembly line reduced the skill and discretion of workers in the labor process, and they now could easily be replaced by the large pool of unskilled and unemployed immigrants that existed in the United States during this period. Given this increased ease of supervision, Ford was able to reduce drastically the number of straw bosses and foremen in the plants until eventually there was only one immediate supervisor for each fifty-nine workers, "an impossible ratio except in the situation where the foremen no longer directed the sequence and pacing of work" (Edwards, 1979: 119). Furthermore, the company was able to dispense with its established practice of giving bonuses in order to stimulate production and individual initiative and reverted to the payment of a flat hourly wage rate that was more or less uniform throughout the work force.

From the beginning, workers hated the assembly line and fought with great intensity against this new form of degradation. Initially, when other auto firms had not fully adopted assembly line techniques, they could simply quit and get jobs elsewhere. Indeed, during this period workers left Ford in droves, and, as a result, annual labor turnover at the company in the years around 1914 approached 400 percent (Gartman, 1979: 204).

Absentee rates climbed to about 10 percent per day, as many Ford workers simply chose to stay home. The crisis was confounded by the halting attempts at unionization made in the summer of 1913 by the Industrial Workers of the World. Ford's reaction to this worker dissatisfaction and unionization drive was to institute new measures to control workers, including a wage of $5.00 per day, announced with much publicity in 1914, and the creation of the infamous Sociology Department whose purpose was to investigate the private lives of workers. This new wage was well above the prevailing rate in the Detroit area and thus gave the company a large pool of labor from which to choose and also made Ford workers more anxious to hold onto their jobs. "The payment of five dollars a day for an eight-hour day," Ford later wrote in his autobiography, "was one of the finest cost-cutting moves we ever made" (Quoted in Braverman, 1974: 150).

The irony of capitalist production, therefore, is that machinery, rather than extending freedom and assisting workers in the mastery of the world, becomes one instrument of more sophisticated domination and the extension of authoritarian work relations. The fact that machines can be paced by centralized decisions offers management the opportunity to control work structurally in ways much more effective than previously could be accomplished through more simple personal controls. Therefore, "the mass of humanity is subjected to the labor process for the purposes of those who control it rather than for any general purposes of 'humanity' as such," concluded Braverman (1974: 193). In addition to increasing the productivity of labor, which would

happen in any economic system, machinery now has "the function of divesting the mass of workers of their control over their
own labor."

Employers were later to discover, however, that the intricate
coordination and interdependency resulting from assembly line
production made them highly vulnerable to disruption by a relatively small number of strikers. At General Motors in 1936–37,
and a few years later at Ford, a handful of dedicated unionists
were able to shut down the plants merely by throwing down
their tools and refusing to budge from the buildings. Confronted
by this new tactic of the "sit-down strike," employers in most
basic U.S. manufacturing industries—steel, rubber, automobiles,
electrical appliances, farm implements—were forced in a relatively few years to recognize and negotiate with employee unions.
The assembly line, which had been so important in winning
employer control over the labor process, by this time also had
become an invaluable resource in the struggle by workers to
organize and win collective bargaining rights for themselves.

Computer-Based Technology and the Extension of Management Control

The Hyatt Regency Hotel in Dearborn, Michigan, which
is part of a shopping complex originally built by Henry Ford II,
was the site of an important event in December 1979. Meeting
only a short distance from Henry Ford's former home and the
Ford World Headquarters, some five hundred local union officials and staff members of the Communication Workers of America held the first conference on workplace technology ever
sponsored by an American labor union.

Although these telephone workers were focusing on issues
relating to the computerization of work, many of their complaints
would have been understandable to the early mechanics and
craftspersons whose traditional skills had been made obsolete by
the assembly line. Workers were losing their jobs because management was replacing them with computers and robots; others
were being given less interesting, lower paying work as the
decision-making parts of their jobs were taken over by computers.
Still other workers were finding their jobs more repetitious, isolated, and stressful as they were forced to sit in front of Video
Display Terminals (VDTs) for their entire eight-hour shifts.
"Members feel that they have lost the challenge of the job, the
authority to make decisions," explained a local union president

at the conference. "Also they have lost their sense of accomplishment, freedom, and overall prestige" (Howard, 1980: 21).

As we have seen, the control over the work process that Taylor sought was vastly strengthened by the adoption of new assembly line techniques resulting in a massive shift from craft to mass production in American manufacturing industries. From management's viewpoint, the value of the computer also lies in its potential for removing still further control of the pace and planning of work from the worker. This is true whether it is a programmed cutting tool in the machine shop or an automatic typewriter in the office that writes a letter while the operator merely inserts a few variable words as directed by a recorded message from the boss. These new automated systems can thus assign work, determine work pace, keep closer tabs on productivity, record unauthorized breaks or deviations from prescribed work patterns, count mistakes, and, if workers get fed up and strike, even help management keep operations going with only the assistance of a few supervisory personnel. Given these tremendous capabilities for redesigning work, therefore, this struggle for control over workplace computer technology promises to be one of the most important arenas of conflict between management and workers in the decades ahead.

With the computerization of industry, different jobs are likely to resemble each other more and more: sitting at a VDT, looking at a television-like screen, and typing in commands and responses. These electronic keyboards and screens are now being used by an estimated 5 to 7 million American workers, and by 1985 predictions are that the number of VDTs in use will more than double. It might be added that in many cases VDTs will eliminate social contact among workers, take away variety in their jobs, and keep track of their work more carefully so that they too will begin to face many of the same pressures to keep up with the machine-paced quotas that presently characterize assembly line production.

The Computerized Factory

As is the case with machinery in general, computer technology itself does not necessarily result in increased domination of workers. Technology merely opens up a range of possibilities; which solutions are selected depends on who does the choosing and for what purposes. Specifically, regarding computer technology these new electronic machines can be used either to expand worker creativity and extend worker control or they can be employed by management to degrade jobs and destroy worker skills.

THE CASE OF AUTOMATICALLY CONTROLLED MACHINE TOOLS. The development of numerical control (NC) technology to automate machine tools provides an illustrative case study of some of the decisions that determine whether the modern machinist will become a more highly skilled craftsperson or merely a "button pusher." Machine tools, such as lathes and milling machines, are used to cut away surplus materials to produce metal parts of certain desired shapes, sizes, and finishes. They remain the fundamental branch of industry because these tools are the means whereby all machinery, including the machine tools themselves, are made. Since most machine parts are created in small batches of fewer than fifty at a time, businesses have not found it profitable to invest in automated machinery to produce these specialized parts. Instead, they have hired skilled craftspersons (about 10 percent of all production workers in manufacturing industries) to run general purpose metal-cutting machines that the operator can adjust and adapt for making many different types of machine parts.

Electronic technology opened up the possibility of automating these general metal-cutting machines, however, and in 1946–47 the "record-playback" method of programming machine tools was first developed.[16] It involved having a skilled machinist make a part while the motions of the machine under his command were recorded on magnetic tape. After the first piece was made, identical parts could be made automatically by playing back a tape and reproducing the machine's motions (Noble, 1979: 22–23). The curious fact is that this promising new technology enjoyed only a brief existence and was never widely accepted in American industry. Rather, from 1949 to 1959 the U.S. Air Force spent at least $62 million on the research and development of NC technology which was based on an entirely different philosophy of manufacturing. With NC, as Noble explained,

> The specifications for a part—the information contained in an engineering blueprint—are first broken down into a mathematical representation of the part, then into a mathematical description of the desired path of the cutting tool along up to five axes, and finally into hundreds of thousands of discrete instructions, translated for economy into a

numerical code, which is read and translated into electrical signals for the machine controls. The NC tape, in short, is a means of formally circumventing the role of the machinist as the source of the intelligence of production.

Record-playback technology was much simpler and cheaper than NC and thus more suited to the small shops in which about 80 percent of the machine parts in the United States were then produced. According to Noble (1979: 28–29), record-playback was also potentially more reliable than the more elaborate NC technology since all the programming was done directly on the shop floor at the machine, which allowed errors to be eliminated during the programming process prior to actual production.

Why, then, did the control manufacturers abandon the record-playback technology in favor of NC? "The defects of record-playback were conceptual, not technical," concluded Noble (1979: 33); "the system simply did not meet the needs of the larger firms for managerial control over production." The control that machinists exercise concerning how they perform their jobs results in a strong sense of independence that is often incompatible with managerial authority. Therefore, "management's intent in the development and use of NC is clear," declared Shaiken (1979: 30): "the elimination of skill, the basis for job control by workers. This in turn saps the power workers have on the shop floor."

The NC technology thus makes it possible for management to assign programming and machine tending to different people and thereby reduce their dependence on skilled laborers. A consulting engineer at General Electric, who had been in charge of developing both technologies, candidly explained this shift by his company from record-playback to NC:

> . . . with record-playback the control of the machine remains with the machinist—control of feeds, speeds, number of cuts, output; with NC there is a shift of control to management. Management is no longer dependent upon the operator and can thus optimize the use of their machines. With NC control over the process is placed firmly in the hands of management—and why shouldn't we have it? (Quoted in Noble, 1979: 34)

Sociologist Earl Lundgren surveyed NC user plants in the 1960s and concluded that the "prime interest in each subject company was the transfer of as much planning and control from the shop to the office as possible." This finding was reinforced by Noble's own 1977–78 study of twenty-five manufacturing firms. "Everywhere, management initially believed in the promises of NC promoters and attempted to remove all decision making from the floor and assign unskilled people to NC machines," Noble explained, "and to tighten up authority by concentrating all mental activity in the office and otherwise to extend detail control over all aspects of the production process" (1979: 36).

The selection of technology is therefore essentially a political, rather than a purely technical, matter. Whenever management is free to use computer automation as it wishes, technology becomes an important weapon in undermining worker control, as is illustrated by the devastating effects of the adoption of NC technology on individual workers. Shaiken, for instance, interviewed a highly skilled aerospace machinist who was deeply frustrated over being forced to run an NC-controlled lathe: "I've worked at this trade for seventeen years. The knowledge is still in my head, the skill is still in my hands, but there is no use for either one now. I go home and I feel frustrated, like I haven't done anything. I want to work, make things around the house" (1979: 30).

ROBOTS. Microprocessors (the development of the computer on a chip that powers a growing variety of modern gadgets) also can be used along with sensing devices as controls for "robots," or general purpose machines designed so that the choice of tasks at any particular moment is determined not only by a preset program but also by some information fed into it from the outside world. By 1979 there were already approximately eight thousand such robots being used in industry, and the number is growing rapidly. As Goldhaber (1979: 20) emphasized, robots may turn out actually to be simpler to build than automobiles and can perhaps one day be mass-produced at similar costs.

The steady cost reductions and rapidly expanding versatility of these automated machines virtually guarantee their widespread deployment in industry during the coming decades. Besides such relatively simple tasks as welding, bolt assembly operations, lifting of heavy castings, and spray painting, General Motors claims that it will soon be using robots for many other relatively detailed jobs such as putting light bulbs into dashboards and fitting armatures into small electric motors. Texas Instruments is currently using camera-assisted robots for watch and calculator assembly operations (*Dollars and Sense*, December 1979: 16).

COMPUTERIZED MANAGEMENT REPORTING SYSTEMS. Although the impact of both NC-controlled machines and robots is considerable, this influence will be dwarfed during the coming years as separate computer systems are tied together into a totally computerized factory. "It is already technically possible to go from the designers' pen in the engineering office to the production of a part with no intervening human skills," emphasized Shaiken (1979: 34). On the shop floor, a large central computer manages armies of smaller computers, which in turn direct and monitor microprocessors that maintain tabs on every worker and operation in the plant. The system routes parts through the shop, controls machine tools, keeps track of inventories, and reports to management the work patterns of the various individual workers.

Already installed in many plants, management data reporting systems tie workers to certain machines while simultaneously gathering and reporting information on their labor activities. One worker commented on the effects of such a system—the Shop Activities Management—which was installed at General Electric's Lynn, Massachusetts, aircraft parts manufacturing plant: "Actually, the system allows the company to keep closer track of each worker and to more easily raise production standards," he emphasized. "It also gives foremen greater access to personnel records, including attendance and tardiness, so if they want to take disciplinary action against somebody, the excuse is a lot handier." Shaiken explained how this integrated management reporting technology functions in the case of a single machine operator making automobile axles:

> The central computer is linked to a mini-computer on the machine. Every time the machine makes a part, or 'cycles,' it registers in the computer. When the machine doesn't produce a part within the allotted time, that fact is immediately obvious: it is both displayed on a video screen in the foreman's office and recorded on a computer printout. The foreman is instructed to go to the machine and investigate the problem. The printout is forwarded to higher management for analysis. Every minute of the worker's time must be accounted for. The record states how many minutes late he returned from lunch or break, how many minutes the machine was down without explanation, and how many breakdown minutes were recorded.

With the advent of the computerized factory, therefore, the potential for the technical control of work will be greatly enhanced. The discretion of individual supervisors, for example, may be much less; instead of making independent decisions about whether or not to discipline workers, they may be obligated to carry out the "automatic" decisions programmed into the computer supervisory system. In this highly structured environment, managerial control will be more deeply embedded in the physical structure of the organization, and the work process itself may not even be open to policy decisions or negotiations by the managers and workers physically present at the production site.

Automating the Office

Taylor proposed that the functions of thought and planning be concentrated in the office in contrast to the shop where all manual labor was to be performed. In its beginnings, then, office work resembled a craft; clerks were often all-around workers who had extended responsibilities that today would be classified as managerial or administrative. "Master craftsmen, such as bookkeepers or chief clerks, maintained control over the process in its totality," emphasized Braverman (1974: 298–99), "and apprentices or journeymen craftsmen—ordinary clerks, copying clerks, office boys—learned their craft in office apprenticeships, and in the ordinary course of events advanced through the levels of promotion." A bookkeeper, intimately familiar with all of the financial details of the firm, might thus readily be consulted by the owner on financial decisions, and in the 1920s one secretary actually ran a business for most of the year while the head of the firm lived in the southwest for his health (Glenn and Feldberg, 1979: 53).

As American corporations grew larger and more complex, however, the demand for clerical workers expanded rapidly. In 1870, for instance, these office employees were only about seven-tenths of 1 percent of the work force; in 1900 they were almost 3 percent; and at the present time they represent nearly one out of every five American workers, or about 18 percent of the total labor force. In office industries, such as banking and insurance, clerical workers are now about one-half the total work force, whereas in public administration they are well over one-third, and in transportation and utilities, one-quarter (Tepperman, 1976: 39).

As office work became a significant expense for companies, efficiency experts began experimenting with ways in which scientific management techniques, previously applied to shop labor, could now be employed in the office as well. As was the case in the plant, primary concerns in this modern office reorganization were the breaking down of work into the simplest possible jobs and then hiring detail workers to perform each of these repetitive tasks all day long. In a typical insurance company, for instance, opening mail, rating policies, coding information for computers, keypunching, checking medical information, filing, and other individual tasks are each performed by separate specialized workers. In fact, as Glenn and Feldberg (1979: 54) observed, one large insurance company had over 350 separate job titles for its 2,000 clerical employees. Offices thus come to resemble factories for processing information.

> Many clericals work in huge rooms, with rows of people sitting at desks or machines. . . . The work is often organized on an assembly-line basis, with each person doing only one step in the whole process. The close working relationship of the private secretary to her boss has grown less common, as huge, impersonal office organizations have developed. One file clerk at John Hancock said, 'My manager has only talked to me twice in five years—once when we were stuck in an elevator together.' (Tepperman, 1976: 41–42)

The standardization and routinization of office jobs also has been both a cause and an effect of the further mechanization of clerical tasks. This new office technology involves several elements: the use of computers to capture, process, and store large quantities of information; the use of electronic communications to transmit information within and between offices; and the application of systems and behavioral sciences to analyze and simulate office procedures in order to automate them. As predicted by the Stanford Research Institute, the investment in equipment per office employee is expected to rise to $10,000 by 1985, which would mean that the "total market for office systems technology could reach $85 billion" by that time (Glenn and Feldberg, 1979: 54, 60).

Like production workers before them, clerical employees are thus increasingly tied to expensive machines that both standardize and dictate the pace and flow of their work. The computerized word processing machine, for example, stores form letters and "canned" paragraphs in memory or on magnetic tapes, typing them out automatically at 160 to 180 words per minute. The typist's task is merely to stop the machine at intervals and insert names or other special information. Exxon Information System's new "Qyx" word processing typewriter can even mail a letter electronically, office to office, in twenty seconds, dialing from the typewriter itself, assuming that there is also another "Qyx" typewriter at the other end of the line (*Dollars and Sense*, November 1979: 13).

In many of the larger offices, there are also increasing pressures to utilize these new office machines in clerical pooling arrangements, eliminating general "private" secretaries, except for high-status managers, and further standardizing clerical tasks. At a public utility company studied by Glenn and Feldberg (1979: 58–59), for instance, IBM's Word Processing/Administrative Support System had been introduced. While managers (called "clients" in the new system) previously had personal secretaries, supplemented by a typing pool, now secretarial work was divided among three pools.

The first of these pools, the Word Processing Unit, is composed of two clerical assistants and eight general service clerks who type on computerized word processing machines. A supervisor receives and parcels out the work assignments and instructions obtained from recording equipment that automatically accepts dictation telephoned in by the clients at any time of the day or night, even from distant cities. Ten to twelve women in the second pool, the Administrative Support Center, handle all the nontyping clerical tasks such as answering telephones, scheduling appointments, ordering supplies, and keeping records and charts. Working for thirty to forty clients, this unit also has a head supervisor and two assistants. Reproduction work, in turn, is performed by a third pool, which consists of four or five men and women.

In secretarial schools, clerical workers are still trained in a wide range of office skills, but many of them find that when they enter the modern mechanized office their extremely specialized jobs preclude their using and maintaining many of these skills. Such traditional specialties as stenography and bookkeeping, which required extensive training, for instance, have been displaced or simplified beyond recognition. The skills now required are more mechanical in nature, such as operating a copying machine, explained Glenn and Feldberg (1979: 61); they tend also to be narrow and low-level skills such as typing addresses on automatically typed correspondence.

The growing job fragmentation means that few office workers really understand the overall nature of their work. This artificially inflates the importance of the office manager, who often is the only one who understands the total office work routine and thus aids in employee control, but it also contributes to worker alienation and the meaninglessness of much contemporary office work.

This simplification of jobs and relative absence of mental activity often make the work more demanding. Glenn and Feldberg observed that "the worker experiences great pressure to work quickly, accurately, and to maintain the pace set by the machines." In their study, these researchers also found that this strain of routine work was demonstrated by clerical workers' emphasis on their need for temperamental qualities rather than skills. For instance, patience was mentioned by fourteen of thirty workers. "You need a lot of patience," stated a twenty-one-year-old typist in Word Processing. "You need to be more or less good-natured, easy going. Sometimes the tension gets really bad" (1979: 62).

Furthermore, the deskilling of clerical labor has reduced the opportunities for upward mobility. More energetic and ambitious employees reach the top of their job ladders in a few years, and, like assembly line workers, they also find the skills they develop on the job rarely qualify them for better positions in new settings. Their dead-end positions and relatively low salaries become associated in the organization with a general lack of respect and job prestige. As one insurance clerk observed,

> I don't think Travelers cares anything at all about their employees. They just don't have any respect for the work we do, they think that any idiot could do it. A lot of it is very technical and time consuming and it has to be very exact. I think that's the thing I hate most. They just don't think we're important at all, that we're *just* clericals. (Tepperman, n.d.: 7)

Like the computerized factory described above, the automated office requires that information be handled in a standardized form. As a result, work throughout the organization is structured by the requirements of the computer. "Although the

clerks may be less directly supervised, they do not gain autonomy," explained Glenn and Feldberg (1979: 56), "the requirements of the machine replace the directives of an immediate
supervisor." Mental choices are therefore limited to predeter-
mined categories and there is little discretion possible on the job.
Managerial control in the office, like the factory, has become
highly impersonal and external in form and deeply embedded
in the technical structure of the organization.

Taming Middle-level and Professional Employees

As we have seen, the two basic tendencies operating in the
capitalist organization of work are the conversion of all other
forms of labor power into wage or salaried labor that is purchased
and sold in the marketplace, and the control of larger and larger
segments of the labor force by more sophisticated and exacting
scientific management procedures. Perhaps the last major grouping of workers to be brought into this new precisely managed
wage labor system are middle-level and professional employees,
a heterogeneous occupational category that embraces scientists,
engineers, and many advanced technical workers, middle-level
managers and administrators, and the traditional professional
practitioners such as lawyers, teachers, and physicians. Until
recently these types of middle-level and professional workers,
who presently make up about 15 to 20 percent of the labor force,
have experienced much independence and exercised considerable
control over their own labor activities. Since World War Two,
however, employers also have developed elaborate systems of
bureaucratic controls designed to regulate the work of these more
privileged employees. These bureaucratic controls, to be discussed below, have been reinforced by more sophisticated technical controls, based on the development of new machinery and
technology.
    "The erosion of the power of the established professions will
be a striking feature of the second phase of the Computer Revolution," declared renowned computer scientist and author
Christopher Evans (1979). The special vulnerability of the
professions to advanced computer technology is related to their
basic strength: they act as exclusive repositories and dissemi-
nators of specialized knowledge.

    The professions guard their secrets closely, insisting on
    careful scrutiny and rigorous training of individuals who

wish to enter their ranks. But this state of privilege can only persist as long as the special data and the rules for its administration remain inaccessible to the general public. Once the barriers which stand between the average person and this knowledge dissolve, the significance of the profession dwindles and the power and status of its members shrink. Characteristically, the services which the profession originally offered then become available [with the assistance of new computer technology] at a very low cost. (Evans, 1979: 122)

The first signs of this appearance of computers in medicine, for instance, may be their use in routine medical interviewing, screening, advice, and diagnosis. Large areas of the legal practice, such as searches for legal precedents and routine brief writing, also may yield its secrets to the computer. This automation of "mental work" by computers is now only in its beginning stages, but over the coming decades it would seem to possess much of the same potential for the control and pacing of work that has already been evidenced in the factory and office.

Technology is also being applied to teaching—closed circuit television, computer-assisted instruction, programmed teaching, systems learning approaches—not merely to complement the work of regular teachers but also increasingly to replace this human labor. From a management perspective this application of teaching technology has many advantages analogous to those we have already witnessed in other occupational areas: reducing labor costs, undermining resistance to management control by breaking down student-teacher interaction, separating students from one another by placing them before machines, providing needed markets for high-technology companies such as IBM, and getting students accustomed to the types of machines they will be associated with in their jobs after graduation. "It affords close political control over the content of instruction," concluded a group of City University of New York researchers, and "it allows for standardized teaching and grading" (Newt Davidson Collective, 1974: 91).

Future of Technical Control

The present trend toward workplace automation reduces the number of skilled workers and weakens America's already weak industrial and craft unions, with the possible exceptions of the organized public sector and technical workers. As we will

see in the following section, this trend is also related to the loss
and relocation of jobs from the northeastern and midwestern
sections of the country where labor organization is strongest and
movements to other parts of the country and abroad where labor
unions are weak or nonexistent.

"If labor does not find ways to control technology, then
management will use technology to control labor," emphasized
Shaiken (1979: 37). As presently constituted, the labor movement
is ill-equipped to cope successfully with issues of advanced technology. "American unions typically do not perceive technology
as a human process whose goals and character they could influence," explained Goldhaber (1979: 28). "With technology viewed
as an external force—which corresponds to the way technological
change is experienced by most workers—union responses have
been limited to resistance or, more commonly, acceptance."

PAYING FOR PAST SUCCESSES.   To a significant extent the
present trend toward automation is a management response to
past labor successes: relatively high wages, benefits, seniority,
and workplace and safety rights. California's farm wages have
risen 20 percent faster than farm wages in any other state in the
last five years, for instance, as a result of a vigorous organizing
drive by the United Farm Workers (UFW). In turn, a major
response by the growers has been the mechanization of farm
jobs. An investment of $200,000 or more for a mechanized har-
vester may seem to be a large expense, but as one grower
explained: "The machine won't strike for more money, and will
work when we want it to." The California State Assembly Office
of Research estimates that over the next ten years mechanization
threatens to displace as many as 120,000 farm workers, which
would be one-third to one-half of the state's entire farm work
force (*Dollars and Sense*, March 1978: 14–15).

The tremendous power of this computer-based automation,
therefore, gives labor organizations like the UFW little alternatives but to challenge management over how the workplace is
organized. Public taxpayers not only pay for much of this research
but are also saddled with many of the "hidden" social costs of
mechanization in the form of higher welfare costs, escalating
crime rates by unemployed workers, and the lost human resources
and contributions of these displaced persons. One unemployed
worker summed up his feelings: "We have worked hard for these
growers all our lives. When they bought tractors to pull the plows,
they cut the horses' necks and ate horsemeat. That might be a

kinder end than the future they are preparing for us" (*Dollars and Sense*, March 1978: 15).

EMPLOYING COMPUTERS TO BRING A ONCE MIGHTY PRINTERS' UNION TO ITS KNEES. Labor relations with the printers became particularly troublesome for *Washington Post* publisher Katherine Graham in the late 1960s, as these skilled craftspersons demanded increasing control over their work activities. First organized in 1852, the printers had long been regarded as one of America's strongest craft unions. A Harvard Business School study described the extent of the power of the *Washington Post* printers:

> Printers would curse their supervisors and had even thrown slugs at them. The stereotypers had responded to the arrival of a new production manager, whom they considered anti-union, by imposing a $10 fine on any member who talked to him. (The ban of silence was only removed eight months after the manager had significantly improved working conditions.) Pressmen had occasionally displayed their disapproval of certain executives by shutting down the presses when those individuals came into the pressroom. (Quoted in Zimbalist, 1979: 118)

Given this power, the printers were able to negotiate successful contracts in 1967 and 1969 by staging slowdowns and in 1971 by disrupting operations for several weeks. Graham countered in November 1971 by hiring a new general manager, John Prescott, and giving him a mandate to assert managerial control over the rebellious union. Prescott, in turn, inaugurated "Project X," which was aimed at countering the union's ability to shut down production. By introducing new computerized technology and sending employees to the *Post*'s own secret school in Virginia, the strategy was to develop the capacity to print a newspaper without craft union labor.

In a 1973 labor confrontation, although only partially successful in introducing the new automated printing processes, the *Post*'s labor relations chief, Larry Wallace, vowed that, when the pressmen's contract expired in 1975, "the company [would] regain control of the pressroom, which meant exempting all salaried supervisors from union discipline" (Zimbalist, 1979: 119). Indeed, the union remained on strike for weeks, but the *Post* was able, with automated processes, to continue production and eventually to decertify the pressmen. Following the lead of newspapers in

Miami, Los Angeles, Portland (Oregon), New Haven, Dallas, and Kansas City, Zimbalist (1979: 121) explained, "the *Post* had successfully used new technology and other tactics to break the pressmen's union."

Internationalization of Capital

Besides technology, a second basis of the contemporary structural controls over work lies in the worldwide system of resources and production alternatives possessed by modern global companies. In the United States, as was described above, this present internationalization of capital had its beginnings in the wave of corporate mergers that took place between 1897 and 1905. Reacting to a sustained period of depression and reduced profits, companies sought during these years to eliminate competition and thereby raise prices through a wave of mergers in which more than 5,300 separate business firms came under the control of 318 emerging giant corporations (Dowd, 1978: 126).

A second wave of business mergers took place in the period from the mid-1920s to the mid-1930s, and this time the trend toward economic concentration also often took the form of vertical mergers in which giant firms absorbed their suppliers, distributors, or both, with financial backing coming from large investment banking houses. It was during these years, for instance, that the major oil companies emerged, "using networks of wholly owned or franchised small companies to control the petroleum industry, from drilling through refining to the retail sale of gasoline" (Bluestone, Harrison, and Baker, 1981: 42).

Beginning in about the mid-1950s the present merger wave has been characterized by "conglomerate" mergers in which the companies bought are often in product areas unrelated to those of the acquiring firms. Between 1953 and 1968, for example, there were over 14,000 mergers of manufacturing corporations in the United States, and the acquiring corporations obtained $66 billion in new assets. By the late 1960s more than four-fifths of all these corporate mergers were conglomerate in nature. This expansion was dominated by eight corporations: ITT, Gulf & Western, Ling-Temco-Vought, Tenneco, White Consolidated, Teledyne, Occidental Petroleum, and Litton Industries, with six of these companies each making acquisitions during the 1960s totaling more than $1 billion (Dowd, 1978: 129–30).

Industrial growth and mergers thus have resulted in an accelerating domination by America's largest corporations. In 1955, for example, less than 45 percent of all persons working in manufacturing and mining industries were employees of the top 500 corporations, but by 1970 this figure had risen to 72 percent. Also during this period these 500 corporations increased their share of all manufacturing and mining assets in the country from 40 to 70 percent. In addition, finance capital is becoming more concentrated, with the top four of America's nearly 13,000 banks—the Bank of America, Chase Manhattan, the First National City Bank, and Manufacturers Hanover Trust—currently possessing more than 16 percent of all the nation's bank assets (Barnet and Müller, 1974: 230, 232).

In 1950 there were 440 beer companies in the United States, whereas today there are only 48, and the five largest producers—Anheuser-Busch, Miller, Schlitz, Pabst, and Coors—control 74 percent of the market. This trend toward monopolization is also reflected in other industries, with a recent survey by the Department of Commerce showing that the four biggest companies control 98 percent of locomotive production, 90 percent of steam engine and turbine production, 83 percent of laundry equipment production, 66 percent of metal can production, 79 percent of typewriter production, 94 percent of telephone equipment production, 73 percent of tire production, 66 percent of aircraft production, 60 percent of steel production, 73 percent of aluminum rolling stock production, 58 percent of computer production, 83 percent of cigarette production, and 99 percent of domestic automobile production (Babson and Brigham, 1977: 42).

The Rise of Planetary Business Enterprises

Accompanying this increased economic concentration also has been the creation of global companies whose productive facilities and marketing operations are integrated on a worldwide basis. The power of these global corporations derives from such sources as their increased control over new technology, their greater ability to borrow and amass large amounts of capital to finance their own expansion, and the ability to create and satisfy a demand for their goods by diffusing a consumption ideology through their control of advertising, mass media, and popular culture. "The global corporation is the most powerful human organization yet devised for colonizing the future," observed Barnet and Müller (1974: 363). "By scanning the entire planet for opportunities, by shifting its resources from industry to industry and country to country, and by keeping its overriding goal simple—worldwide profit maximization—it has become an institution of unique power."

The most revolutionary aspect of these new world companies is that, rather than viewing overseas factories and markets merely as adjuncts of their home operations, they have succeeded in integrating their widely dispersed productive operations and facilities into single organic structures in which each part is expected to serve the whole. Based on the opportunities opened up by new computer and telecommunications technology, for example, success and failure in these global enterprises is no longer measured by the balance sheet of an individual subsidiary, the sales of a particular product line, or the social impact of the company on a particular country but rather in the growth of wealth and market shares on a worldwide scale. Before the product reaches the consumer, therefore, it may bear the stamp of several countries: the capital of one, the natural resources of a second, and the labor of a third. For example, Massey-Ferguson, a Canadian-based global company, assembles French-made transmissions, Mexican-made axles, and British-made engines in a Detroit plant for the Canadian market (Barnet and Müller, 1974: 27–28).

Private Power Versus the Public Interest

Conglomeration and the creation of world companies usually creates little or no new productive capacity; capital assets are merely shifted from one organization to another without creating new products or providing new employment opportunities. "The 'increased efficiency' and 'rationalization' of the operation of widespread businesses which is usually heralded as a principal benefit of mergers is in fact something of a myth," declared Bluestone, Harrison, and Baker (1981: 43). "Often the result is duplication of services and functions and great inefficiency; for acquired companies whose assets are drained off, the result—which we can see with alarming frequency—is a rapid decline in profitability and a sudden sale or shutdown."

The competitive edge held by global corporations over their smaller business rivals, therefore, would appear to be largely a result of political rather than purely economic factors. Contrary to the model of perfect competition, for instance, companies such as the automobile makers, the steel firms, and the cigarette producers may compete with one another through innovations and advertising but rarely do they compete through direct price competition. Generally such price cutting is regarded as an antisocial practice, and, once started, the process of retaliatory price cuts could spiral out of control and reduce drastically the profits for all firms in the market area. Prices for large monopoly corporations tend thus to be administered rather than being solely a result of market forces, and studies of the profits of these giant companies show them to be as much as 30 percent higher than their smaller competitive sector counterparts. Research also demonstrates that the prices of goods and services provided by these monopoly sector firms over the past two decades have risen two to three times faster than the overall American inflation rate.

Since the mid-1960s the U.S. government has shown a declining ability—and with the Reagan administration, a declining motivation—to regulate the activities of global companies. It is impossible for the Internal Revenue Service to tax properly a company like Sears, Roebuck, for instance, which can make worldwide investments by means of its own offshore bank located conveniently just outside of IRS control. Through "creative" accounting methods, such as "transfer pricing," global companies can artificially enhance the value of their subsidiaries, thus deducting heavily for their operating costs while, at the same time, they may be milking them of their profits.

Companies often give their stockholders a much rosier picture of their overall financial situation than they do to the tax assessors. In 1966, for example, the oil industry showed profits of $3 billion on their own books but reported only $1.5 billion to the IRS. According to Barnet and Müller (1974: 279–80), some companies employ up to five different sets of books in their foreign subsidiaries: set one is to keep track of the costs of production, set two is for the local tax collector, set three is for the IRS, set four is for worldwide accounting purposes, and set five is for currency transactions. "Because of their ability to take advantage of certain provisions of the Internal Revenue Code, especially those which permit deferral of tax on foreign earnings and a credit for foreign taxes," continued these authors, "a U.S. based global company is likely to keep a greater share of a dollar earned abroad than a dollar earned in the United States."

Corporate income as a percentage of total income earned in the United States has remained relatively constant during recent years, but corporations are now paying a significantly reduced share of total taxes. The effective federal income tax rate paid by U.S. corporations, for instance, has declined from 51 percent in 1960 to only 28 percent in 1974 (Bluestone, Harrison, and Baker, 1981: 46). Since overall federal spending has increased substantially during this period, the result has been a new type of "corporate welfarism" in which higher taxes on individual taxpayers have been used increasingly to subsidize services previously paid for by the companies. Moreover, as a result of their political power, the largest global firms pay considerably less taxes than do their weaker competitors. Large companies can win greater tax concessions from cities, states, and even countries because of the significant number of jobs and greater capital investment involved. Thus, statistics show that in 1969, for example, the top 100 giants paid a federal tax rate of only 26.9 percent, while all corporations below the top 100 were paying at the average rate of 44 percent (Barnet and Müller, 1974: 273–74).

New Forms of Labor Control

During the 1960s, U.S. multinational corporations began opening increasing numbers of plants in low-wage countries in Latin America and Asia, transferring their production to these foreign locations. In 1971 the world's twenty-seven major electronics companies employed 3,940,833 persons, and the twelve world leaders of the automobile industry had a worldwide work force of 2,401,223. The largest American-based global corporations, such as Ford, ITT, Kodak, and Procter & Gamble, employ more than one-third of their work force outside the United States. As of 1966, U.S.-based global firms employed overseas 3,324,321 non-Americans, approximately 30 percent of their total payrolls. The figure is unquestionably much higher today, as demonstrated by ITT, which currently has a world payroll of 425,000 employees in seventy countries (Barnet and Müller, 1974: 303).

As a result of this migration of jobs out of the United States, Bluestone, Harrison, and Baker (1981: 13) reported that between 1969 and 1976 at least 15 million jobs were destroyed in this country as a consequence of plant closings and shutdowns, an average of 2.1 million jobs each year. On a regional basis, there also recently has been a mass exodus of industry from the northern tier of old industrial states—the so-called "frost belt"—to the more nearly union-free environments of the southern and western states. From 1960 to 1976, for instance, southern manufacturing capital stock grew almost twice as fast as that of the Northeast, and 65 percent faster than in the North Central region. This does little to diminish the problem of foreign flight by corporations, however, since the rate at which manufacturing plants closed and escaped the country is actually greater at the present time in the South than anywhere else in the United States (Bluestone, Harrison, and Baker, 1981: 13).

LOWER WAGES.   One major reason global companies are moving production to foreign countries is their constant search for cheaper labor. As an outgrowth of Taylorism, the labor process has now become so fragmented that the most unskilled workers can perform much of the labor associated with even the most technologically advanced products. This deskilling of the machine operator allows low-skilled assembly jobs to be separated from the more sophisticated research and engineering tasks and thus be shipped to wherever in the world workers can be hired most cheaply. These recipient nations are primarily economically underdeveloped countries in the Third World, with particular emphasis at the present time on Asia (see Table 2). Wages remain so low in these countries because all are ruled by dictatorial governments, backed in most cases by U.S. intelligence and military support, which suppress all political opposition, unions, and other types of working-class movements.

It therefore makes sense for General Electric to ship components to Indonesia where they can be assembled at 17¢ per

Table 2. Hourly Wages for Unskilled Workers in Asian Countries to Which U.S. Plants Have Moved

Country	Hourly Wage	Country	Hourly Wage
Indonesia	17¢	Malaysia	41¢
Thailand	26¢	South Korea	52¢
Philippines	32¢	Hong Kong	55¢
India	37¢	Singapore	62¢
Taiwan	37¢		

Source: This table is taken from Brecher (1979: 220). These are average wage rates calculated for unskilled workers in 1976 U.S. dollars as an average of monthly high- and low-wage rates for a standard forty-six-hour week.

hour rather than producing them in the Ashland, Massachusetts, plant for $5.50 per hour. As a consequence, between 1957 and 1967 GE built sixty-one plants overseas, with a number of these moves being made as a response to threatened strikes and labor disputes with American workers. Today, Fairchild Camera, Texas Instruments, and Motorola have settled in Hong Kong to take advantage of the 800 to 900 percent labor savings and seven-day working week conditions there. Timex and Bulova make an increasing portion of their watches in Taiwan, where they share a union-free labor pool with RCA, Admiral, Zenith, and a large number of other American corporations (Barnet and Müller, 1974: 29). Just how profitable these moves have been was explained by the manager of a plant in Malaysia: "One worker working one hour produces enough to pay the wages of 10 workers working one shift plus all the costs of materials and transport" (Sivanandan, 1979: 122).

LABOR AND CAPITAL IN THE SILICON AGE. It is sometimes said that the microprocessor is to the modern industrial revolution what the steam engine was to the old except that, where the steam engine replaced human muscle, microelectronics replaces the brain. However marvelous they may be, microcomputers are still produced by old-fashioned industrial methods involving the exploitation of labor, partly in the United States and partly in sweatshops in Asia. Their manufacture, therefore, provides an illustration of the worldwide division of labor initiated by modern global companies.[17]

Different types of workers perform each of the several stages of microcomputer production. The initial research and design of the circuits is complex technical work, and for this reason microcomputer companies have usually sprung up around major American universities. One cluster of such companies is located on Route 118 around Boston, a spin-off of MIT and Harvard. Because the Boston area electronics workers are strongly unionized, however, the industry has grown more rapidly in the Palo Alto-San Jose area of California near Stanford University and the University of California, Berkeley.

The first stage of production involves cutting pure silicon wafers, three or four inches long, into several hundred computer chips. The circuit designs are then photographed, reduced to a small fraction of their original size, and photoengraved onto the wafers. Since this stage of production requires complex, expensive equipment, much of the work is done in the companies' home plants, many of which are located in a six-square mile area south of San Francisco, popularly known as the "Silicon Valley." Today, 500 electronics facilities are located in this area, employing more than 160,000 people.

The assemblers, who are usually minority women often working without the benefits of minimum wages, Social Security, or workers' compensation, also face unhealthy working conditions. Silicon wafer production and photoengraving involve elaborate chemical reactions, and the industry now employs 10 percent of the chemicals used in the United States, including some of the most dangerous: corrosive hydrochloric and hydrofluoric acids, toxic solvents such as xylene, dangerous poisons including arsine gas and cyanide, and known and suspected carcinogens like vinyl chloride and trichloroethylene (Martinez and Ramo, 1980: 12). Consequently, according to recent government statistics, the growth of the electronics industry has been accompanied by a 20 percent increase in the death rate in the Silicon Valley area over the last eight years, and job related illnesses in these firms are reported to be more than four times that of industry as a whole. Workers complain of physical problems after using these chemicals, ranging from nausea, headaches, dizziness, skin rashes, respiratory problems, and liver and kidney ailments. Many employees, however, are not aware that they are working with known carcinogens and toxic substances with long-range health effects, and some people have even brought these materials into their homes.

Because the final stage of microcomputer production involves extremely repetitive manual work that requires little equipment other than a microscope, most of this work is shipped to Asian countries where labor is cheaper. California-based microcomputer companies have at least sixty-five Asian plants, mainly in Malaysia, Singapore, Hong Kong, Taiwan, and South Korea. Wages range from $90 per month in Taiwan to $43.20 in Malaysia, and almost all the work force are women between the ages of sixteen and twenty-five.

FUTURE OF GLOBAL CONTROL. The ability of global corporations to open and close plants rapidly and to shift their investments from one country to another has greatly strengthened their control over labor. Through strategies such as "parallel production," world companies protect themselves against the strike by employing different plants in various countries to produce the same components. Companies such as Chrysler, British Leyland, Goodyear, Michelin, and Volkswagen are among the many firms that use these parallel production techniques to

make themselves independent of the labor force in any one plant
(Barnet and Müller, 1974: 309). Similarly, in the purchase of
goods, corporations also can enhance their own power by playing
off suppliers against each other by refusing to grant sole source
arrangements, even to subcontractors who might offer a slight
competitive advantage.

Illustrative of one of the many difficulties workers encounter
in dealing with large global corporations is the massive power
these world companies possess over their employees, as exem-
plified by the defeat of the Royal Typewriter strikers by Litton
Industries.[18] After its incorporation as a small electronics firm
in 1953, Litton acquired more than one hundred other companies
within twenty years to become the thirty-fifth largest U.S. industrial corporation. One important merger in the overall development of this conglomerate was the 1965 acquisition of Royal
Typewriter, the second largest U.S. firm in the industry. During
the next three years Litton also bought three European typewriter manufacturers, including Triumph-Adler, West Germany's largest. In February 1969 the management at Royal
Typewriter's Springfield, Missouri, plant refused to renegotiate
an expiring contract, precipitating a general strike by Local 469
of the Allied Industrial Workers. Two months later Litton offered
striking workers a new contract with a modest pay raise, no extra
fringe benefits, no job security provisions, and the elimination
of the union shop. Royal's strikers unanimously rejected the
company's offer, and management reacted the following day by
permanently shutting down the plant. Litton transferred part of
the Springfield operation to Royal's Hartford, Connecticut, plant
and part to Litton's European typewriter divisions. A few years
later Litton also closed the Hartford plant, transferring all its
typewriter manufacturing operations out of the United States.

Since it is easier to move capital than to move workers and
their families, global companies such as Litton Industries have
immense advantages over labor. By 1968 the company had twenty-
six separate labor contracts with eleven different unions, making
a company-wide strike nearly impossible to organize. In addition,
typewriters accounted for less than 8 percent of Litton's sales in
1969, so the loss of Royal's production barely dented Litton's
profits.

During the last few years several unions have successfully
negotiated contract provisions to protect jobs and wages, or at
least to guarantee severance benefits in cases involving runaway
corporations. For example, the major electrical unions have won

an agreement from the Westinghouse Corporation for two years' prior notice in the event of a partial or complete shutdown. This agreement also covers layoffs connected with changes in production lines and gives the unions limited access to the company's records pertaining to long-term investment and production plans. Other new contracts between the United Food and Commercial Workers and several meat-packing firms prohibit the companies from closing a plant and then reopening it on a nonunion basis within five years (Bluestone, Harrison, and Baker, 1981: 81–82).

Because of their higher living standards, however, American workers play a diminishing role in the global corporate work force. In effect these world companies have succeeded in creating an integrated planet-wide proletariat and also a global reserve army of surplus unemployed workers. In the intensifying class struggles of the coming decades, labor has no choice but to aggressively organize within and, more importantly, across regional and national boundaries. Recently some labor unions, mostly in Europe, have experienced modest successes in negotiating international labor contracts, but there nevertheless persists tremendous obstacles to transnational labor organizing.

Bureaucratization

The nineteenth-century craft production system was based on workers' training and skills, training that for the most part was received on the shop floor from other workers. Taylor recognized that this system of divided control was inherently unstable and must be abolished if employers were ever to dominate production. The key to Taylorism thus was a strategy for removing control over the work process and the planning of work from shop floor employees. A new group management was to be created which would learn what the workers already knew—how to plan and direct the details of the work process—and would use this knowledge to issue detailed specific orders to each individual worker. This required an increase in the size of management (amounting to perhaps one-third of the entire work force), but in this way workers could be made to obey employer directives and increase output.

The brainwork that had previously been spread throughout the work force was now to be concentrated on by managers who would be socialized primarily in schools and colleges rather than on the shop floor. Since they do not produce goods, these managers are not themselves productive workers, but rather they organize work in such a way that production workers would have as little need as possible to use their own skills and initiative. "The work which used to be united in one group is now split in two," explained Clawson (1980: 253), "but it is important to understand that both parts—the bureaucratic apparatus and the routinized deskilled production work—are aspects of one unity." Production workers who mindlessly obey detailed orders are thus the flip side of the coin of an expanded management force that now has usurped the right to organize and plan the entire work process.

Controlling employees through this enforced split between the conception and execution of work was enhanced, as we have seen, through machine pacing and the development of more sophisticated technical controls. The internationalization of capital also has magnified greatly the power of these global corporate structures over the lives and futures of their individual employees. Especially since World War II these two sources of management power have been reinforced by the development of increasingly elaborate and effective bureaucratic controls over work.

As Edwards (1979: 131) described it, these bureaucratic controls also developed out of the formal structure of the firm rather than emanating directly from the personal relationships between workers and bosses. Whereas the earlier structural controls over production workers were a result of such things as plant architecture and the design of machines, these bureaucratic controls are "embedded in the social and organizational structure of the firm and are built into job categories, work scales, definitions of responsibilities, and the like." Bureaucratic control establishes the impersonal force of company rules or policy as the basis of control.

Bureaucratic control thus institutionalizes the power of the employer by making power appear to emanate from the formal organization itself. Authoritarian work relations are transformed from relations between particular bosses and employees to formal bureaucratic rules and procedures. The power of the employer remains the power to establish the rules in the first place, but within this maze of formal policies and procedures the hierarchical nature of the work relations tends to be somewhat more hidden from view. In fact, bureaucratic controls have the potential of being even more totalitarian than earlier less sophisticated management systems because they can often more nearly dominate the total personality and behavior of the worker. "In bureaucratic control," concluded Edwards (1979: 148), "workers owe not only a hard day's work to the corporation but also their demeanor and affections." Conscientious work therefore is no longer enough; the worker must also internalize the enterprise's goals and values. "Now the 'soulful' corporation demands the worker's soul, or at least the worker's identity."

5
Schools and the Imperialism of Culture

Urban public school systems present a curious amalgam of inherent structural and ideological defects; it is no wonder that they have failed. They have not reformed society; they have not won the allegiance of the poor and the black; they have not bound Americans to each other in affection and respect. They have been erected first and foremost upon a soft, evasive intellectual base; they have depended on a continued reluctance to compare their actual and official functions or their stated and operative purposes. They have developed organizational structures that moved them even farther away from interaction with the communities they served, and, finally, they even refused to accept responsibility for educating anybody successfully in anything. Once granted a captive audience, they have had little need to succeed; it has been easier to develop a battery of excuses that place the blame for educational failure outside the school and on the home.

—MICHAEL KATZ

I see human perfection in the progressive elimination of the institutional intermediary between man and the truth he wants to learn.

—IVAN ILLICH

Learning to talk is perhaps the most difficult and complex task we will ever be asked to perform, but by the age of five or six years, almost all of us have learned to utter more than fifty distinct sounds that have been designated as meaningful in the

151

English language and combine these various sounds into a complex vocabulary of several thousand words. In turn, we use these words to construct phrases and sentences that can express virtually an infinite number of thoughts and feelings. At the mechanical level each such utterance involves a subtle and complicated coordination of lips, tongue, teeth, palate, jaws, cheeks, voice, and breath. "Simply as a muscular skill," remarked Holt (1967: 56), speech is "at least as difficult as the skill required to master a serious musical instrument."[1]

Moreover, such childhood learning appears to be remarkably effective since virtually all children master the language or languages spoken in their native environments; it is cost effective since it does not require school buildings, curricular materials, or highly paid professional educators; and it is humane since the learning is self-initiated and accomplished in most instances without the threat of external rewards and punishments. Such learning also demonstrates that children are eager and competent learners, acquiring long before they begin schooling a vast quantity of knowledge "without being taught." Besides learning to speak, for instance, they also learn the intuitive geometry needed to get around in space and enough logic and rhetoric to get around their parents.[2]

The infant does not have periods set aside for "learning talking," and the efficiency of these natural childhood learning processes contrasts markedly with the clumsiness and ineffectiveness of the instructional techniques commonly employed in schools to teach the far less complex cognitive skills associated with reading and writing. Students are forced to spend hundreds of hours in these formal institutional settings and are drilled, evaluated, bribed, cajoled, intimidated, tested, threatened, begged, and badgered into becoming literate human beings. The children themselves become confused, discouraged, humiliated, or fearful, and often either learn to read on their own time anyway because there are comic books or other materials they find worth reading, or else take refuge in deliberate failure and silence, refusing to acquiesce to this outside domination.

Numerous research studies show that the number of illiterate men and women in the United States is rising at the present time. One government analyst for the U.S. Office of Education, for instance, concluded that 57 million Americans were unequipped to carry out even the most basic reading and writing tasks, a figure that is over 35 percent of the entire adult population. Another research study reported that 14 percent of the adults sampled made errors when asked to fill out a check in a business transaction, errors that were so serious it was unlikely that the check would clear the bank. Thirteen percent did not address the envelope well enough to guarantee that it would reach its destination, and 24 percent did not place a return address on the same envelope. Twenty-eight percent of the sample population could not calculate the amount of change that they should get back after paying for a purchase with a twenty dollar bill.[3] With these statistics in mind, then, it is perhaps with some justification that school critics have charged that, if we taught children to speak in schools, as we have attempted to teach them to read and write, many of them would probably end up stuttering, despising conversation, or simply choosing to remain mute.

Similarly, if we base our opinions of the ability of children to learn to speak German on their performances in high-school or college classrooms, we might conclude that German is an extremely difficult language that can be mastered only by a select few "smart" students. However, we know that all normal children learn this language relatively easily provided that they happen to live in Germany. We must therefore ask why some learning that takes place so early and spontaneously in everyday life becomes so difficult or completely impossible if imposed through compulsory school instruction.

Talking and other natural childhood learning is perceived by children as having intrinsic value. It empowers them to perform personally meaningful projects that would be impossible without this new knowledge and skill, and it helps them better communicate with their parents and friends. Traditional school classrooms, by contrast, are authoritarian environments where learning has become medicine that must be forced down with external rewards (good grades, promotions, gold stars, or the teacher's approving smiles) and punishments (bad evaluations, the teacher's dirty looks, or other disciplinary measures).

The predictable result of this dissociated instruction is alienated and divided students who are routinely forced to employ inauthenticity and repression as methods for coping with school pressures. There also develops among young people a school-fearing culture in which beating the system becomes the name of the game, and the ambivalent relationships between students and school authorities produce familiar defense mechanisms such as identification with authority, compulsive rebelliousness, and resignation. Another outcome is greatly restricted learning which, in turn, accentuates the growing disillusionment with contemporary education. Some parents react by withdrawing their children from schools and attempting to educate them at home, but for most there is simply the gnawing sense that schools are not doing as good a job as they should be doing.

Why, then, has the obligatory confinement of children in authoritarian schools become such a pervasive feature of American society, occupying as it does most of the waking hours in the first quarter to one-third of most people's lives? Why have we not come to rely more heavily on natural, nonformal learning environments, or upon more democratically structured schools?

In this chapter, schools are portrayed as institutions that developed to bring persons out of a traditional hierarchy dominated by the patriarchal family, as described in Chapter 3, into a new industrial hierarchy, characterized by such things as wage labor and managed working conditions, as described in the previous chapter. The development of schooling thus has elements of *liberation*, as students are introduced to ideas and alternative ways of living which they might not have been exposed to in their own father-dominated homes. Schools, however, also promote *dependency* and *alienation*, as they are employed as sorting machines to reproduce and perpetuate the existing social class structure. Thus, the sons and daughters of the wealthy are provided with more and better education, while schools brand poor children as "failures," and their low test scores and unfavorable teacher evaluations are employed as justifications for tracking them into lower paying jobs that require little skill or originality.

In terms of personal growth, schools also take students to a certain level of development but no further. Formal education facilitates the growth of the consciousness and cognitive skills necessary to manage and productively contribute to the maintenance of the modern bureaucratic industrial system. Schools also submerge students in a "culture of silence" in which they are programmed for passivity, dependency, fear of freedom, and generally become incapable of critically evaluating and transcending the logic of the authoritarian system of which they are such an essential part (Freire, 1970: 15), or, in Greer's words:

> The fact of the matter is that American public schools in general, and urban public schools in particular, are a highly successful enterprise. Basic to that success is the high degree of academic failure among students. Attitudes and behavior patterns such as tolerance of boredom, learning as memorization, competition, and hostility are learned and

> reinforced in the classroom. The schools do the job today
> that they have always done. They select out individuals for
> opportunities according to a hierarchical schema which runs
> closely parallel to existing social class patterns. (1972: 152)

The triumph of Taylorism in the workplace resulted in the vast expansion of alienation as work was progressively deskilled and rendered meaningless and growing numbers of workers were systematically separated from both the products and planning of their own labor activities. The extension of compulsory education, in terms of increased hours each day and in added years of obligatory schooling, further contributed to this general alienation process by making persons more dependent on existing institutions and expert knowledge. During the twentieth century, as the school assumed increased responsibilities for the whole child, for example, larger areas of human actions were brought under the expertise of outside authorities and subjected to external school criteria. Students learned in schools that thinking, acting, dressing, and even playing, in the form of "creative leisure," could be evaluated on a scale of value and that, if one wished to do them properly, then one must search out expert advice.

Driver's education, sex education, child-rearing education, and death education are now all rapidly becoming standard areas of school expertise. "It is not beyond the realm of possibility," exclaimed Spring (1972: 152–53), "that sometime in the future people will not engage in sexual acts until 'properly' taught the most valuable response and the most scientific method." Moreover, in the field of geriatrics there is already a growing body of literature concerning the techniques for assisting individuals on how to die "properly."

This increasing dependence on outside authority is further expanded as educational institutions provide extension courses on a variety of human activities ranging from aerobic dancing to Zen Buddhism as well as extending educational credit for community activities, vacations, foreign travel, and virtually every other form of "life" experience. "In the future, individuals might only participate in activities if the school approves them and gives them credit," remarked Spring (1972: 153). "As a student once suggested to me, people will start demanding three hours credit for being born."

In school, the ability to act is no longer an individual matter but is turned over to outside authorities who grade, rank, and prescribe. Perhaps as a consequence, schooling often seems to produce people, as Fromm (1960: xi) lamented, who feel free and independent but who are nevertheless willing to do what is expected of them, people who will fit into the social machine without friction, who can be guided without force, who can be led without leaders, and who can be directed without any aim except the one of "making good." It is not that authority itself has disappeared, nor indeed that it has lost its strength, but that it has been transformed from the highly visible and direct authority of the father to the anonymous authority of modern persuasion and suggestion. Thus, whereas people in the nineteenth century lost control over their productive endeavors, in the twentieth century they have lost much of their ability and motivation for self-direction. "In order to be adaptable," concluded Fromm (1960: xi), "modern man is obliged to nourish the illusion that everything is done with his consent, even though such consent be extracted from him by subtle manipulation." The following sections of this chapter, therefore, focus respectively on the development of schools as colonizing institutions, the resulting crisis in modern schooling, and some future alternatives for democratizing education in American society.

THE RISE OF COMPULSORY SCHOOLING

Today, the word "learning" often evokes the accompanying word "teaching," reflecting the growth of organized instruction in the popular mind as the dominant model of education. Historically, however, purposive classroom teaching can best be viewed as the development of a particular type of artificial and relatively inefficient learning environment made necessary by the failure of natural informal learning situations in everyday life. Since prior to the nineteenth century the main job of upbringing and training children was performed almost totally by the patriarchal family—supplemented by the local church and sometimes by craft apprenticeship activities—formal schooling in preindustrial America played a rather inconsequential and marginal role in the overall child-rearing process.[4]

Schooling was strictly voluntary in most cases, with children attending schools for relatively short periods of time until they had mastered basic literacy and ciphering skills. Attendance also varied enormously from day to day and season to season, depending on the weather, the need for labor at home, and the affection or terror inspired by the teacher (Tyack, 1974: 16). As recently as 1870, for example, less than one-half of the children from ages five to seventeen attended school and, among those enrolled, the school year averaged only about seventy-eight days (U.S. Bureau of the Census, 1960). Curriculums were seldom standardized, and classes were typically ungraded with no regular progression among levels of schooling. Instructional materials often consisted of whatever textbooks lay at hand, with much of the instruction of younger children being conducted by the older pupils.

The structure of the school was also relatively simple and uncomplicated by today's standards, with teachers being hired and supervised directly by local community patrons and school administrative tasks being performed by local people on an informal and voluntary basis. This direct community control often made the position of teachers rather tenuous since they were accountable to the school trustees who hired them, to the parents and other community taxpayers who voluntarily supported the school, and to the children whose respect they needed to keep out of trouble with these other two groups.

Rapid social and economic change during the early nineteenth century, however, radically altered the relationship between the family and work and, as a direct consequence, caused a drastic restructuring of the American school system as well. With the expansion of the factory system, as we have seen, small shopkeepers, independent craftspersons, and self-employed farmers were often forced out of business. Faced with declining opportunities for an independent livelihood, workers were increasingly compelled to relinquish control over their own labor and begin to work for wages. In New York City, for example, there was a fourfold increase in the relative number of wage workers between 1795 and 1855, accompanied by a reduction by two-thirds in the relative number of independent merchants and proprietors (Bowles and Gintis, 1976: 157).

The decline of the family as the dominant unit of production meant that work was now carried on in large industrial organizations in which the employer directed and evaluated the work process and also owned the products created by the workers. In this new managed labor system, as we saw in Chapters 3 and 4, training within the family became increasingly inadequate, for the parents no longer possessed the knowledge or skills demanded by the emerging factory system. Moreover, work typically was routinized and, in any case, often performed merely to obtain a wage rather than to be intrinsically motivating. A new system of control was thus needed to ensure that work tasks were performed correctly under these new alienating factory conditions.[5]

> Employers in the most rapidly growing sectors of the
> economy began to require more than obedience and punc
> tuality in their workers; a change in motivational outlook
> was required. The new structure of production provided
> little built-in motivation. There were fewer jobs like farming
> and piece-rate work in manufacturing in which material
> was tied directly to effort. As work roles became more com
> plicated and interrelated, the evaluation of the individual
> worker's performance became increasingly difficult.
> Employers began to look for workers who had internalized
> the production-related values of the firms' managers.
> (Bowles, 1978: 319)

Development of the Urban Education System

The substitution of factory wage labor for the older system
of home industry and the dissolution of the village social structure
led to numerous urban riots, rapidly escalating crime and divorce
rates, and a general urban crisis in the United States during the
latter part of the nineteenth century. This threat to hierarchical
control led to the rise of mass education in this country and the
other industrializing nations of Europe as well. Schooling proponents argued that public mass education would help "Americanize" immigrant and working-class children, thereby
controlling crime and the threatened breakdown of the urban
social order as well as socializing these poor children for work
in the rapidly expanding factory system.

> Compulsory, free public education was given many jus
> tifications, but among the most common was the argument
> that families—especially immigrant families—simply could
> not educate their children for a productive role in the grow
> ing, increasingly complicated American economy. Schools,
> it was claimed, could do what families were failing or unable
> to do: teach good work habits, pass on essential skills, form
> good character, and in short, Americanize. (Keniston, 1977:
> 15)

One possible solution to the disruption caused by capitalist
industrialization was to adapt the existing rural school system

to these newly emerging urban conditions. "Democratic localism," as Katz labeled it, was a movement during this period which attempted to bring the rural neighborhood or community school into the cities. The democratic localists wanted to keep the American government decentralized; the people of the district would have the right to provide any kind of education they wished and they could not be overridden by the state. "If we ever expect to root deeply this system in the affection of the people," warned a delegate to the Pennsylvania convention, "we must make the system voluntary—entirely so. But if we force it upon the people, it will be taken with an ill grace, and will be made use of, if used at all, with reluctance and suspicion" (Katz, 1975: 19).[6]

Professional educators rejected this democratic localism, however, in favor of a bureaucratic model that would centralize control of schools in the hands of administrators who shared the interests of the urban merchants and manufacturers in industrialization.[7] Impressed with the order and efficiency of modern factories, early school reformers sought to transform the local community-controlled rural school system into a standardized, professionally managed urban institution.[8] Like managers of factories, school administrators would supervise the teachers, and in turn the teachers would supervise the students to ensure efficient academic production and the maintenance of consistently high and uniform standards of teaching and learning.

As William T. Harris, superintendent of schools in St. Louis, explained, "the first requisite of the school is *order*: each pupil must be taught first and foremost to conform his behavior to a general standard." Since in modern industrial society "conformity to the time of the train, to the starting of work in the manufactory" required great precision and regulation, urban schools must therefore be models of those central attributes: "The pupil must have his lessons ready at the appointed time, must rise at the tap of the bell, move to the line, return; in short, go through all of the evolutions with equal precision" (Tyack, 1974: 43).

Complementing the older relations of domination based on patriarchy, therefore, was this new bureaucratic authoritarianism based on the "correspondence" between the social relations within the school and the emerging wage labor relations within the office and factory. Thus, within the school, like the factory, social relations were organized in terms of hierarchy (obeying the teacher/foreman), individual advancement (obtaining grade promotions/job promotions), and motivation by outside rewards (grades/wages).[9]

The institutional crisis caused by the emergence of industrial capitalism was thus dealt with by a variety of mechanisms such as the establishment of the family wage, the development of urban welfare and police institutions, and the creation of a mass public school system. In their own way, schools "are imperial institutions designed to civilize the natives," emphasized Katz (1975: xvi). "Their main purpose is to make these children orderly, industrious, law-abiding, and respectful of authority." Katz further argued that by about 1880 American schools had acquired their fundamental structural characteristics, and that these central attributes have not been fundamentally altered since that time. "Certain characteristics of American education today were also characteristic nearly a century ago," observed Katz (1975: xvi); "it is, and was, universal, tax-supported, free, compulsory, bureaucratic, racist, and class-biased."

Testing, Tracking, and the Illusion of Meritocracy

In the early twentieth century the bureaucratic hierarchy of the modern corporation increasingly replaced the simplified boss-worker hierarchy of older entrepreneurial firms. This led to an increasingly stratified labor force with finely differentiated job classifications ranging from top managers through multiplying layers of middle managers and white-collar employees, down the chain of command to those who worked under conditions of detailed supervision by their immediate bosses. In this regard, the number of nonmanual employees grew rapidly, and clerical and sales workers, who were only 5 percent of the labor force in 1900, accounted for one-quarter of the increase in total employment over the next three decades (Bowles and Gintis, 1976: 185).

This growing stratification of workers in modern business firms also led to an increasing incompatibility between the democratic ideology of the nineteenth-century common school and the new realities of the emerging twentieth-century class structure. Social efficiency, declared school reformers, demanded a new relationship between the school and society. Schools should better prepare working-class children for the roles they were likely to face in life, and the old idea that a common school grounding in the three Rs would suffice for all children, from future manual workers to prospective bank presidents, was clearly absurd.

Crucial to this task of sorting students for different occupations and status levels in society was the problem of efficiently and objectively classifying or grading students. Responding to these pressures, school leaders like Horace Mann in Massachusetts, Calvin Stowe in Ohio, and John Pierce in Michigan urged communities to begin replacing the heterogeneous grouping of students with a systematic plan of gradation based on the highly regimented Prussian school model. In Boston, school administrator John Philbrick convinced the school board to build a new type of building (popularly dubbed the "egg crate school") in which each of the teachers had separate classrooms for the one grade they taught and each of the students had their own desk. The students, Philbrick said, should be divided according to their tested proficiency, and "all in the same class should attend to precisely the same branches of study" (Tyack, 1974: 45).

Measuring IQ

The school's ability to classify and evaluate students was given a large boost after World War I by the spread of "intelligence" testing in the United States. Even though, as we will see below, the validity of these new measures was—and still is—highly questionable on strictly scientific grounds, IQ tests nevertheless performed useful functions for school systems. These tests provided the illusion of objectivity which, on the one hand, served the personal needs of school administrators to appear professional and scientific and, on the other hand, served the needs of the system for a myth that would convince the lower classes that their meager station in life was part of the natural order of things.

Working in Paris, Alfred Binet in 1905 had developed the first intelligence test. The French government gave Binet the task of discovering ways to identify children likely to fail in grammar school. Binet and his colleagues tested and rejected many proposed physical correlates of intelligence, such as arm length, head size, and facial features, and even attempted to predict intelligence by means of palmistry. However, the investigators found that, if children were asked to perform simple tasks like those they performed in school, then performance on these tests could predict with moderate accuracy how well children would actually do in school. The Binet-Simon intelligence scale was published in 1908 and was compiled of items appropriate for children ages three through twelve.

For Binet, scores on IQ tests were interpreted as measures of how well children had adapted to schooling: whether they had learned more or less than most other students their age. Binet insisted that intelligence was not fixed biologically, and he advocated a system of instructional exercises to improve the performance of children with low scores. More particularly, he clearly did not view IQ scores as indices of general mental capacity, and he made no claims about what the tests could measure outside the classroom setting (Blum, 1978: 57).

More exaggerated claims for IQ tests were made, however, when the Binet-Simon scale was translated and imported into the United States. This new test was given enthusiastic support by eugenics advocates of the day, who generally believed the poor were poor because they had inferior nervous systems and the rich, in turn, owed their wealth to their superior hereditary intelligence and morality. One ardent advocate of this eugenics position, for example, was the steel magnate, Andrew Carnegie, and his tax-exempt Carnegie Foundation invested approximately $6,424,000 in advancing the testing movement in the United States up to 1954.[10] Like Carnegie, the wealthy generally favored this eugenics movement which made it possible for testing advocates to obtain large-scale philanthropy during the early decades of the twentieth century.

Psychologist Lewis Terman was one of the original translators of the Binet-Simon intelligence test in the United States. It was clear to Terman that America was a land of opportunity where the best excelled and the inferior must learn to accept their lower stations in life. In Americanizing the IQ test, Terman developed questions based on the "presumed progressive difficulty in performing tasks which he believed were necessary for achievement in ascending the hierarchical occupational structure. He then proceeded to find that according to the results of his tests the intelligence of different occupational classes fit his ascending hierarchy" (Karier, 1972: 163). Terman said:

> Preliminary investigations indicate that an IQ below 70 rarely permits anything better than unskilled labor; that the range from 70 to 80 is preeminently that of semi-skilled labor, from 80 to 100 that of the skilled or ordinary clerical labor, from 100 to 115 that of semi-professional pursuits; and that above all these are the grades of intelligence which permit one to enter the professions or the larger fields of business. Intelligence tests can tell us whether a child's native brightness corresponds more nearly to the median of (1) the professional class, (2) that in the semi-professional

pursuits, (3) ordinary skilled workers, (4) semi-skilled workers, or (5) unskilled workers. This information will be of great value in planning the education of a particular child and also in planning the differentiated curriculum here recommended. (Karier, 1972: 164)

The early advocates of using IQ tests in school administration urged that these measures be employed to segregate students by ability, to aid in vocational guidance, to detect unusually able and retarded students, and to diagnose learning problems. The work of Terman, Edward Thorndike, and other intelligence testers was extensively supported by the federal government and by foundations, with Thorndike, for instance, receiving approximately $325,000 from the Carnegie Foundation from 1922 to 1938 (Karier, 1972: 166). Thorndike, in turn, called for the sterilization of the "socially inadequate," the closing of immigration to inferior races and nationalities, and a school tracking system that would encourage acceptance of inequality and social class divisions. Based on the claims of such influential psychologists, testing quickly became a major industry in the United States. Between 1912 and 1936, for example, over 5,000 articles on mental measurement appeared in print, by 1939 no less than 4,279 mental tests were in circulation, and a national survey in 1940 showed that virtually every major school system in the country had a full program of IQ and achievement testing (Cohen and Lazerson, 1972).

Tracking and Vocational Guidance

As working-class children began attending high schools in growing numbers in the early twentieth century, testing was increasingly used as a basis for "tracking" them into "suitable" vocational areas. The tracking systems that arose in most large American cities typically separated students into such program categories as college preparatory, general, vocational, and basic. A different curriculum for each track was then designed to best meet the needs of the children in that school category. Such a system clearly favored those who managed at an early age to be placed in the higher tracks, and it was precisely children from the more affluent homes who were usually given these initial advantages in placement.

Conversely, these tracking systems often resulted in a type of "programmed retardation" for the poor. "To determine how infrequently poor children do well and are rewarded for it," observed Howe and Lauter (1972: 232), "one need only observe how disproportionately the children of the poor are placed in the lower tracks of public schools." For example, Virgil Dickson, a student of Terman and a research director in Oakland, California, carried out a massive tracking program in that city beginning in the 1920s. In a study of why children failed to be promoted, Dickson observed that "mental tests given to nearly 30,000 children in Oakland proved conclusively that the proportion of failures due chiefly to mental inferiority is nearer 90 percent than 50 percent." The obvious solution, he concluded, was to track students, and "it was the invariable testimony of teachers in charge of special limited classes, where pupils of similar mental ability have been grouped together, that these pupils behave better, work better, and accomplish more than they did under the former classification with regular grade pupils" (Tyack, 1974: 210).

Dickson's method was to "find the mental ability of the pupil and place him where he belongs," which meant in practice to direct him into one of five tracks from "accelerated" (or fast) to "atypical." The standards for placement were based on the student population of the entire city so that one school in a poor section of Oakland had more than 50 percent of students in "limited" (or slow) classes and only an occasional child for an accelerated class, while another school in a rich neighborhood had over one-half in fast classes and only 3 percent in limited classes (Tyack, 1974: 209).

Since students with inferior intelligence were those who usually dropped out of the junior high-school grades, special tracks were devised which would give them "instruction aimed definitely toward civic and social relationships required of useful members of society" and hold them in school by offering them vocational training in subjects like sheet metalwork, agriculture, sewing, and cooking. Removing these pupils "from the regular classes relieves both the teacher and the class of a great weight." Dickson added that this "policy of segregation" should continue in senior high school since secondary education faced the responsibility "of educating a large number of pupils who are of high school age but are admittedly unable to cope with the requirements of the standard high school curriculum" (Tyack, 1974: 209–10).

The incorporation of vocational training in the schools alongside academic courses really meant that educators were giving up the concept of equality of opportunity. According to that conception, rich and poor alike would attend high school together, exposed to a common curriculum, and would participate equally in the upward mobility of the community. These tests and guidance programs, as will be demonstrated below, often served, however, to "objectify" the existence of biased and unfair selection processes in a way that made people think they were being given the best deal possible within their own limitations.

The Meritocratic Illusion

To appreciate more fully the underlying foundations of intelligence testing and of schooling in general, it is necessary at this point to describe briefly the ideology of meritocracy that accompanied the nineteenth-century rise of industrialization in the United States. Once the broad significance of test scores was asumed, it then became possible to equate test results with pure ability, or all-around talent, and to see people with high IQ scores as deserving high-status, well-paying jobs. Since test scores correlate with social class, it was a short step to believing that the upper classes deserved their privileged positions and that the lower classes were capable of nothing more than unskilled work. The test scores obtained in school thus became a further justification for hierarchy and inequality in society (Blum, 1978: 162).

"Meritocracy," therefore, refers to a philosophy and general perspective promoted by schools and testing which assumes that people are inherently unequal in their talents and abilities and therefore should be accorded a station in life corresponding with their differential capacities.[11] Advocates of meritocracy advance two related arguments to defend the class structure of American society. First, they portray society as providing opportunities for all to rise in the occupational hierarchy. Inequalities of wealth, power, and status exist because people differ in how intelligent and industrious they are. Inequalities in society are thus natural and to be expected because of these inherent differences in people's natural abilities.

Second, meritocratic proponents argue that society benefits by recruiting the most capable individuals into higher status and more responsible jobs. These occupations, in turn, must offer much greater prestige and salaries than others if they are to attract the most capable people. Hence, the existing inequalities in American society perform the necessary function of conserving scarce talent and directing it to where it is most needed. Persons employed in upper-class occupations deserve their wealth and privileges because their contributions to society are equally valuable. Conversely, the poor are poor because they are lazy and/or unintelligent. They merit nothing better than bare subsistence living because they contribute little to society, and, to keep alive the incentive to rise and contribute more to the community, it is absolutely necessary that their position not be substantially improved (Blum, 1978: 162).

Schools are therefore important because, by employing intelligence and achievement tests, they separate students on the basis of ability, allowing the clever ones access to the advanced training that equips them for high-status jobs. Dumb students, on the other hand, do poorly in school, receive less education, and as a result are consigned to low-status employment. Intelligence and achievement test scores, being the principal measures of general ability, predict academic performance as well as potential competence in professional and managerial occupations. By channeling students on the basis of their IQ scores and scholastic achievement, schools are helping to create a society where people's place in life truly depends upon merit.

Meritocratic ideology first became important in American society in the mid-nineteenth century as a convenient apology for the recently acquired wealth of the rising capitalist class of urban merchants, financiers, and manufacturers. As was also the case earlier in Europe, this class of newly wealthy capitalists found itself in a position of waging a two-front struggle with remnants of the inherited aristocracy (the "old wealthy class in America") from above and with the new industrial working class from below. Members of the capitalist class thus argued that they should have access to positions of power in society, and that these positions should be allocated to all with talent rather than being a special privilege derived from noble birth. Therefore, "the capitalists' opposition to the aristocracy led them to favor a formal equality represented by slogans like equality of opportunity and equality of all under the law," emphasized Blum (1978: 164).

However, the prosperity of this new capitalist class, on the other hand, was acquired through foreign plunder and the inequalities in society which made available plentiful sources of cheap labor power. Like the old aristocracy, the new capitalist class was itself increasingly an hereditary class; wealth and position were passed directly from fathers to offsprings. Increasingly in the latter part of the nineteenth century, as we saw in Chapter 4, unions and organized protests by workers compelled the capitalists to justify their inherited wealth. This conflict with the old aristocracy constrained them from using any concept of birthright directly. However, what they needed was "some mysterious notion of talent or virtue which theoretically anyone could possess, but which in practice usually coincided with possession of property and wealth" (Blum, 1978: 164). Meritocratic ideology thus arose as a way of reconciling these concepts of formal equality and actual existing substantive inequality in American society.

With the emergence of corporate capitalism in the early twentieth century, we also see the growing importance of school certification as a necessary prerequisite for success. The middle class now included a greater proportion of salaried employees who occupied positions in the middle and upper strata of occupational hierarchies. As a result, middle-class status depended less upon ownership of capital and more upon having the kinds of certification that made one eligible for professional, technical, and managerial jobs. This, in turn, promoted the rapid expansion of public education. As opportunities for upward social mobility through education increased, other opportunities for upward mobility diminished, for example, owning one's own farm or business; therefore, the essential competition for middle-class positions came to be housed more and more within the school system.

The general meritocratic conclusion that social standing is an accurate index of personal merit and innate talent depends upon three highly questionable assumptions: 1) the validity of the "general intelligence" concept, 2) the validity of IQ tests as a measure of that concept, and 3) the equality of opportunity for people both to do well in school and to become rich and famous in society. Since the analysis of the problems of contemporary schools and the future possibilities for education in American society depend on the correctness of these essential assumptions, they will be examined below in relation to present knowledge and educational research.

THE VALIDITY OF GENERAL INTELLIGENCE.   IQ tests explicitly or implicitly assume that it is possible to measure a person's general capacity for intellectual achievement and professional success. The only way to validate this construct scientifically, however, would be to discover consistently high correlations between IQ scores and reliable ratings of performance in a wide variety of artistic, scientific, and professional activities. Thus far, as Blum (1978: 71) concluded in his definitive work on the subject, "such data have never been obtained," and attempts to obtain such data have "produced negative results."

Since grades in school are determined primarily by performance on examinations, most of which are somewhat similar to IQ tests, moderate correlations between IQ scores and scholastic achievement have been found. This correlation, however, would only be meaningful if in turn school performance were somehow related to achievement in subsequent occupational endeavors. Hoyt (1965: 36), for example, summarized the results of about forty separate studies, correlating the college grade point average with different measures of occupational performance, and concluded that college grades "have no more than very modest relationships to measures of research performance."[12] Other studies not summarized by Hoyt also support this essentially pessimistic conclusion.[13]

This lack of correlation between grades and occupational achievement also appears not to depend upon how performance is measured. "Peer ratings, supervisor's ratings, direct measures of productivity, and monetary income all point in the same direction," concluded Blum (1978: 77); "college grades predict occupational achievement very little, and in most cases not at all." In this regard, Walter Lippmann (in Karier, 1975: 290–91) suggested that IQ tests were like an attempt to measure general athletic ability with a one-hour test of running, jumping, pulling, and throwing. Such a test might give some clue to differences in athletic prowess but would tell us much less than could be learned by examining performance in the different sports separately, forgetting the notion of athletic ability in general.

The concept of intelligence thus has no clear definition, and the available evidence hardly justifies using IQ as a measure of all-around talent or general ability. It subsumes too many fundamentally different types of behavior and, in practice, becomes merely a labeling device for justifying an existing social structure based upon differential privilege and wealth.

THE BIASED NATURE OF IQ TESTS.   Intelligence tests discriminate against working-class and minority children indirectly by what they leave out and more directly by what is included, as demonstrated by at least one intelligence test specifically designed so that minority students typically score higher than do nonminority students.[14] On a recent version of the Stanford-Binet intelligence test, for example, children are asked: "Which is prettier?" and must select the picture of the Anglo-Saxon child to be correct. If, however, those taking this test happen to be black or southern European, for example, and also have reasonably good self-images, they may select the wrong answer. "Neither Blacks nor Southern Europeans are beautiful according to the authors of the Stanford-Binet," remarked Karier (1972: 166). "The test, then, discriminated in content against particular groups in the very questions that were asked as well as the questions that were not used with respect to particular minority experiences."

The "poor are dumb" theories of inequality thus are reinforced by the schools' seriously biased methods of measuring intellectual ability. The evidence suggests that often children may be sorted more on the basis of wealth and social class background than on the basis of their own natural abilities. This is not particularly surprising since in designing the Stanford-Binet intelligence test, for instance,

> Terman developed questions which were based on presumed progressive difficulty in performing tasks which he believed were necessary for achievement in ascending the hierarchical occupational structure. He then proceeded to find that according to the results of his tests the intelligence of different occupational classes fit his ascending hierarchy. It was little wonder that IQ (as measured by this test) reflected social class bias. It was, in fact, based on the social class order. Terman believed that, for the most part, people were at that level because of heredity and not social environment. (Blum, 1978: 164)

IQ TESTS AS SELF-JUSTIFYING PROPHECIES.   One effect of merit selection, as we have seen, is that it shifted the responsibility for individuals' productive capabilities to the individuals themselves and away from the authoritarian structure of society. If persons were convinced that they are not capable of doing well, then they are less likely to rise up against the social system than if people believe that it is the system itself that is unfair and based on social class. "The definition of democracy has changed from rule by the people to rule by the intelligent," declared Carnoy (1974: 253). "The intelligent, as defined by the designers of tests and vocational guidance counselors, were those of higher social classes, who were at the same time more 'moral' and had the characteristics necessary for leadership in America."

Schools are thus not simply neutral proving grounds for individual talent and diligence but rather are agencies that work to fit children into their proper occupational roles. Working-class children, in particular, are a product of fifty years of testing. They have been channeled through an intricate bureaucratic educational system which, in the name of meeting their individual needs, classified and tracked them into an occupation appropriate to their class status. The tragic character of this phenomenon is not only that the lower class learned to believe in the system but also, by internalizing that set of beliefs, made it work. It worked because the lowered self-image that the school and society reinforced on the child resulted in lower achievement. "A normal child objectified as subnormal and treated by the teacher and the school as subnormal will almost surely behave as a subnormal child," concluded Karier (1972: 167). "Likewise, the lower class child who is taught in many ways to doubt his own intelligence can be expected to exhibit a lower achievement level than those children who are repeatedly reminded that they are made of superior clay and, therefore, are of superior worth."[15]

In challenging the school tracking system existing in Washington, DC, schools in 1967, for example, U.S. Circuit Judge Shelly Wright warned that "a system that presumes to tell a student what his ability is and what he can successfully learn incurs an obligation to take account of the psychological damage that can come from such an encounter between the student and the school; and to be in a position to decide whether the student's deficiencies are true, or only apparent" (Karier, 1972: 170–71).

While one farsighted judge might outlaw a given school tracking plan and outraged blacks in a ghetto community might do away with standardized IQ or achievement tests as a protest against the middle-class values reflected in them, these persons do not possess the power to eliminate the hierarchical occupational and political system that required these debilitating educational measures in the first place. Since the various levels of jobs within the system still have different entrance requirements, abolishing one oppressive school practice tends merely to be replaced by another, just as in individual schools one authoritarian teacher is inevitably replaced by an equally authoritarian successor. The roots of this outward repression lie in the requirements of the authoritarian class structure itself, and schools, far from challenging the unfair system, were established in the first place to defend this hierarchical social order.

THE MODERN SCHOOL CRISIS

Formal education expanded during the last century, with one layer of schooling continually being placed upon another. Before the Civil War most Americans received no formal instruction, and it was not until the last two decades of the nineteenth century that compulsory primary schooling emerged as a general pattern of urban life. In the early twentieth century, universal schooling through twelfth grade was generally available and free, but still many students dropped out and few entered college. As late as 1910, for example, there were nearly 2 million employed youngsters aged seven to thirteen. College education did not become widespread until after World War II, with the emergence of an extensive network of two-year colleges which placed campuses within commuting distance of almost every household.

Today, by contrast, about 99 percent of all eligible preteen children are in school, and there are almost as many persons attending school full time in America as there are those working in full-time occupations. One study estimated that upwards of 100 million persons are currently enrolled in schools, with 50 to 60 million adults attending postsecondary classes alone.[16] As Shor (1980: 2) emphasized, schooling in America is still spreading, with a new concept of "life-long learning."

As schools have grown in size so have the problems associated with them, and at the present time it seems that the educational system does not completely satisfy anyone's expectations. Although there have been many waves of school reforms in the United States since Colonel Francis Parker first attempted to humanize the Quincy, Massachusetts, school curriculum in 1875, such efforts usually have been short-lived and have almost always failed. After an initial flurry of intense activity, the reforms fall out of fashion, reaction sets in, most of the few schools that attempted to make the humane changes give them up, and usually the failings of the schools are then blamed on the reformers themselves. During these reforms, the educational process may become somewhat less painful and humiliating to students, but the overall hierarchical structures remain intact and they continue to perform their primary domesticating functions. Thus, schools have been resistant to change not because they have failed to perform their tasks well but because they have undertaken to perform the wrong tasks, ones that are contradictory to each other.

Producing Dependable Citizens/Workers Versus
Producing More Fully Developed Persons

Almost nobody wants children around; they exist as a major problem in modern societies. Parents do not want them in the house, merchants do not want them on the streets, and workers do not want them taking their jobs. There is nothing for youngsters to do so schools become institutions for warehousing this surplus labor power and for baby-sitting until they can be properly absorbed into the adult work force. Moreover, while they are in school, students become a flexible, surplus labor pool, and they typically are underemployed even while they are in schools engaged in the process of becoming undereducated.

Because this artificial elongation of schools makes them into warehouses instead of growth centers, they become an illegitimate imposition on students' freedom and time. These student development contradictions run even more deeply, however, as John Dewey (1916) perceptively argued more than a half century ago. In a hierarchical society such as our own, Dewey emphasized, schools cannot foster full student development while simultaneously preparing students for full adult participation in society. To prepare students to be dependable citizens/workers in a hierarchical and bureaucratic society, for example, means to teach them how to give and receive orders, respond to extrinsic rewards, and relinquish control of their lives to others. At the level of school social relations this in turn means an emphasis on such things as obedience to outside authority, grades, and hierarchical control.

The central prerequisite for personal development, however, lies in the capacity to control the conditions of one's own life. Thus a school system—and a society—can foster personal growth roughly to the extent that it allows and requires personal interactions that are democratic, participative, and based on equality. As we have seen, American schools cannot perform their citizen/worker integrative missions without undermining these relations of dialogue, social equality, and personal development. To reproduce the labor force, therefore, the schools are destined to legitimate inequality and limit growth.

Overeducation and the "Cooling-out" Process

Schooling in twentieth-century America served many of the same functions provided by the western frontier in this country during the nineteenth century. Rapidly expanding educational opportunity helped to reduce conflicts resulting from the injustices inherent in the natural functioning of industrial capitalism by holding out the hope of increased opportunity for becoming successful and making it within the framework of the present system. Developing a career, rather than owning land or starting a business, became the new version of the American dream, as millions of young persons attempted to adapt to modern industrial realities (Bowles and Gintis, 1976: 3–4).

The educational attainment of Americans continued to rise each decade of the twentieth century, with the percentage of young people graduating from high school increasing from about 6 percent in 1900 to almost 75 percent in 1980. More years of schooling became necessary for occupational success, however, with a high-school diploma qualifying many people earlier in this century for jobs in which a college degree now became essential. In 1920 a high-school diploma was sufficient to put a person in the educated elite of the country since at that time only 16.8 percent of the population had gone that far in school. By 1970 one-half of the children in each age cohort was attending college, and a bachelor's degree had become increasingly necessary for most professional occupations (Squires, 1979).

College graduates during the 1950s and 1960s typically had a choice of numerous good jobs upon the receipt of their degrees. Thousands of companies recruited on the major college campuses, searching for desired technical, managerial, and professional workers. However, this college employment bubble burst in the early 1970s when, for the first time since the Great Depression, the number of college-educated persons began to outnumber the available job openings. In these new depressed labor market conditions, increasing numbers of college graduates sought a relatively shrinking number of high-level jobs and at times were lucky merely to obtain positions in their own areas of study. Moreover, this collapse of employment opportunities forced an unprecedented number of these persons into noncollege-level jobs, often very different from those for which they had prepared themselves in school.

"By every indicator, the graduates of 1972 were worse off than those in 1958," reported Freeman (1976: 20), "despite relatively better overall labor market conditions in the latter year." In the class of 1972, for example, only 46 percent of males with bachelor's degrees obtained professional jobs, compared with 71 percent of men in the class of 1958; 65 percent of women in the graduating class of 1972 were employed as professionals, compared with 81 percent in the class of 1958. Additional data on bachelor's and master's graduates from this survey also revealed that in 1972 over 30 percent of the men and 25 percent of the women ended up employed in nonprofessional, nonmanagerial jobs as compared with approximately 5 percent of the 1958 degree recipients. "However measured," concluded Freeman (1976: 21), "the job situation for graduates by the mid-1970s was bad."

This problem of the increasing gap between student aspirations and available employment is heightened by the fact that few jobs in modern society really demand, or are even fully compatible with, a liberating education. Experts currently estimate, for example, that perhaps as many as 80 percent of the jobs that will be filled during the next decade will be jobs for which a college degree is not needed (Holt, 1976: 158). As a result of Taylorism, employers continuously seek ways to break down complex work tasks into more simple chores that can be performed by lesser skilled and lower paid workers. Modern work is thus repetitive and moronic by design, with few decisions left to challenge the intelligence and judgment of the worker. To the extent possible, then, the worker should be turned into a machine, performing over and over again the simplest possible series of operations, always the same way and exactly as prescribed by management.

The predictable result of increasing school attendance in a society predicated on such job performance is an increasingly overeducated general population relative to the actual requirements of existing occupations. Berg (1971: 46), for instance, estimated that, whereas 1.4 million jobs in the United States require a college graduate, at the present time the number of college graduates has actually increased to more than 6 million workers. Similarly, based on an analysis of 450 professional and technical occupations, Rawlins and Ulman (1974) concluded that the increasing educational attainment required over the past decade for most occupations bears little relationship with the actual expertise or training needed in these jobs. During this period, for example, the educational requirements for such dead-end jobs as letter carrier, truck and/or tractor driver, and railroad conductor have increased dramatically even though the actual job requirements for these occupations have remained essentially the same.

While employers often extolled the value of education as a screening device in recruiting better workers, Berg (1971) surveyed many studies that found no relationship or even an inverse relationship between educational attainment and job performance. In samples of both blue-collar and white-collar workers, for instance, Berg found that, given the present degradation of work, the better educated employees were often the least productive and had higher rates of absenteeism and job turnover. In other words, without realizing it employers in many cases have actually used schooling to eliminate their better workers.

A 1976 government report showed that 44 percent of the country's high-school students aspire to professional jobs, despite the fact that only 14 percent of the national employment slots are in these more prestigious occupational categories.[17] Schools become increasingly important in an overeducated society; therefore, in this process of picking "winners" and "losers" in the job race and in lowering the expectations—or "cooling-out"—the majority of students are destined to be tracked into nonprofessional jobs. This process of cooling-out persons is a sophisticated type of thought control which transfers the locus of failure from the institutional structure to the individual. "At issue is the student's setting of goals and the student's perception of who is responsible for the place he or she reaches in society," explained Shor (1980: 17). "When 'cooling-out' works, the student feels that she or he blew the chance to make it, and what choice is there but to settle for less." To lower sights and to prevent alienation and rebellion, batteries of scientific tests, elaborate tracking schemes, and an army of counseling specialists are employed by school systems. For peace and stability, the multitude of losers in the job race must be persuaded that the judging process was fair, and that they indeed deserve to lose. The system is rigged, as we saw in the last section, so that most of the winners selected in schools just happen to be the children of winners, and the losers are children of working-class parents whom society already had determined to be losers.

Failing is thus essential for the functioning of the meritocratic society. The best schools are those that can boast that their standards are so high that almost no student is good enough to meet them. By a "quality education," many parents want the schools to provide whatever learning will advantage their children relative to other children. The goal, therefore, is not for all students to be winners but rather for their children to be winners in a race where most of the other kids lose.

From a human development perspective, the concept of overeducation is rather ridiculous. In a society dedicated to the development of every individual's full human capacities and potentials, overeducation would be without meaning. However,

in a class-dominated society in which social power and privilege
are passed from one generation to the next through sophisticated
mechanisms of school certification and educational credentials,
preservation of the status quo demands that educational attainment be reserved primarily for the wealthy. Learning thus cannot
be distributed uniformly across the general population, and the
schools at some point must become an obstacle to the self-actualization and growth of their students. Ranking, not self-reliance,
becomes the basic function of schools, and the compulsory school
system itself ultimately becomes the general enemy of human
learning and freedom.

The Atrophy of Consciousness

Particularly since the late 1950s schooling costs have escalated in this country, and increasingly school critics have cast
doubts about the cost-effectiveness of the American formal educational system.[18] According to one analyst, for instance, "the
cost of elementary and secondary public education has risen from
$15.9 billion in 1960 to $100.2 billion in 1980, and the average
expenditure per pupil is $2,400. Each year, we pay about $450
per person (or $749 per taxpayer) to support schools. All told,
education consumes 7 percent of our entire Gross National Product" (Johnson, 1982: 128). Although new buildings and better
facilities account for part of this astounding rise in schooling
expenditures, growing personnel costs are responsible for a much
larger share of these increases. Salary and fringe benefit gains
achieved by workers in the private sector, which during the last
two decades have been primarily offset by corresponding rises
in labor productivity, also have generally been passed along to
teachers and other public sector employees whose jobs are such
that comparable increases in productivity have not been
achieved.[19]

As a direct result of the bureaucratic model adopted by
schools, administrative costs since World War II also have escalated at an even faster rate than have teachers' salaries. A recent
survey by the National Education Association demonstrated that
this is both a result of the fact that the salaries of administrators
have risen even faster than those of teachers and that the proportion of administrators in school systems has grown rapidly
during recent years. Whereas in 1945 the administrator/teacher
ratio was about one administrator for every five teachers, it is

one administrator for every four teachers at the present time and is projected to be one administrator for every three teachers within a decade.[20] As opposed to the early nineteenth-century rural school system, where much of the school administration was performed voluntarily by parents and other community patrons, the current school bureaucracy is characterized by little free or voluntary community labor. As a professionally administered institution, it has in fact increasingly become a power unto itself, moving even further apart from the community which it serves. This augmented professionalized staff is in turn more expensive, and thus modern schooling expenditures continue to skyrocket, causing widespread tax revolts and local taxpayer dissatisfaction.

The New Illiteracy

As argued in this chapter's introduction, these recently rising school expenditures have not been translated directly into increased student learning. On the contrary, numerous studies document a steady decline of basic intellectual skills among today's students.[21] The College Entrance Examination Board, for example, has revealed that college applicants' scores on the Scholastic Aptitude Test (SAT) have been declining. High-school seniors in 1966 scored an average of 467 points on the verbal section and 495 points on the mathematical part of the test, whereas a decade later students scored an average of only 429 and 470 points, respectively.

Studies by the National Assessment of Educational Progress (NAEP) also have shown that an overwhelming majority of American students cannot write a coherent analysis of what they read. In another NAEP study, researchers reported that seventeen year olds as a group knew less about the natural sciences, wrote worse essays, made fewer accurate inferences from what they read, and were less adept at using reference works in 1973–74 than in 1969–70. "Even at the top schools in the country," observed Lasch (1978: 129), "students' ability to use their own language, their knowledge of foreign languages, their reasoning powers, their stock of historical information, and their knowledge of the major literary classics have all undergone a relentless process of deterioration." Thus, each year 40 to 60 percent of the students at the University of California find themselves required to enroll in remedial English. Only one-quarter of the students in the class entering Stanford in 1975, for instance, managed to pass the university's English placement test, even though these students had achieved high scores on their SATs.

NAEP also reported that students' knowledge about politics and their rights as citizens had declined during recent years. In a study of seventeen year olds, 47 percent of the sample did not know that each state elects two U.S. senators, and more than one-half of the students could not explain the significance of the Fifth Amendment protection against self-incrimination. One of every eight students believed that the president does not have to obey the law, and one of every two students thought that the president appoints members of Congress. Only a few students could explain what steps the Constitution entitles Congress to take to stop a president from fighting a war without congressional approval. "If an educated electorate is the best defense against arbitrary government, the survival of political freedom appears uncertain at best," explained Lasch (1978: 129–30). "Universal public education, instead of creating a community of self-governing citizens, has contributed to the spread of intellectual torpor and political passivity." Thus, while compulsory schooling has succeeded in achieving unprecedented rates of formal literacy, it also has produced new forms of illiteracy.

Mutilization of the Spirit

The growing criticism of schools has not been confined to the area of declining cognitive skills, however, as many parents and students have rejected as well the values and personality traits reinforced by the structure of school systems. After reviewing several studies of the personality traits rewarded and punished by schools, for instance, Bowles, Gintis, and Meyer (1975) concluded that schools create students with authority dependent character structures by generally reinforcing precisely those attitudes and personality traits that are necessary for functioning in alienating and hierarchically controlled bureaucratic organizations. Thus, in one study conducted in a New York high school, for example, those personality traits penalized by the school included independence, aggressiveness, and creativity. Rewarded student personality traits, on the other hand, included perseverance, dependability, consistency, identification with the school, willingness to take orders, punctuality, ability to defer immediate gratifications, motivation by external rewards, predictableness, and tactfulness. In a second study these authors also demonstrated that these same personality traits were the ones generally rewarded in bureaucratic work organizations, thereby reinforcing the notion of a general correspondence between authoritarian school and work social relations. At least for the schools and workplaces sampled, concluded Bowles and Gintis (1976: 138), "the personality traits rewarded in schools seem to be rather similar to those indicative of good job performance in the capitalist economy."

The feelings of powerlessness and confusion that are intrinsic features of daily life in modern society can be understood only through critical thinking which attempts to get at the roots of one's discomforts and problems. However, the authority dependent character promoted by schools, as portrayed in these studies, operates as a barrier against such popular awareness and deep understanding. Hierarchical classroom relations are thus irreconcilable with human development, and attempts to be fully human within the institutional context of modern schools inevitably produces frustration and struggle.

STUDENTS' DIVIDED SELVES. Authoritarian school relations cut students off from their own human potential and force them to divide their energies between their conflicting needs to develop their personal capacities and to be successful as college students. As we have seen, to develop their potentials, students must engage in authentic self-disclosure, receive honest feedback, and be motivated to appropriate their own personal experiences and observations. The conditions, however, that govern traditional classrooms make these types of growth-producing activities very difficult to achieve.

> In schools, the student is obliged to present a 'false-self' in order to survive the contradiction of his or her education. Outside the class, the student is a lively, verbal, critical, and motivated human being. In class, the student dissimulates, frowns, masks anger and/or delight, and dissociates from the student role as fast as possible. This produces a self increasingly divided as one makes further commitment to educational institutions until the original self is lost to consciousness and the cynical false-self dominates behavior and reproduces itself in the classroom for another generation of students. (Young, 1975)

The problems of students are further compounded by the fact that they typically carry into the classroom scars from their past educational oppression. Having seldom in the past been responsible for planning their own learning and having been continually rewarded in schools for their submissiveness, dependability, and willingness to obey rules, most students quite naturally lack confidence in their abilities to govern their own education. As Freire (1970: 32–33) observed, students in this situation tend to suffer from a duality that has been established in their innermost being. With regard to their education, they discover that without freedom they cannot exist authentically, and yet they tend to resist and fear this freedom.

SEPARATION BETWEEN STUDENTS AND TEACHERS.   At some level most students have a somewhat general awareness of their own divided selves. The fact that participation in the classroom puts them into contradiction against themselves produces resentment and sometimes open rebellion. To the extent that teachers faithfully perform their roles as school functionaries, they represent an oppressive force in the lives of students. Solidarity with students requires such things as dialogue, community, power equality, and freedom. Traditional educators are simply not often in a position to provide these types of growth-producing social relationships.

TEACHERS' DIVIDED SELVES.   Because of their power in the classroom, teachers tend to be cut off from both honest disclosure and trustworthy feedback from students. Since, as we have discussed previously, teachers as persons are also dependent on self-activities and growth-producing social relationships as a basis for their own development, they tend to be separated from their human potentials within the context of teacher-student relationships.

There is thus little reality in most classroom encounters between teachers and students, as Holt observed:

> The teachers are not themselves, but players of roles. They do not talk about what is real to them, what they know, are interested in, and love, but about what the curriculum, the teachers' manual, and the lesson plan says they must talk about. . . . They do not respond naturally and honestly to the acts and needs of the children, but only as the rules tell them to respond. They ask themselves all the time, 'If I do this or say this, or let the students do this or say this, will I get into trouble?' and act according to the answer. Not that their fears are groundless, or these dangers imaginary. Far from it. The newspapers often tell of teachers who were fired for saying things the community did not like.

No one is fired for hiding the truth from children, but many
are fired for telling the truth. (1976: 24)

Like students, therefore, teachers are forced to divide their energies between their conflicting needs to develop their own personal
capacities and to be successful as teachers.

Toward Total Confinement

In many ways schools have become less blatantly restrictive, painful, and humiliating as teachers and school administrators have learned additional sophisticated management and
disciplinary techniques, but schools also have become more
harmful in other ways. They take up a greater portion of people's
time which gives individuals even less leisure to pursue their own
interests. Schools increasingly control children's futures because
there are now fewer paths to success and a fulfilling life that do
not involve school degrees and diplomas. The struggle for the
few winner slots in the hierarchical occupational structure may
actually begin as early as three years old when the parents select
their child's first nursery school.

Schools are also more effective in their labeling of children
than they used to be. Whereas previously school records were
usually temporary and easily misplaced or destroyed, modern
technology has made them much more permanent. "Throughout
his entire life people may be reading whatever his second-grade
or other teachers had to say about him, things which in earlier
days teachers would never have thought of saying or been allowed
to say," explained Holt (1976: 146). "My report cards were *cards*,
with nothing on them but grades. But today, as any number of
reports have pointed out, the school records of children are full
of the most gossipy, malicious, damaging pseudopsychological
observations and diagnoses, often about the parents as well as
the children, and made in most cases by people wholly incom-
petent to make them." With the growth of special education,
increasing numbers of children also are being labeled as "weird,"
"stupid," or as having some type of "learning disability."

Schools today make greater, larger, and vaguer demands
on students. There are few parts of the child's life or personality
that teachers do not consider as areas in which they can meddle,
judge, or shape behavior. Modern behavioral science has given

school authorities more sophisticated techniques for manipulating and controlling students' behaviors and opinions. "As the school expanded and gained a greater role in social control there was more and more talk about allowing freedom in the school," reported Spring (1972: 162–63). "Looking at the phenomenon in retrospect it appears that calling the activities of the classroom 'free' was one way of avoiding the fact that less and less of the child's life was free."

The same types of control can be seen in continuing or adult education which is today the new schooling growth industry. "Adult education programs in industry and the professions, in universities, community colleges, public schools, and other establishment institutions now command tax, corporate, and personal dollars that may rival the money spent on education for children and young people," emphasized Lisman and Ohlinger (1978: 35).

Although adult education is usually characterized as voluntary, the growing demands of employers and many recent state and federal laws have in actuality made this adult schooling compulsory for millions of Americans.[22] Besides the military and public school teaching areas, where mandatory adult education is most firmly established, some form of continuing education is required in at least fourteen professions in forty-five states, and most other states are considering such laws and regulations. At the present time, for example, at least seventeen states require continuing education for doctors, eight for dentists, and eleven for nurses. Thirty-seven states have additional schooling requirements for nursing home administrators, forty-five for optometrists, fifteen for pharmacists, and eighteen for veterinarians.

Outside the health care field, twenty-three states now subject certified public accountants to continuing education, and seven states require it for lawyers. Many local, state, and federal employees, such as policemen, firemen, and agricultural extension agents, are also compelled to enroll in courses to qualify for pay raises, promotions, or tenure. There are similar pressures on architects and even on members of the clergy. "All indications are that mandatory continuing education will become a fact of life for every professional subject to licensing," concluded Lisman and Ohlinger (1978: 36), making cradle-to-grave schooling an even more unforgettable and total life-consuming experience.

Next to the right to life itself, perhaps our most fundamental right in a free society should be to control our own minds and thoughts. This means the right to decide for ourselves how our talents and abilities will be challenged and shaped, the types of new experiences we will choose to examine and explore, and all the other multitude of decisions we will make in constructing our own educations. Whoever takes this right away from us, as schools have been created to do, attacks the very center of our being and does us a most permanent and lasting injury. School authorities tell us, in effect, that we cannot be trusted even to think, that we must come to depend on others to tell us the meaning of our world and our lives, and that any meaning we may make out of our own experience has no value.

BEYOND SCHOOLING

During the last century, we have witnessed in the United States and other industrialized countries the steady trend toward universal compulsory schooling in government-supported and regulated schools. The purpose of mass schooling has been to train the citizens and workers for a modern industrial society. The dream of schooling enthusiasts has been that tax-supported public education would also result in a literate and informed populace capable of self-government. However, as we saw in the previous section, the effects of compulsory school attendance have been very different. "The enforced, threatening quality of education in America has taught people to hate school, to hate the subject matter, and tragically, to hate themselves," observed Farson (1974: 97). Instead of learning to read, for example, students learn in school not to read. Most children are so adverse to reading that by the time they have finished their compulsory schooling they seldom pick up a book after graduation.

American children have no choice but to attend school. When compared with other involuntarily confined persons in society, such as criminals and the mentally ill, for example, children represent the largest incarcerated group; moreover, they typically are incarcerated for a longer period of time than persons in these other groups. In every state except Mississippi compulsory school attendance is enforced by law, and children and their parents can be jailed for noncompliance. Schools are compulsory at the present time for reasons even more basic than mere legal sanctions: if children do not complete their schooling, they are threatened with unemployment, poverty, loss of self-esteem, and exclusion from adult society.

School reformers over the years have proposed revisions of virtually every aspect of the schooling process including curriculum, teacher training, grading, and institutional development. These reforms have typically failed, as suggested above, because they have been based on the faulty assumption that schools are not working properly. At the most fundamental level, however, we have seen that the school system does not function primarily to liberate children but to maintain and perpetuate the present system of domination. It has not been so much concerned with humane learning and growth, for example, as it has with keeping our way of life intact. Schools thus function to keep children in their places, socially, politically, and economically.

This indoctrination probably has less to do with the subject matter being taught in schools than with the teaching methods themselves. The "hidden curriculum" of schools therefore resides in the authoritarian classroom rituals: the punishments, bribes, threats, grades, and guilt-producing mechanisms that are employed to gain student compliance.

> Education, with its supporting system of compulsory and competitive schooling, all its carrots and sticks, its grades, diplomas, and credentials, now seems to me perhaps the most authoritarian and dangerous of all the social inventions of mankind. It is the deepest foundation of the modern and worldwide slave state, in which most people feel themselves to be nothing but producers, consumers, spectators, and 'fans,' driven more and more, in all parts of their lives, by greed, envy, and fear. My concern is not to improve 'education' but to do away with it, to end the ugly and anti-human business of people-shaping and let people shape themselves. (Holt, 1976: 4)

Authoritarian pedagogy also teaches us to distrust our own abilities and to put our faith in experts who somehow know better than we do what is important and best for our lives. If we want to learn something of any significance, we must get it from a teacher in school. The hidden school curriculum also reinforces the importance of competition as a fundamental value and the corollary idea that the world is comprised of winners and losers, of which, naturally, there must be many more of the latter. Learning becomes separated from doing, with education being a commodity that can be purchased from another. Schools also breed reward- and punishment-oriented people who are taught to live by fear and greed. Despite their talk of cooperation and sharing, however, schools teach that nobody ever does anything important except to gain a reward, escape a penalty, or take advantage of someone else. Teachers may disagree or be unaware of the values they teach, but the authoritarian classroom relations ensure that the lessons nevertheless will be instilled effectively.

Worst of all, perhaps, is that schools do not teach freedom as a process within which people can work and live their lives. In traditional compulsory schools, students have so little experience of freedom, except in the most trivial situations, that they can hardly imagine how it might work or how they might use it in their everyday activities. The authoritarian model of social organization—of bosses and the giving and taking of orders—thus becomes the only model of society which they know, trust, and with which they feel comfortable. Democracy at its best becomes merely a complicated and alienated process for choosing bosses whom all must obey once they are selected.[23]

Compulsory Schooling Versus Noncompulsory Learning Resources and Alternatives

For the present discussion, the total educational resources provided in American society can roughly be divided into two basic types: compulsory schooling and noncompulsory learning resources and alternatives. Thus far we have focused on compulsory schooling as represented by primary and secondary schools, in which attendance is required by law, and higher educational institutions, in which attendance has become a sought after ticket to job security and a comfortable life. In addition to the compulsory school system, however, there are also at the present time other learning resources and educational alternatives in our society. These include libraries, museums, theaters, and televised courses, as well as many other voluntary schools and classes which were created to assist persons in developing their own self-understanding and abilities—for example, dancing classes, Berlitz language schools, gymnastic centers, ice-skating rinks, and karate lessons.

In these voluntary learning environments there typically are no exams, rules requiring attendance, or corporal punishments. Persons judge the worthwhileness of their endeavors in terms of their own self-improvement and the importance of the new understandings and abilities which they are developing. Instead of holding their students by promises or threats, these noncompulsory educational institutions provide them with opportunities to explore the world as they choose to explore it, as an aid to self-directed and self-motivated learning activities.

The general argument presented here is that in the future there is little that can be done to improve the effectiveness of compulsory schooling, and, indeed, many of our reform efforts will unfortunately make these involuntary institutions even worse. Herndon (1971), for instance, found that students would rather do "all that creative stuff" in their classes rather than traditional teacher-directed classroom activities. However, when he developed a special creative arts class and told the students they could do whatever they wanted to do, he discovered that students did not really want to do the creative activities either. These "creative" tasks they had previously performed only as the best option they had among their small set of uniformly bad choices. If given the chance to decide among different penitentiaries, for example, the inmates would likely choose the one that was most pleasant and attractive, but no matter what decisions they made, the prison, like the school, would still be a prison.

Through the authoritarian school ritual, children become fair game for imposition of whatever values and superstitions currently are prevalent in the adult community, but the ownership of self implies freedom from such outside domination. It means that children should be able to choose whatever belief systems happen to comfort and inspire them and not necessarily the systems that adults would have them choose. "Political liberty has little meaning if an individual's actions are guided by an internalized authority from which there is no escape," explained Spring (1976: 33). Rather children must be able to plan, direct, control, and judge their own actions; it is they who must decide what they will say, hear, read, write, think, and dream. Such self-directed individuals would shape and control the society in which they lived instead of being shaped and controlled by it. "People would be busy *doing interesting things that mattered*, and they would grow more informed, competent, and wise in doing them," proposed Holt (1976: 6). "They would learn about the world from living in it, working in it, and changing it, and from knowing a wide variety of people who were doing the same."

Discussed in the next section, therefore, are methods for abolishing, or at least reducing the impact of, compulsory schooling. Although currently rich and powerful, the school establishment has not been ordained by nature; instead, schools were originally constructed during the past century, as we have seen, by people who believed it was necessary to create obedient children who would become productive factory workers and feel comfortable in the newly emerging industrial hierarchy. As society's needs change, however, so too can people abolish the institutions that they have created previously. Like patriarchy and capitalism, schooling is part of our institutional heritage which now limits our growth and freedom and which therefore must be transcended.

The Withering Away of Compulsory Education

Schools currently serve as jails for the young and increasingly, through compulsory adult education, for many of the rest of us as well. Difficulties associated with reforming schools thus are not basically problems in providing more or better school facilities, improving the various instructional materials and techniques used in these authoritarian settings, or even developing new sugarcoated or child-centered pedagogies. Instead, as long as schools remain compulsory, effective teaching methods must at some level remain either manipulative or directly coercive and the classroom atmosphere that of involuntary servitude. Given the coercive nature of their assigned tasks, schools have no choice but to bribe and punish students into compliance and to rank, certify, label, and domesticate them in the service of the current social hierarchy.

If schools are taught to become places for honest communication and thought, declared Katz (1975: 145), they "should be voluntary; compulsion should be removed on principle, wherever possible." Compulsory school attendance should therefore be abolished, along with the accompanying mechanisms and procedures that allow schools to rank, certify, and label students. If some schools are allowed to rank, all schools will be forced to follow this practice since to give no rank will then be to give the lowest rank of all.

School Equivalency Examinations

There is little likelihood that the institution of public schooling, which in this country took more than a century to develop, will in fact be abolished within the next decade. Fortunately, there are a number of other more limited school reforms that, while falling short of the complete elimination of schools, would nevertheless reduce many of the destructive effects of compulsory education. One such reform is based on the idea of extending the high-school equivalency examinations that currently exist in all states of the union.[24] These equivalency exams allow persons who have never finished high school to pass a test and obtain the equivalent of a high-school diploma. Unfortunately, at the present time, individuals are not allowed to take these examinations until they have reached a certain age, usually about seventeen to twenty-one years old. Typically, the state regulations thus are constructed so as to require that students be a year or two older than when they would normally have finished high school.

The notion of equivalency examinations also could be applied at other levels of schooling. There might be college equivalency exams, junior high equivalency exams, doctoral degree equivalency exams, or perhaps, better yet, equivalency examinations for every grade in school. In this latter instance, once students passed the relevant examination for a given grade, they no longer would be required to spend time at that grade in school. Rather, they could then choose either to go into the next school grade, do independent study in school, or not to go to school at all. Many children already have shown that they can learn what the schools teach more effectively and much more rapidly in other ways, and, if the law allowed, those who wanted to finish their schooling quickly would be permitted to do so. Some students might use this additional time to stay out of school, to work, or to move much sooner into more advanced training.

Equivalency exams would break the monopoly of schools over educational credentials, and particularly attractive would be the prospect of lowering schooling costs. Why should taxpayers' money be spent to keep children in certain grades in school when they already have learned what is being taught in those grades? How can we justify holding back children who want to improve themselves and be more productive citizens? These reforms also would make schools less alienating by providing opportunities for students to escape classes that were especially useless and boring for them. At the level of self-confidence such individual accomplishments would undoubtedly provide many children with paths to achievement which would not be completely monopolized and controlled by the present school bureaucracy.

Destroying the Schools' Monopoly Over Job Credentials

Another way of reducing the arbitrary power of schools might be to take away their current near monopoly powers over job and career credentials. It would not help, for instance, to tell children that they did not have to attend school if schools were the only places where they could get the licenses, diplomas, and other credentials they needed to obtain the best kinds of work in society. The problem thus would be to take away from school systems their more or less exclusive right to provide job and career tickets.

Job credentials and licenses themselves might continue to be necessary in modern society. If we want to drive a car, fly a plane, play in an orchestra, act in a play, or be capable of doing other things that affect the lives of people, we would probably need mechanisms and procedures for determining whether or not persons were competent at doing what they claimed they could do. These demands, however, are much more specific and directly tied to the actual tasks to be performed than are the general educational credentials and licenses provided by traditional schools.

Unnecessary credentialing could therefore be eliminated and alternatives to school credentials provided. We could probably protect ourselves quite well against most of these dangers related to job incompetence, for instance, if we were not so early in life made into expert worshippers and if we could easily find out the truth about such occupational dangers. Friedman (1980), for example, has suggested that even medical doctors should not be licensed. If persons think they can heal others, they should say so and get what patients they can, but they should also be required to make open to everyone both their methods and the results of their work, including the names and addresses of all their past clients so interested persons could check up on them.

Increased freedom might also be provided by passing laws that stated that whenever credentials were needed for given types of work there must be ways to obtain these credentials without going to schools. These alternatives might involve home study and the passing of formal examinations, such as the bar exams for lawyers and the medical exams for doctors that presently exist, without, however, the current formal schooling requirements that merely duplicate the materials certified by the examinations. In many other cases it might be more appropriate for

job credentialing to require practical experience and apprenticeship activities.[25]

The evidence cited previously demonstrated that researchers have generally found no consistent relationship between school
achievement and occupational success. Therefore, it would seem
preferable in many instances to select job-credentialing criteria
that are more closely related to the jobs themselves. Such changes
might not only provide more relevant criteria of occupational
accomplishment but also help break the death grip of schools
over people's career training and choices.

Limiting the Schools' Labeling Powers

Short of abolishing compulsory schools, practical steps could
be taken to limit the powers of these authoritarian institutions
to rank and label children. At the present time, for example,
schools routinely keep detailed files on children and these contain
many types of damaging, libelous, and pseudopsychological
observations about the child's character and personality. Moreover, it is often left to the discretion of school officials to determine
which school employees, government bureaucrats, prospective
employers, and others will have access to these records and evaluations. There is a need for stiffer laws that would place restrictions on the types of tests and records which a school system
may create and keep about students and also to specify that all
such records, even if only grades, should be the property of those
students and must be turned over to them when they leave the
school.[26]

The Extension of Choice

Paradoxically, compulsory schooling has both a captive
clientele and in turn is itself a captive to the larger political
processes in the community. Dissatisfied parents and children,
in theory at least, can protest school actions with which they
disagree. However, in actual practice, mounting an effective campaign to change local public schools requires an enormous investment in time, energy, and money. Few persons have the political
skills or commitment necessary to engage in such a struggle. As
a result, effective control over public schools is largely vested in

educational administrators, school boards, and state legislators and not in the parents and children themselves.

Giving parents and students more choice in the selection of schools would ease somewhat these dilemmas facing compulsory school systems. Writers like Goodman (1962), Jencks (1972), and Friedman (1980) have proposed the use of "educational vouchers" which parents could use to enroll their children in any school that agreed to abide by the rules of the voucher system. Each school would convert its vouchers into cash, and parents would no longer be forced to send their children to prescribed neighborhood schools. Despite the limited nature of this reform, such a voucher system would probably encourage some diversity and choice within the public education system. "Educators with new ideas—or old ideas that are now out of fashion in the public schools—would also be able to set up their own schools," stated Areen and Jencks (1972: 241). "Entrepreneurs who thought they could teach children better and more inexpensively than the public schools would have an opportunity to do so."

Even more schooling choices are advocated by Illich (1970) who proposed that an "educredit" card be issued to children at birth, which would permit entrance into many different learning resources and programs, not all of which would be schools. A variety of institutions in the community, such as libraries, museums, hospitals, factories, banks, construction firms, lumber yards, insurance companies, theaters, and labor unions, could develop different kinds of educational activities that would make them eligible for educredit reimbursements. Almost all community businesses and organizations, therefore, could offer important learning experiences, not only in the specific functions of those particular organizations but also in basic educational skills such as measuring, alphabetizing, and counting. As with the voucher proposals, the schools and other institutions that qualified for educredit reimbursements would compete for students, and the most attractive alternatives would undoubtedly receive the largest number of applications.

A variety of other proposals have been made that would increase the number of schooling choices from direct cash payments to parents to spend on their childrens' educations to proposals for reducing the total number of days per year, or even the total number of years of required school attendance. Schools could also be required to offer more flexible hours so that students could work or be engaged in other activities during the day and get their school credits in the evenings or even on weekends.

Students could be allowed to take different classes at various schools and be given credits for a variety of alternative nonschool work.[27] None of these suggestions will erase all of the destructive effects of compulsory schooling, however, but, given the entrenched character of the present educational system, they could provide a transition from the present "schooled up" society to a more free and open society in the future.

The "Free Learner"

The withering away of schools is not a popular topic with some people because they cannot imagine what would be done with children in modern society if they were not incarcerated in institutions of formal learning. Immediately one visualizes scenes of chaos: children running wild in revolutionary bands, playing endlessly, drugging themselves, not accomplishing or achieving, not contributing to society, engaging in crime, and generally making life impossible for others. Up until the last century few children had to be involuntarily confined in schools, and these images in people's minds actually may say more about their own beliefs and authoritarian upbringings than about basic human nature or the probable effects of eliminating compulsory schooling.

Nevertheless, one cannot define the world negatively simply in terms of removing schools and putting nothing in their place. Ending compulsory education raises the prospect of many children entering the labor force at an early age and of youngsters having much more time to engage in nonschool learning activities. One product of the past century of school indoctrination, therefore, is that people often have problems with the notion of self-directed learning. They do not see that independent, unconstrained, noninstitutional learning is real education. They assume that the right way to learn is in a classroom from a teacher and from textbooks through listening to "expert authorities," reading assigned work, taking tests, and getting grades.

A becoming free society thus would not merely be dedicated to the abolition of compulsory schooling but also to providing alternative educational resources and enhanced opportunities for lifelong learning. "It means acquiring new skills and powers," proposed Gross (1977: 16). "Each day becomes an adventure in discovery, challenging you to add to your experience and knowledge. Rather than a struggle within well-worn ruts, the passing

weeks and months become milestones in your constant exploration, inquiry, and development." True lifelong learning, therefore, is not consciously studying all the time, having to memorize
something someone tells you to learn, or pursuing a certain set
of subjects which school authorities consider important. The
lifelong learner is rather a "free learner," impelled toward self-
development and self-directed growth. "True higher learning,"
commented Buckminster Fuller, "is self-administered unlearning
of most of what we've been taught in school."[28]

Some Principles of Free Learning

If education is to be truly liberatory, then children have a
better chance to grow into maturity having developed their values on the basis of personal experience and self-determined growth
activities rather than as a result of adult indoctrination. Increased
resources and opportunities for free learning should therefore be
a basic policy goal in American society. Given the analysis of
human development presented in Part One, below are suggested
some general free-learning principles that might serve as guides
in creating these increased resources and opportunities for self-
exploration and growth.

ALL LEARNING IS SELF-LEARNING.   In reality, we cannot
teach another person important things, any more than we can
eat for another person or love for another person. "I have come
to feel that the only learning which significantly influences behavior is self-discovered, self-appropriated learning," claimed Rogers
(1961: 275). "To learn is an active verb," Gross (1977: 17) added;
"your education is something you must tailor to yourself, not
something you can get ready made."

PEOPLE LEARN PRIMARILY WHAT THEY THINK IS WORTH
LEARNING.   When persons have goals they wish to achieve and
see the materials available to them as relevant to achieving these
goals, learning takes place naturally and often with great rap-
idity. "We need only to recall what a brief length of time it takes
for an adolescent to learn to drive a car," explained Rogers (1969:
158–59). "There is evidence that the time for learning various
subjects would be cut to a fraction of the time currently allotted
if the material were perceived by the learner as related to his
own purposes." There thus cannot be a prescribed time or grade
level for all persons to learn standardized subjects, as is often
assumed by current school authorities. Rather, "the prime time

to learn is when your own need, curiosity, taste, or hunger impels you in a particular direction," observed Gross (1977: 18). This rule holds for adults in their developing interests and capacities as it does for children's miraculous learning of walking and talking.

LEARNING CANNOT BE SEPARATED FROM DOING.   People learn important things when they are asserting themselves, trying to perform significant tasks better, and working in a self-directed purposive fashion. One reason traditional schooling is often so destructive is that it forces students to labor so hard at memorizing information and storing the knowledge deposits entrusted to them by "experts" that they have little time left to develop their own personal abilities and to relate what they have learned to their own everyday activities.

IN SOCIAL SITUATIONS LEARNING INVOLVES DIALOGUE. Democratic social relations, as we have seen, involve genuine two-way communication and patterns of mutual influence. Dialogue among persons is thus a description of democratic relations viewed from the perspective of social process. In democratic teaching/learning environments, the teacher is no longer merely the one who deposits information into students' minds but now also becomes the one who is taught in a two-way dialogue with these other persons (Freire, 1970). Such democratic relations facilitate mutual growth because they provide opportunities for such things as modeling, leveling, disclosure, and social support, all of which are necessary in the growth process.

BEING WELL EDUCATED IS NOT A MATTER OF SCHOOLING. There is no prescribed curriculum that everybody must, should, or can learn in order to be well educated, observed Gross (1976: 17). In fact, a narrow academic notion about what constitutes education can be a major block to growth. "The scope of free learning stretches far beyond the subjects taught in schools and colleges. The worth to you of any particular subject or field is for you to decide on your own terms. Virtually every aspect of your life has the latent power to enhance your 'second education,' if you can find or create the ways to learn it" (Gross, 1977: 18).

Increased emphasis in society on principles of free learning such as these would have the dual effect of reducing the ability of adults to indoctrinate children while at the same time providing both youngsters and adults with more resources for self-learning and growth. In previous generations, learning has involved primarily the young learning from the old. The information, history, values, and culture have been passed along from the elder to the younger. However, in a free learning society, we may begin to see a reversal of this situation: for the first time a more genuine exchange of values and information between children and adults is created. Such a "pre-figurative" culture, as Mead (1970) referred to it, would be one dedicated to the progressive achievement of democratic relations between the generations in every major sphere of life.

Learning Without Schools

Several recent surveys have suggested that most Americans engage in at least one significant independent learning project each year and that the amount of such independent learning has increased substantially during the past decade.[29] Moreover, these studies show that most of this self-education is not undertaken for academic credit, and for this reason many of the people surveyed at first hesitated to believe that what they had been doing could be called "true education."

From his own research, Gross (1977: 54) observed that the personal character of free learning typically involved "each person doing what he is uniquely equipped to do—determining precisely what he wants, when and how and where he wants it." These individuals frequently used other people as resources, although in these free-learning situations they were usually colearners rather than "authorities." "Though occasionally they may be paid experts, they are more often friends, neighbors, relatives, or colleagues," noted Gross (1977: 54). "Chances are most of us prefer to learn *with* other people, if not necessarily *from* them."

The "Invisible University"

As portrayed by Holt, Gross, and others, the "invisible university" consists of the total wealth of resources and opportunities in society which are available to the free learner, including book clubs, libraries, local support groups, churches, museums, art galleries, theaters, television programs, records, tape cassettes, games, films, newspapers, magazines, correspondence courses, and lifelong education classes sponsored by community schools and colleges. Generally speaking, this invisible university offers much more flexibility than is possible in pursuing conventional schooling. Persons can start whenever they want, learn at their own pace, backtrack and review as much as they like, and change direction on short notice. Individuals are also free to combine resources from different institutions and augment any particular offering with others.

Furthermore, free learners can determine the amount of time and money they spend, measure themselves against their own standards, and shape their learning activities in terms of their own unique needs and personalities. By so doing, "each of us finds his own style," explained Gross (1977: 89).

"Learning Exchanges"

Libraries represent the learning resource centers that have been, and undoubtedly will continue to be, at the heart of a free-learning system. Here persons seeking information are able to avail themselves of a variety of learning resources without testing, external evaluation, bureaucratic hassles, or the heavy time commitments and costs that encumber formal education. More than forty American cities also have experimented with types of "learning exchanges" which are educational matching services that facilitate the coming together of persons possessing certain types of knowledge and skills with other people seeking to learn.

A model for such a service is provided by the Learning Exchange, which began operation in 1971 in the Chicago suburb of Evanston, Illinois. This matching service was designed according to suggestions popularized by Illich (1970) for providing those who wanted to learn with access to available instructional resources. When individuals contacted the Learning Exchange regarding a given activity, they could register either as a teacher, a learner, or merely as a person who wanted to meet other people who shared a particular interest. Persons who wanted to learn to speak Spanish, for instance, could call the Learning Exchange and indicate their interest as learners. The Exchange would then give the callers the names and phone numbers of those who had offered to teach Spanish, and it would be the responsibility of these learners to call the Spanish teachers and work out mutually agreeable arrangements.

Even though the Learning Exchange in the early 1970s offered courses in more than 3,000 subjects, served over 20,000 persons each year, and employed a staff of six part-time and six full-time people, costs nevertheless remained low (Gross, 1977: 101). The Exchange provided education in an atmosphere more supportive and congenial to many people than the traditional teacher-controlled classroom, and one evaluation study found that 97 percent of the exchange's clients who met with teachers expressed satisfaction with the arrangements they had made (Squires, 1975: 21). Through such arrangements some of the wasted human resources which exist in communities can be more fully utilized.

Thousands of informal networks, newsletters, and learning groups exist at the present time on topics and issues ranging from progressive or reactionary politics to oriental religions. "The freshest voices in the press today belong to the thousands of local newsletters, community publications, and broadsides by activist groups," declared Buchsbaum (1980: 63). These lively and widely circulated alternatives to the current homogenized mass media reflect the impressive vitality of grass-roots activism, as these local publications seek to inform, challenge, and inspire civic and political action.

A few communities also have initiated tool exchanges in which the implements needed for many projects such as gardening and car repairs can be obtained either free or at a nominal charge. In the past, billions of dollars have been spent on highly structured learning bureaucracies, but only recently have we begun to experiment with public support for informal learning resources, which are open to all and which place themselves at the disposal of every interested learner. "I would like to see an upsurge in offerings and options for learners through the burgeoning of all kinds of fresh initiatives," suggested Gross (1977: 167): "learning exchanges, free universities, study and action groups, social change alliances, special interest networks, small publications and newsletters, open access media, catalogs, and expanded library services."

Free Schools and Educational Alternatives

The free school movement spread across the United States in the late 1960s and by the early 1970s, at the movement's height, a total of perhaps 15,000 to 25,000 students were attending privately financed and controlled free schools. Although there were many differences among these schools, they tended to share a general antiauthoritarian educational philosophy that emphasized, among other things, student participation in government, parent and community involvement, work in the outside world,

student choice in curriculum, more social and personal relevance
in classroom activities, and opposition to external rewards and
punishments as a basis for student learning. The accomplishments of many of these utopian institutions did not live up to
the reformer's expectations, however, since parents were forced
in most cases to support these schools in addition to the public
school systems already existing in their communities. As a consequence, this free school movement began to level off and actually
declined in the mid-1970s.[30]

The number of people involved in educational reforms
incorporating a free school perspective, however, has continued
to grow, and today actually is much larger than during the
heyday of the free school movement. Much of the schooling
reform impetus though has now moved inside the public school
system, with the concept changing to that of alternative schools
rather than free schools. "Instead of starting their own schools,
parents, teachers, and students who shared the educational and
cultural ideas of the small band of free schoolers worked to establish the idea of parent and student choice in the kind of education
provided by the public system," explained Graubard (1979: 50).
These alternative schools are often called "schools-within-
schools," "open schools," or "schools-without-walls."

Coping with Schools

Compulsory schooling is tyranny; it involves the colonization of the human mind and spirit. The long-run solution to this
deeply entrenched despotism, as described above, must be a
general encroachment program aimed at weakening, and ultimately abolishing, the arbitrary ranking, credentialing, and
labeling powers of schools. Only when schools become purely
voluntary institutions, not only in a strictly legal sense but also
in terms of people's economic livelihoods and job aspirations,
will it be possible to humanize and democratize these educational
bureaucracies. Such a "deschooling" program must also be
accompanied, as we have seen, by a positive program to increase
the free-learning resources and educational alternatives in American society.

As previously discussed regarding the family and work environments, however, the immediate problem for students, parents,
teachers, and others is one of coping with the present educational

system. What can be done, then, in dealing with these author-itarian structures and the limitations on freedom and human growth which they do impose?

What Professional Educators Can Do

This chapter was not written to oppose teaching; rather, it is an analysis of some of the ways significant teaching and learning are defeated by the structure and functioning of contempo-rary schools. Language, interaction, and social relationships are necessary for human growth, and people can obviously learn many, many things from other people, but modern schools are domesticating institutions based on domination and power rela-tions. Under these circumstances, then, what can teachers and school administrators do to reduce the destructive effects of authoritarian schooling?

The struggle to stay alive and renew oneself is a particularly difficult one for teachers within large school bureaucracies. "Trying to do justice to crowds of children is exhausting," stated Featherstone (1979: 2); "teachers notice signs of routinization in the curriculum and in themselves." Given the number of unem-ployed teachers and lack of alternative career possibilities, "most teachers stay in the classroom, weary or not, and look for some form of support in their working lives."

Professional support from school administrators can be especially crucial to the mental health and growth of teachers. Whereas some school principals and superintendents allow or encourage bureaucratic intimidation, other school administra-tors help teachers resist these structural forces which would limit their teaching effectiveness. School administrators thus can use their authority to promote teacher communication and teacher autonomy. They also can resist the pressures to manage schools in an increasingly sophisticated top-down manner and help teachers and students achieve more control over the teaching/learning process. It is only through this type of "class suicide" that school administrators can become a part of the solution of the modern school crisis rather than merely functionaries per-petuating further bureaucratic domination and dehumanization.

Although severely restricted in the context of compulsory school relations, teachers can nevertheless improve their own abilities for facilitating student growth. The work of democratic teachers really begins when students have problems or questions they themselves want to solve. If there were no such questions or problems, then there would be no teaching since significant learning can never be imposed on students from the outside. Even when there are such questions, teachers still do not give students knowledge in any simple or straightforward way.

> A teacher does not give knowledge with his answer. Knowledge cannot be *given*. If you ask me a question all I can do in my reply is try to put into words a part of my experience. But you get only the words, not the experience. *To make meaning* out of my words, you must use your own experience. If you have not seen or done at least some part of what I have seen and done, then you cannot make any meaning from my words. There is no way we could explain bicycles or cars or gears or pulleys to someone who had never seen a wheel or a circle. (Holt, 1976: 85)

Teachers instead must work to stimulate the openness to experience, self-confidence, and other features of democratic character structures discussed previously. Teachers can *model* complex behaviors and show students by example how things can be done. They can provide *feedback* to students, which helps them better understand their own actions and experiences. Master teachers can often break down large tasks into smaller ones that students are able to perform and also pace students in the accomplishment of progressively more difficult tasks. In terms of growth-producing social relationships, teachers may facilitate the students' *self-disclosure* necessary to help them formulate their own ideas and mental perspectives. Equally important is the teacher's ability to provide *social support* for students to take the risks that accompany the expression of new ideas and activities. The task of the true teacher, therefore, is not to make students more dependent but rather to help them become more autonomous and self-reliant persons.

Teachers can also help one another by forming teaching centers, seminars, and other kinds of support networks that regularly bring them together and allow them to discuss common problems and concerns. "Such seminars are a good sign that the process by which children learn is being taken seriously, and that teachers are being encouraged to look closely at the specific issues that arise in every classroom situation," exclaimed Featherstone (1979: 3). These types of support activities are more than mere handholding; they offer the types of intellectual and emotional support teachers need to operate in these anti-intellectual, top-down, bureaucratic settings.

In addition, teachers can work to improve schools through their teacher unions, which in many states currently exist as the most effective and influential educational lobbies. Unfortunately, in the tradition of pragmatic unionism, teachers' unions have usually "defined their role as bargaining for increases in teacher salaries, higher nonwage benefits, and improved promotion policies and job security. None of these issues affects the conditions of teaching in the schools, however, which are determined from above" (Carnoy, 1976: 284). Teachers must therefore work to change the limited nature of most academic union bargaining, expanding it to include control over all aspects of the school work situation.[31]

It is crucial that this increasing teacher control of the curriculum and classroom relations be won at the expense of central management and does not merely increase the domination of students by teachers. True teacher autonomy is itself unachievable within the bounds of the present school system, but, even if it could be achieved, such teacher control would only be one step in the overall task of placing school power in the hands of the direct participants in the teaching/learning process.

What Parents Can Do

Depending on their specific circumstances, parents with children stuck in the compulsory school system can pursue any one, or some combination, of the following options: 1) help their children better cope with schools, 2) give their children alternatives to public schools, and/or 3) participate in the growing movement for increased community control over schools. For children who are active and contented with schools, for instance, the best advice to parents often may be to help their children get along better in school. Even though parents may personally dislike the hidden curriculum of schools as well as the values implied by these authoritarian organizations, children are fortunately amazingly resilient and often much harder to fool or brainwash than many parents believe. It is also difficult for parents to judge the actual impact of particular teachers or classroom situations on their children's lives. The most crude and authoritarian teacher, for example, may also be enthusiastic and competent in some particular academic area, and children may identify with these good qualities while ignoring the other negative traits that happen to upset the parents.

HELPING CHILDREN COPE WITH SCHOOLS.   Parents can often assist their children in coping with schools by helping them understand how reward/punishment systems work and how language often becomes distorted in these authoritarian environments. Many teachers, for example, will use the concept "self-discipline" to apply to situations in which children are willing to obey their orders, and thus the self-disciplined children become the ones who turn in their math or reading assignments on time.

What is really being referred to in this situation are internalized social controls rather than self-discipline, which in self-regulated children would refer to their being able to stick with and complete self-initiated tasks. Parents can also help children cope with schools by sharing with them their own studying methods and test-cramming techniques and by providing study implements such as calculators, good study facilities, and, as the costs come down, with home computers and computerized software and study aids. "The most important trick in beating the school game is to know that it *is* a game, as abstract, unreal, and useless as chess, and that beating it *is* a trick," observed Holt (1967: 217).

ALTERNATIVES TO SCHOOLING.   Schools hurt children, however, and, despite parents' best efforts to help them adapt, education will not be a pleasant experience for a lot of youngsters. Many children are defeated by the abstractness, fragmentation, and disconnectedness of classroom subjects, and others are offended by the school motivational systems based on bribes and threats of failure. They cannot adjust to the mean-spirited competition of the classroom and the fact that for them to win other children are required to lose.

What children often need, therefore, are ways to escape schools and educational alternatives in their lives. Holt (1976: 218) suggested, in this regard, that students need a "Children's Underground Railroad" analogous to the system devised in the last century to assist blacks in escaping from slavery. Why, then, not now organize a new Underground Railroad to help children escape from schools? "The Children's Underground Railroad, like all movements of social protest and change, must begin small; it will grow larger as more children ride it," explained Holt (1967: 218). "Beyond that, as was the case with draft refusal, keeping one's children out of school is not likely to become legal unless a good many people do it even when it is illegal. Only as more people do this can they show convincingly on a large scale what the experience of a few has already shown—that the children are not hurt by it, and are usually very much the better."

The safest and most legal way for parents to keep children out of school is to persuade the schools to let them keep their children out. In some states if one of the parents has a teacher's certificate, they have a legal right to teach their children at home. Even in states where they have no such right, parents are more likely to obtain the needed permission if they have a certificate. If the children's test scores keep above their grade level, many school systems will remain satisfied with such home arrangements.

In some states it may be legal and possible for parents to hire a certified teacher to tutor their children and to supervise a home study program. Also, some states allow anyone with a teacher's certificate to start a school and, if the school is small enough (six children or less), many houses may be equipped to satisfy the government's health and safety requirements. If these options are not possible, parents may elect to enroll their children in a local alternative school, or even send them to live with relatives, friends, or other sympathetic adults in communities where such an arrangement is possible. "If people cannot persuade their local school to approve a home or work study program for their children," suggested Holt (1967: 219–20), "they may be able, for a very small fee, to enroll them in some alternative school, perhaps nearby, perhaps in another district or state, which will approve such a program."

Unfortunately, as we have seen, the public school system in 1980 cost more than $100 billion per year and currently has great political power and support. Therefore, none of these alternatives to compulsory education are particularly easy ones. The present system, based on forced consumption, will not be defeated without a difficult struggle. "By the time enough children have escaped school so that the schools feel they have to close the escape routes, we may have enough evidence to convince the courts and legislators that they should be kept open," concluded Holt (1976: 222). "In short, we may be able to show that children out of school learn much faster and better than children in them, at vastly less public expense, and that for reasons of public policy as well as liberty and justice we ought to let parents and children together decide how much (if any) and what kind of schooling they want."

COMMUNITY CONTROL OF SCHOOLS. At the community level parents, worried about the destructive impact of schools, can participate in movements for school decentralization, whose goal is to make these public institutions more responsive to the particular populations that they serve. The unwieldiness of the present highly centralized administrative structures prevents this type of accountability. Parents can hope by making schools answerable to local, rather than city-wide governing boards, for instance, that these new localized institutions will improve their students' learning environments. As Levin argued, "the direct impact of decentralization on schools would be derived from the ability of each community to select the curricula, materials, programs, and personnel that were most appropriate to the specific needs of its students."

> Experimentation and innovation, then, might lead to school environments more receptive to students and more successful in stimulating intellectual and emotional growth than are the present schools. In addition, decentralization would enable schools to handle logistical problems more efficiently by obtaining textbooks and other supplies in appropriate quantities at times when they are needed. Decentralization could also enable schools to obtain outside consulting on specific problems, utilize new types of personnel, such as artists and writers, and contract certain services that might be supplied more efficiently by private firms. (1972: 203)

Greater participation by parents in the operation of schools would undoubtedly reduce alienation and lead to a more total involvement in education by community residents than is possible under the present bureaucratic system. Currently, the schools appear as impenetrable and alien fortresses to many community residents. The inability of parents to have any meaningful influence in modifying rigid and anachronistic school policies has certainly led to parental frustrations and hostile attitudes that are easily transmitted to students. With greater community control, however, parents could pressure school boards to provide their children with more diversified educational experiences such as the schools-within-schools and other alternative programs already described.

What Students Can Do

One problem in the analysis thus far is the possible implication that most educators and parents actually want to reform schools. The truth is that many adults, once they have survived the school system themselves, now are actually in a position to profit from that autocratic system. The schools provide a much-needed child-sitting service for parents and relieve them of the additional burdens of helping to educate their own children. For teachers and administrators, this system affords a comfortable, relatively prestigious, and taken-for-granted way of life. Like other areas of society, the authoritarian school structures will probably only change when those who are exploited and oppressed by them—the children—demand such a change. Much of the hope of abolishing compulsory education and reforming the educational establishment, therefore, lies in the achievement of more general children's rights in society, of which, as discussed in Chapter 3, one of the most important is the right to educate oneself.

At the present time, school children typically are seldom granted the rights of free speech, free assembly, free dress, free thought, or freedom from cruel and unusual punishment that supposedly are the birthright of all Americans. They also typically do not have the right to participate in planning their own education or in setting policies and goals within their own schools. Moreover, students can be suspended or expelled, in most instances without the right to due process or a trial by a jury of their peers. So few opportunities are provided in the public schools for students to exercise free action and thought that they gain little experience in applying these concepts to their daily lives. Consequently, they often grow up being ambivalent and actually fearing freedom.[32]

However, many in our society are slowly becoming aware of this issue, and the court system has finally begun addressing the civil rights of students. For instance, in the case of *Tinker v. Des Moines Independent School District*, which has popularly been hailed as the "magna carta" of students' rights, the Supreme Court for the first time spelled out the free speech rights of students. In effect, the Court upheld the general principle that, in a democratic society such as America, the processes in our schools also must be democratic. Speaking for the majority of the Court, Justice Abe Fortas wrote: "It can hardly be argued that either students or teachers shed their constitutional rights to freedom of speech or expression at the schoolhouse gate" (Hentoff, 1981: 5). Students, therefore, should demand involvement in the planning of their own educations. They should be in control of their own school newspapers, for instance, and have guaranteed financing for these media even when their views happen to be unpopular with school administrators or other adults. Supporting the liberties and democratic rights of students is indeed a step in the right direction.

However students decide to cope with schools, they should realize sooner or later that they must take responsibilities for designing their own educations. They should begin by paying attention to themselves as changing, developing, and growing persons and tune in to how they might most effectively develop new skills, interests, and capacities. Gross observed that "though your goals may change over time, you must begin somewhere. Start with exploring how you learn best and what's most worth learning for you right now. You're the boss as a free learner; you can take command of your own education: what, where, when, how, and with whom you will learn" (1977: 64). To help pay closer attention to their own thoughts and ideas, some students also might choose to write personal journals or "learning logs," for example. "Your learning log will help ensure that nothing valuable is wasted and that your learning becomes cumulative, enabling you to take full advantage of every kind of experience," concluded Gross (1977: 64). Students also can endeavor to take greater advantage of the invisible university, as described previously. Fortunately, modern society offers many alternative ways to learn and to develop our individual human talents and potentials.

Education and a Democratic American Future

"A people who mean to be their own governors," wrote James Madison, "must arm themselves with the power which knowledge gives." Unfortunately, the modern school system is not in tune with these revolutionary ideals as expressed by our nation's Founding Fathers. Rather, education has become an instrument of domination in evaluating and ranking students, in labeling and tracking them into appropriate jobs, and in indoctrinating them with approved values and motivations, excluding "independence of thought" which is difficult to teach through such coercion.

School reform, in turn, must be analyzed in terms of the contribution it makes to eroding hierarchy and putting control of American institutions in the hands of the people who use them. New educational resources and alternatives also must be designed to create and reinforce such a democratic social order in which people no longer have the right to dominate one another. We must work to develop constituencies for a process of lifelong learning. Employers should be encouraged to become less interested in mere credentials and more concerned with the actual competencies and skills of their job applicants. Educational institutions should be directed to see their roles less as compulsory institutions externally shaping students and more as resources for personal self-exploration and growth. Finally, people themselves must be encouraged to take responsibilities for their own learning and growth. "Most important of all, we Americans as individuals seem to be developing a fresh hunger for experience, for growth, for personal cultivation," wrote Gross (1977: 169). "Men and women of all ages today feel the urge to seek more in life—to shape a larger self." This, then, is the hope and the promise of the becoming free society.

6

Authoritarian Dreams and Other Assorted Nuclear Nightmares

> The last three elected Presidents . . . have found the country ungovernable. None succeeded in carrying through a major domestic program. Each spent time making and unmaking foreign commitments, ordering weapons, and performing other tasks more amenable to Presidential initiative than solving the energy or water crisis in the U.S. or resurrecting the decaying cities.
>
> —RICHARD J. BARNET

We worked hard, educated our children, trusted the "experts," and believed that in America everything would always get better, but somehow this did not work out. The economists promised a managed prosperity and continued economic growth, but their policies only succeeded in producing escalating inflation, galloping unemployment, and a deteriorating natural environment in which the gross national product was increasingly dependent on waste and inefficiency, environmental pollution, the perpetuation of poverty, and the expansion of a costly and dangerous military war-making apparatus. Instead of the boundless frontiers promised by scientists, environmental and social limits popped up everywhere.

> Burn gasoline, scientists advised, and cities choke in fumes. Burn coal, and the delicate ecological balance of the earth is jeopardized. Take the nuclear route, and you court catastrophe. Mechanize agriculture to make it efficient, and it takes forty calories to produce and deliver a calorie of food. Develop miracle pesticides and you produce miracle pests

209

who seem to thrive on them. There is a misfit between
politics and the natural order which neither economists nor
scientists nor corporate executives nor government bureaucrats quite understand. To be sure, it is not written anywhere that leaders understand, much less have vision. But
the contemporary crop of leaders, surely as bright and as
well schooled as any, seem to lack even the competence to
manage disasters well. (Barnet, 1980: 16)

Slowly we have come instead to learn that our present mode
of life is without future. If we continue down this road of expert-
directed planning, as we will discuss below, nuclear war becomes
increasingly likely, and even if through accident or sheer luck
such wholesale destruction is averted, within a generation the
oceans and rivers will likely be sterile, the soil infertile, the air
unbreathable, and the world stripped of much of its oil, iron ore,
bauxite, and many other precious minerals upon which our civilization remains dependent. Over the past century we have succeeded in looting natural reserves whose existence required
millions of years to create, and it is clear that disregarding these
natural limits sets off a backlash resulting in new diseases, declining life expectancy, and a decreasing quality of life despite ever-
increasing levels of material consumption.

THE CRISIS OF AUTHORITARIANISM

As we have seen in capitalist factory production, managers have
systematically attempted to remove most elements of skill and
judgment from all but a handful of jobs and to substitute general,
abstract, interchangeable labor for the individual labor of the
nineteenth-century artisan. Workers produce in order to work
rather than working in order to produce. Jobs become devoid of
sense, or that which occupies workers and perpetuates the social
relations of subordination and domination upon which the present hierarchical system depends. Workers are increasingly proletarianized while being associated in ever larger enterprises in
huge metropolitan centers. Technical specialization and global
economic concentration have destroyed the autonomy of local
productive units, and work has become a process of masking
from the workers themselves their own unemployment.
    As control and decision making are systematically concen-
trated in upper management and bureaucratic rules proliferate,

an increasing number of supervisors and "guards" are necessary to ensure that the rules are followed. Unlike their nineteenth-century craftsperson forebearers, however, modern workers are no longer the masters of the work process in which they are implicated, nor do they necessarily possess either the political skills or the vision that would lead to the transformation of the wage labor system which degrades their lives.[1] Workers lose interest in their labor and invest themselves to living outside of work. Alienation and inefficiency creep into the production process as even the most sophisticated scientific management systems are unable to produce workers who are degraded by their work but who nevertheless are conscientious and proud of their labor. This results, then, in "an unbearable discrepancy between the stupidity, fragmentation, irresponsibility, regimentation of work and the actual or potential creativeness of workers" (Gorz, 1967).

Besides work we also have seen that authoritarian school relations further contribute to the shrinking sphere of personal competence. In schools, students are taught that there is an authority for every question and a paid specialist for every task. Technicians and state-certified professionals thus grow and prepare our food, build our houses, tailor our clothes, raise our children, guard our neighborhoods and defend our country, cure our illnesses (whether real or imagined), fill our emptiness with electronic entertainment, and provide us with our ideas in prepackaged form. Schools, remarked Gorz, do not

> . . . teach us how to speak foreign languages (or even our own, for that matter), how to sing or use our hands and feet, how to eat properly, how to cope with the intricacies of bureaucratic institutions, how to look after children or take care of sick people. If people do not sing any more but buy millions of records to have professionals sing to them, if they don't know how to nourish themselves but pay doctors and the pharmaceutical industry to treat the symptoms of an improper diet, if they don't know how to raise children but only how to hire the services of childcare specialists 'certified by the state,' if they don't know how to repair a radio or fix a leaky faucet or take care of a strained ankle or cure a cold without drugs or grow a vegetable garden, etc., it is because the unacknowledged mission of the school is to provide industry, commerce, the established professions, and the state with workers, consumers, patients, and clients willing to accept the roles assigned to them. (1980: 35)

The apparatus of bureaucratic domination is more pervasive than that of particular businesses or schools, however, and now encompasses virtually our entire way of life. In an aging industrial system we have witnessed an institutional sclerosis of domination, such that power often flows from institutional positions and organizational charts rather than from persons themselves. Bureaucrats have become basic figures in society, plying themselves to administering the rules and procedures that have been developed by others. Individuals thus become identified and subordinated to the specialized roles they play and variously become generals, chauffeurs, engineers, politicians, salespeople, managers, or students as prescribed within their particular hierarchical pyramids. Power is made structural and has no subject; it is personal only in its appearance. The personal power of the top executive, for instance, is largely an optical illusion that exists only in the eyes of those subordinates who receive orders directed to them from those on high.

At the personal level this bureaucratic sclerosis means that self-regulation is increasingly replaced by outside domination. Today, few social and cultural activities can be initiated from below by those directly concerned without the authorization, regulation, or supervision by someone in authority. Without the proper permit or certificate, most people cannot conduct a public picnic or parade, add a room to their houses, fix the plumbing or electrical circuits in their own homes, build a fence, or raise rabbits. With needs determined by a series of institutions, professions, prescriptions, and rights, the citizen is invited to behave primarily as a consumer, patient, customer, or client who is legally entitled to a series of services, facilities, and forms of assistance. Citizens no longer consume those goods and services that correspond to their own heartfelt needs and desires but to those that correspond to the heterogeneous needs attributed to them by professionals and experts from various institutional areas.

The basic problems of modern society thus tend to revolve around issues of outside institutional domination, as opposed to personal self-regulation. Some critics focus primarily on one or another of the manifestations of these general problems; for example, concerns of proliferating government or of corporate domination and control. While these are important issues in themselves, their real significance can best be gleaned in terms of the larger clash in contemporary American and world culture between natural self-regulating social systems and systems relying upon professional experts and outside bureaucratic controls. "The development of voluntary cooperation, the self-determination and freedom of communities and individuals," observed Gorz (1980: 19), "requires the development of technologies and methods of production which can be used and controlled at the level of the neighborhood or community, are capable of generating increased economic autonomy for local and regional collectivities, are not harmful to the environment, and are compatible with the exercise of joint control by producers and consumers over products and production processes."

In this chapter, therefore, we will consider some of the escalating problems caused by these systems of outside domination as reflected at the current time by four levels of general crisis in American society: 1) economic, 2) ecological, 3) military/nuclear war, and 4) American democratic institutions. It is suggested here that underlying each of these modern crises is a developing system of authoritarian control in which certain specialists or experts have been granted the authority to make decisions that affect the lives of others, and these specialists, in turn, are largely left unaccountable for the consequences of their actions. Each of these types of crisis thus becomes a facet of the more general crisis of modern authoritarianism, and these authoritarian contractions will become even more pronounced as we move into the final part of the twentieth century.

With regard to nuclear war, for instance, hawkish politicians, generals, and weapons procurement experts work in an environment where public knowledge about the real issues of national security and military spending are almost nonexistent and where most national security debates are terribly oversimplified and distorted; in fact, they are often conducted at the symbolic level of asserting that America is good and the Soviet Union is evil. This means that the political and military experts on defense matters are largely unaccountable to society in making their plans for the greater glory of the United States and their own careers. Public opinion, which is largely ungrounded in fact or evidence, can be manipulated with skillful military propaganda. If we presume that the same set of factors operates in the Soviet Union, then we can see that the modern problem of nuclear war is at its core a problem of authoritarianism, of experts with uncontrolled power, with personal ambitions and needs that are often different from society's needs, and with few checks on their personal decision making and power.

It also will be argued in the following sections that analogous problems of authoritarianism underlie the ecological, economic, and democratic political crises which are discussed. In each of these areas, people's power and authority have been delegated to specialists whose personal needs often work at cross-purposes with the interests of society. It will be suggested, in each of these instances, that the solutions to this authoritarian crisis lie in moving toward more self-reliant and comutual environments in which people are increasingly responsible for their own lives, decision making is governed by nonpower relations, and control is jointly shared among people.

The conclusions made in the second part of this book thus reinforce those of the first part: overcoming the serious problems facing our society at the institutional level, as was true at the personal level, requires that we overcome relations of domination and develop democratic relations in all major institutional areas which vitally affect our lives. In the last part of this chapter, therefore, some general thoughts will be proposed about problems of transcending these systems of outside authoritarian domination and establishing more self-regulated communities and living arrangements in American society.

DOWN THE LONG ROLLER COASTER

After World War Two the United States enjoyed a period which C. Wright Mills has called the "American Celebration," a time "beyond ideology" when economic prosperity was taken for granted, institutional stability seemed assured, and the American way of life was widely emulated by other countries. The economic crises of the 1970s were to shatter this myth of U.S. economic stability, however, and severely shake the foundations of American institutions and values. By the early 1980s the evidence of our nation's economic decline was unmistakable: crumbling industrial cities, technologically outdated steel mills, corporate giants lobbying for government bailouts and wage concessions from their employees, high unemployment, sustained inflation, low rates of investment in basic production, huge consumer debt, and the disappearance of entire domestic industries, such as television manufacturing, as overseas competitors not only undersold American goods but also offered better design, higher quality, and more advanced technology. As Naisbit has emphasized, in 1960 American companies produced 95 percent of the world's automobiles, steel, and consumer electronics but today the United States no longer dominates the international economy.

- Between 1973 and 1981, productivity growth decreased to about 0.4 percent per year. And in 1979, productivity growth declined 2 percent.
- In 1979 the U.S. share of world manufacturing slipped to just over 17 percent.
- In 1979 American companies' share of the domestic market dropped to only 79 percent in autos, 86 percent in steel, and less than 50 percent of the consumer electronics sold in the United States. These slippages continued into the 1980s. (Naisbit, 1984: 53–54)

The per capita growth rate of the gross national product fell as well, from 3.3. percent in the 1960s to 2.2. percent in the 1970s, with increases in labor productivity also dropping by more than one-third during this period. Moreover, the American terms of trade with foreign countries declined in the 1970s, leading to further decreases in the value of U.S. goods and services. Combined with a rising effective rate of taxation, these developments, in turn, caused the real take-home pay to the average American worker to fall during the 1970s.[2]

Furthermore, during this decade the nation also experienced the longest sustained period of inflation since price statistics were first systematically recorded around 1800. Moreover, the average rate of increase in the Consumer Price Index was nearly three times higher in the 1970s than it had been in the 1950s and 1960s. By the early 1980s the inflation rate was more than 10 percent each year, approximately twice as great as it was in the early 1970s. Most families, however, actually felt inflation even more sharply than these figures indicate. Households in the bottom 80 percent of the income distribution spend an average of 70 percent of their incomes on food, shelter, medical care, and energy, and between 1970 and 1976 the cost of these four basic necessities increased 44 percent more rapidly than the cost of other goods and services.[3]

Americans also began to experience increasing levels of forced joblessness. Rates of unemployment grew from approximately 4 percent in the 1950s, to more than 6 percent in the mid-1970s, to around 10 percent—about 10 million persons unable to find work—in the early 1980s. These were the highest annual rates of joblessness since the Great Depression, and most observers agree that the real rates of U.S. unemployment are perhaps nearly double these official rates.[4] Women, young persons, and minorities were especially hard hit, with unemployment in central cities often approaching 40 to 60 percent of the working populations.

Why, then, after twenty-five years of generally increasing U.S. prosperity has this precipitous economic decline occurred? Most importantly, how might this economic deterioration be reversed? Post-World War Two American prosperity was based on a number of crucial factors such as the growing use of machinery to increase worker productivity, the global superiority of American military and political power in the world economy, the availability of a plentiful supply of basic natural resources and raw materials used in the production process, and the capacity of the earth to receive the waste products of industrial production without serious environmental deterioration. After two decades of rising prosperity, however, the general destructiveness of this industrialization process became increasingly clear, and, during the early 1970s, the system began to run into trouble as growing internal contradictions developed.

Overaccumulation and Falling Profits

"As advanced capitalism develops," explained Gorz (1980: 22), "more and more sophisticated and costly machines are operated by fewer and fewer workers, who are less and less skilled." Businesses become more capital intensive, and this increased use of machinery in the production process tends to restrict the basis from which profits are extracted. Profits, after all, arise essentially from the difference between the amount employers must pay workers and the amount received from the sale of the workers' output. As the share of direct wages decreases as a proportion of the overall costs of the production process, the amount of profit which must be made in order to pay off and renew the machine increases. The decreased reliance on labor in the production process therefore tends to restrict the rate of profit unless there is a concomitant growth in the profits generated for the employer by each worker.

An increasing amount of capital thus is used in producing the same volume of commodities, and businesses must produce a larger mass of profits to replace and renew the ever more costly machines. Under these conditions, Marx and other economists have demonstrated that sooner or later the average rate of profit must decline: "the more capital is used to produce the same volume of commodities, the more the profit which can be derived from this production diminishes in relation to the mass of capital employed."[5] Thus, this invested capital cannot keep increasing without eventually reaching a limit.

> But from the moment that the rate of profit begins to decline, the whole system is jammed: the machines cannot be made to turn out goods which yield the usual profit, nor, consequently, can they be replaced at the same rate as before; hence the production machinery (amongst other things) begins to fall off and the decline in production progressively spreads. In Marxist terms, there is 'overaccumulation': the share of capital in production has become so great . . . that it cannot reproduce itself at a normal rate. The 'productivity' of capital declines. The value of the fixed capital, which cannot be made to yield a sufficient profit, declines to zero. This capital will, in fact, be destroyed: machines are discarded, factories closed down, workers laid off. The system is in crisis. (Gorz, 1980: 22–23)

Several consequences follow from this overaccumulation and the resultant falling rate of profit, including the problems of unemployment and increasingly wasteful production processes.

Increasing Unemployment

Joblessness is a perpetual feature of capitalism since full employment would inevitably lead to increased wage demands by workers and thereby reduce profits. Hayden (1980: 51), for instance, has shown that historically in American industry when unemployment has risen so have the profit rates, and, when unemployment has fallen, profits have done likewise. The current search for profits, however, has led employers to increasing levels of mechanization and to greater foreign investments in countries with cheap labor, lower taxes, antiunion policies, and weak environmental and health regulations.

Like the energy crisis of the 1970s, Barnet (1980: 273) declared that the employment crisis is likely to be the time bomb of the 1980s. Automation destroys jobs without creating anything approaching equivalent opportunities for new employment. "In an industrializing world in which the principal activity is getting and spending, more and more people are becoming irrelevant to the productive process," stated Barnet (1980: 266). "Almost a billion people cannot find work at wages adequate to provide food for their families. Every sign suggests that the number will increase dramatically. It is the monumental social problem of the planet, the cause of mass starvation, repression, and crime." Modern production is thus job-displacing, and the overaccumulation crisis operates as both a cause and effect of this general worldwide trend.[6]

Increasing Waste and Destruction

To avoid crisis, modern employers must constantly work against this tendency toward a declining profit rate. Besides attempts to sell more goods at higher prices, these pressures lead to planned obsolescence, less durable goods, more elaborate and expensive goods, unnecessary duplication of competing brands of identical goods, and generally higher levels of waste in society. Thus, as Gorz observed,

> We have seen tin cans replaced by aluminum ones, which require fifteen times as much energy to produce; rail transport replaced by road transport, which consumes six to seven times as much energy and uses vehicles which must be replaced more often; the disappearance of objects assembled with bolts and screws in favor of welded or molded ones, which are thus impossible to repair; the reduction of the durability of stoves and refrigerators to around six or seven years; the replacement of natural fibers and leather with synthetic materials which wear out faster; the extension of disposable packaging, which wastes as much energy as non-returnable glass; the introduction of throwaway tissue and dishes; [and] the widespread construction of sky-scrapers of glass and aluminum, which consume as much energy for cooling and ventilation in the summer as for heating in the winter. (1980: 23–24)

The problems of overaccumulation have not only led to planned obsolescence and waste but also to greater emphasis on stimulating new demand through more advertising and sales-personship, as analyzed by Baran and Sweezy (1966: 112–41), and through additional military spending, as analyzed below. These efforts to boost sales artificially have become increasingly necessary in modern society, even though the volume of resources absorbed by these unproductive activities has led to ever-increasing levels of irrationality and waste. Industrial efficiency thus is diminished as business organizations consume more for their own needs and deliver less finished products to the consumer. This, in turn, has left fewer resources for such things as social services and private consumption. "Some people will obviously have to do with less," declared the editors of *Business Week* (October 1974), "yet it will be a hard pill for many Americans to swallow—the idea of doing with less so that big business can have more."

Heightened International Competition

A second cause of the current economic crisis in this country is the declining dominance of both American global corporations and of political and economic power. After the Second World War, Japan and the Western European countries were able to rebuild rapidly and by the 1960s were becoming effective trading rivals of the United States. Spurred ahead by relatively low wage rates and an overvalued American dollar, foreign goods became competitive with U.S. products in a growing number of areas. In 1959, for instance, an American company was the largest in the world in eleven of thirteen major industries—aerospace, automobiles, chemicals, electrical equipment, food products, general machinery, iron and steel, metal products, paper, petroleum, pharmaceuticals, textiles, and commercial banking. By 1976, however, U.S. companies were dominating only seven out of the thirteen, and in each industry the number of companies appearing among the world's top twelve corporations declined, except in aerospace. Thus, of the 156 companies that dominate these thirteen industrial groups, the United States controlled 68 of them in 1976, compared with 111 in 1959 (Barnet, 1980: 241). More recently, there is also considerable evidence of a trend in the 1980s toward growing manufacturing power in the Third World.

- Singapore is second only to the United States in its current backlog of oil rigs.
- Hong Kong and Taiwan are moving out of textiles and light electronic assembly and into more complicated computer technology.
- South Korea is challenging Japan's position in home electronics. The reason we hear so little about it, though, is

because their products are marketed in this country under
familiar trade names, such as Sears, J. C. Penney, and
Sylvania. (Naisbit, 1984: 61)

The decline of America's economic dominance has occurred
for several reasons. Developmental costs are less for nations that
have industrialized later because the available technologies can
merely be copied, licensed, or adapted. In their early phase, these
latecomers also had lower wages and better worker productivity
rates. Ironically, the nations defeated in the Second World War—
Germany and Japan—were forced to replace older industrial
plants with more modern factories and equipment which contributed to their long-range productivity and competitiveness.[7]

As the self-appointed world's policeperson, the United States
also assumed a greater military burden than these other countries, which sharply cut into the resources that could be used for
industrial development. In the late 1970s, for instance, as much
as 60 percent of all federal research and development money
went to the military, severely shortchanging civilian research.
Comparing thirteen major industrial countries from 1960 to 1979,
for example, DeGrasse (1982) concluded that the United States
suffered from less rapid growth, slower increases in productivity
and higher unemployment in part because it devoted more of its
gross national product to the military. "Federal spending on
military production at the expense of other programs narrows
the focus of U.S. manufacturing, which abandons subway cars
in favor of missiles," concluded Moberg (1982: 2) "It yields fewer
jobs, because the money goes primarily to higher-paying craft
or engineering jobs. Those, in turn, are siphoned from civilian
work, depriving those industries and creating inflationary
bottlenecks."[8]

In the 1980s newly industrializing countries will undoubtedly further challenge American economic domination. Thirty-
four of the *Fortune* "overseas 500" companies now have their
headquarters in underdeveloped countries. Companies such as
the Taiwanese Steel Company, which is building mills in Nigeria;
the Filipino beer monopoly, which operates breweries in Spain
and New Guinea; and the Korean construction firms in the Middle East, which have more than $4 billion in contracts, will give
U.S. multinationals increasing competition, exclaimed Barnet
(1980: 250). "It is a new development that reflects the absorption
of transferred technologies and the unique opportunities companies from small countries have to take markets away from the

giants. 'We favor investors from small places like Hong Kong,' says the trade minister of Sri Lanka, 'because nobody can talk about a sell-out to imperialism in the case of a country that is as small or smaller than we are.'"

Environmental Limits

Most importantly, however, sustained economic prosperity also has undermined the environmental conditions necessary both for further economic growth and for human life itself. As described in the following section, the rapid growth in U.S. production in the post-World War Two years has put increasing pressure on the world's limited supply of raw materials and nonrenewable resources. Over the past century our industrial civilization has developed through the accelerated looting of natural reserves and borrowing from the resources available to future generations.

These ecological factors thus play an aggravating role in the current economic crisis for several reasons. First, it now becomes necessary to reproduce what was previously abundant and free. Billions of dollars must be invested in equipment to produce breatheable air and drinkable water, fertilize the land, and replenish the forests and seas. Second, searching for new oil, gas, and other increasingly scarce natural resources requires deeper wells and more expensive exploration than was previously the case. High-grade ores that offered 50 to 100 pounds of copper per ton have long since been used up, for instance, and one large U.S. mine is now using ore that has only 5.8 pounds of copper per ton. Getting copper from such low-grade ore requires large machines and tremendous amounts of energy to handle the vast piles of rock, dig the ore out of the ground, transport it, crush it, process it into copper, and haul away the spent ore (Johnson, 1978: 70). Finally, it becomes increasingly expensive to get rid of waste products, the chemicals, radioactive materials, and other toxic by-products of our industrial civilization. Each of these trends is exacerbated by the wastefulness and lack of conservation of nonrenewable resources promoted by industry in an attempt to boost the sagging sales effort.

Thus, our present civilization is built on the twin assumptions of growth and waste, and both of these assumptions are contradicted by an increasingly threatened ecological system and by the approaching environmental limits. "Would it not be more rational," asked Gorz (1980: 13), "to improve the conditions and the quality of life by making more efficient use of available resources, . . . and by refusing to produce socially those goods which are so expensive that they can never be available to all, or which are so cumbersome or polluting that their costs outweigh their benefits as soon as they become accessible to the majority?" Lack of realism at the present time is not a result of advocating a nongrowth-oriented society but rather the result of believing that such perpetual growth can continue to happen without paying a greater and greater economic price for such destructive social tendencies. "What should be crystal clear," concluded Baran and Sweezy (1966: 141), "is that an economic system in which such costs are socially necessary has long ceased to be a socially necessary economic system."

Revitalizing the Economy

Our present affluence is based on the rapid exploitation of the world's abundant virgin resources, and, as these natural resources become depleted, our present way of life is necessarily doomed. Although we might wish it to be otherwise, the higher prices of raw materials during the 1970s have begun to signal the onset of a new era of scarcity, within which the perpetuation of our affluent society is increasingly an uphill struggle. "To maintain the heavy flow of raw materials now being cranked through our economy will become an increasingly laborious and ultimately desperate task," explained Johnson (1978: 9). "Affluence will grow less comfortable, and there will be less peace and security in it."

We therefore have passed through the frontier era of the eighteenth and nineteenth centuries, the affluent era of the twentieth century, and are now headed into this new age of scarcity. Given limited world resources, affluence cannot increase indefinitely, and scarcity, therefore, will ultimately be the mechanism that diverts our industrial society from its self-destructive goals of constant growth and rising wastefulness. Most unpleasantly for us, this era of scarcity undoubtedly will be reflected in recurring cycles of steadily rising prices, declining numbers of full-time and well-paying jobs, and falling real incomes. In general, the 1980s will likely be an ambiguous decade in which environmental resistance gradually builds. During this period both optimists and pessimists can read the economic fluctuations as supporting their respective forecasts, until the environmental resistance builds to the point where irreversible contradictions set in. Often against our wishes we will be compelled to make life-style changes and learn to adjust to declining incomes. We will also be forced to develop attitudes and values that support frugality and the conservation of resources (Johnson, 1978: 202).

Return of the Lowly Paid Worker

In the era of affluence, labor was an expensive commodity when compared with machinery and energy. Therefore, the industrial trend, as we have seen, was toward the replacement of human labor with machinery and automated production processes, that is, toward capital intensity. With the onset of the present age of scarcity, however, the balance is beginning to shift, and gradually labor costs are becoming relatively less expensive than the costs of machines, transportation, and energy. Already in the United States research evidence indicates that labor-intensive industries are becoming more profitable than capital-intensive ones.[9] Therefore, in this country we are witnessing a situation in which basic capital-intensive industries, such as rubber, steel, and aircraft and automobile manufacturing, are declining, and more labor-intensive service industries like Disney Productions, McDonalds, and Coca-Cola are relatively more prosperous.

Low transportation costs have greatly aided the development of mammoth multinational corporations that are able to manufacture and distribute their products on a global scale. However, an estimated 30 to 40 percent of the prices of many of these manufactured goods are the result of the global distribution process itself, and in recent years, since the beginning of the energy shortage, these prices have been escalating rapidly. Large centralized manufacturers can still undersell smaller scale producers in many markets, but their traditional advantages are eroding. As energy and machinery prices soar, local and regional firms have an increasing number of advantages over their larger competitors; for instance, they are located much closer to their consumers, can maintain smaller inventories, have fewer less highly paid managers and administrative bureaucrats, and are often more adaptable to changes in their local markets.

New Opportunities for Self-reliance

It is important to challenge those who argue that our current free enterprise system provides greater freedom than other ways of life. In actuality, as we have seen, capitalism has substituted one set of personal constraints for another. In preindustrial America the constraints on people's lives flowed primarily from tradition, the local community, religion, and particularly from patriarchy, while under capitalism the constraints have shifted more toward those established by the market. To be successful, modern persons therefore must spend the first quarter of their lives leaping teacher-directed hurdles; dedicating themselves to their careers; moving where work is available; being loyal, dependable, and manageable in the eyes of outside authorities; being ambitious and somewhat narcissistic; and competing constantly with other persons. Whether these new obligations are more or less restrictive than the old can be debated, but they nevertheless remain as significant obstacles to full human development.

As time passes and incomes begin to fall, major changes in people's life-styles will be required. This new age represents a breakdown of the present industrial order, an inability of the system to live up to its own promises of constantly increasing levels of goods and services for its citizens. This new scarcity in American society may lead either to a more centralized and expert-managed society or to one with greater autonomy and individual self-governance. The real impact of these changed circumstances on freedom and full human development in people's lives thus will depend on which of these alternative paths is ultimately pursued.

Under current circumstances, *more* is not necessarily *better*, and much present consumption may actually be destructive. We might get along just fine in our lives, for instance, with less sales manipulation and commercial distractions. While the prospects for sustaining a high-level, industrial society are declining, the chances for creating a simple, decentralized way of life are correspondingly enhanced. Institutional passivity might well give way to community involvement as people are forced to learn to pull together at the local level. Without large incomes, people might begin to experiment with various forms of barter and develop mutual assistance associations and cooperatives.

Jobs might start to appear in people's neighborhoods when wages became low enough, relative to machinery, transportation, and energy, to allow small-scale, labor-intensive businesses to compete effectively with their global corporate rivals. Habits of frugality could prove valuable, and persons who were able to get by with less might be able to better survive this new scarcity. The renewable resources and simple technology necessary for greater self-governance and more independent life-styles are already available. As the reality of these new trends toward scarcity becomes better understood and grudgingly accepted, it may be possible to move away from the expert-dominated society that has developed over the past century toward one more truly approximating the Jeffersonian ideal of multitalented, well-rounded, and autonomous persons living in self-governing communities.

THE BETRAYAL OF THE EARTH

Events during the 1970s, such as the oil shortage of 1973 and the 1979 near catastrophe at Three Mile Island, may turn out to be warning signals of a protracted environmental crisis. Modern wealth and productivity have been gained from the rapid short-term exploitation of the environment and thus have created a large debt to nature. "In effect, the account books of modern society are drastically out of balance, so that, largely unconsciously, a huge fraud has been perpetrated on the people of the world," exclaimed Commoner (1971: 295). "The rapidly worsening course of environmental pollution is a warning that the bubble is about to burst, that the demand to pay the global debt may find the world bankrupt."

The environmental crisis should not be seen merely as one part of the economic crisis, as discussed above, but also as posing fundamental problems with regard to energy, food and water supplies, and life itself. To survive on earth, human beings require the stable, continuing existence of a suitable environment. The evidence, however, is overwhelming that the way in which we now live on this planet is driving its thin, life-supporting surface, and ourselves with it, to destruction (Commoner, 1971: 14). Approximately 35 million tons of hazardous wastes, for example, are generated in the United States each year and, according to federal estimates, perhaps 90 percent or more of these materials is disposed of improperly. The Environmental Protection Agency also identified 51,000 sites where hazardous waste materials have been stored or buried and suggested that potentially "significant problems" exist at anywhere between 1,200 and 34,000 of them. Among other effects, watercourses and drinking wells are being poisoned by these problem dump sites, forcing the closing of drinking wells in such states as New Jersey, New York, Maine,

Connecticut, Tennessee, Texas, Michigan, and California (Ridgeway, 1982: 305–06).

"The false assumption that the frontier environment was both a source of unlimited resources and a sink for unlimited disposal of toxic waste has given us a landscape pockmarked with poison," observed Hayden (1980: 125–26). Besides the 9 million cubic feet of high-level radioactive waste stored since the Second World War, the nuclear industry also produces an average of thirty tons of radioactive waste per reactor every year, and as yet there is no known technology for the safe disposal of this radioactive waste.

Environmental problems are further compounded by the inefficiency of American industry. As Schumacher (1973: 110) pointed out, if the entire world's population were put into the United States, the population density of our country would then be just about that of contemporary England. Despite abundant resources and a low population density, the United States cannot subsist on internal resources alone; with only 5.6 percent of the world's population, we seem to require about 40 percent of all global primary resources to keep going (Reece, 1979: 14). "Given present resource consumption rates and the projected increases in these rates, the great majority of the currently important non-renewable resources will be extremely costly 100 years from now."[10]

Instead of conserving natural resources and developing a transition strategy, American companies have tended to operate under a set of incentives that push them to speed up production to meet the demand for ever more expensive goods. Despite the fact that nine-tenths of the world's population presently use no fossil fuels at all, it is estimated that this generation could consume 80 percent of the oil and gas left on earth. American consumption of energy thus has tripled since World War Two, with the United States currently consuming over 250 billion gallons of oil each year, a figure that comes to about 1,200 gallons annually for every American. Since 1945 total automotive horsepower also increased sevenfold in this country, energy-consuming air conditioners and home appliances have become commonly available, new commercial buildings have incorporated artificial and energy-wasteful designs, airline travel has expanded, and thousands of miles of highways have been constructed. After consuming fossil fuels as though they would never run out, we are now faced with the task of undoing the damage of this last forty-year binge (Rodberg, 1982: 541).

Food and World Hunger

Malnutrition is the hidden holocaust of our day, declared Barnet (1980: 160), because it is so avoidable. At the present time, for instance, authorities estimate that 462 million people are starving, over one-half of them children under five years of age, with perhaps 1.3 billion persons on earth who are chronically undernourished (Barnet, 1980: 152). Confronted with these facts, most people believe that there is just not enough food to go around; yet, despite the tremendous wastage of land, there is currently produced in the world each day two pounds of grain, or more than 3,000 calories for every person on earth. Moreover, this estimate does not include the enormous amounts of meat, fish, vegetables, and fruits produced each year. This is about what the average American consumes every day and is considerably above the 2,700 calories recommended for moderately active adult males by the Food and Nutrition Board of the National Research Council. Therefore, on a global scale, the idea that there is not enough food produced to go around just is not accurate (Lappe and Collins, 1977: 13).

The primary obstacle to people feeding themselves is not insufficient production, poor climate, inappropriate technology, discriminatory trade practices, or insufficient capital but rather the result of food maldistribution. Most people are hungry not because there is insufficient food grown in the world but because they no longer grow it themselves and are poor and do not have the money to buy it. Around the world, food self-sufficiency is declining. People who used to grow food for themselves and their families no longer can do so because their land has acquired value for growing export crops. At least fifteen of the poorest countries in the world, for example, devote more acres to cash crops for export than for fruits and vegetables that could feed their own hungry populations (Barnet, 1980: 153).

As subsistence agriculture declines worldwide and more countries lose the ability to feed themselves, they become dependent upon the international grain traffic. Increasingly, this international food production and distribution system is under the control of a relatively small number of multinational corporations. Five major grain companies, such as Continental and Cargill, for example, effectively control the world traffic in wheat, corn, barley, and soy; two farm machinery companies control 60 percent of this industry in the United States and also have a major influence on the world market; and a small number of

grain and chemical companies now control the world seed market. More concentrated even than the oil companies, the power
of these multinational firms is derived from their control over
the entire process of growing, transporting, milling, and consuming grain (Barnet, 1980: 169).

One of the most lethal and environmentally unsound aspects
of multinational agribusiness, for instance, is its heavy reliance
on pesticides. "Despite the lessons of DDT, Agent Orange and
other chemicals originally deemed 'safe,' there is still a disquiet-
ing casualness about the 1.2 billion pounds of pesticides in 35,000
varieties that are sprayed each year on American farms and
forests," reported Burton (1981: 6). Even though food producers
credit pesticides with doubling U.S. food production since they
first were sold in 1945, critics respond that today pests destroy
twice as many crops despite a tenfold increase in the use of
chemical controls. As more and more pests become resistant to
pesticides, even more toxic poisons must be created to keep them
in check.

Exporting pesticides is also big business for U.S. companies.
Pesticide sales abroad have nearly quadrupled in the last two
decades, with the chemical industry now exporting about
20 percent of the pesticides it produces, shipping 400,000 tons
per year to the Third World. Many of these chemicals exported
to other countries are already lethal enough to have been banned
or severely restricted by the government in this country. According to the World Health Organization, a pesticide-related death
occurs about every two hours in the Third World, and about
500,000 people become seriously ill from pesticide use each year
(Weir and Schapiro, 1981).

Since large pesticide companies such as Dow, Shell, Bayer,
Stauffer, and Velsicol operate on a global scale, they are difficult
to control by any one nation. Velsicol Chemical Corporation's
marketing of Phosvel provides a case in point. The government
of Colombia banned the pesticide after tests revealed that expo-
sure to the chemical caused serious disorders of the central nervous system in workers. Velsicol, however, "simply moved its
stock piles of Phosvel to a free trade zone technically outside of
Colombian jurisdiction and proceeded to ship the stuff to countries where it was not yet banned."

Seventy percent of the total value of Central American agricultural production is shipped to industrial countries such as the
United States. According to the Food and Drug Administration,
approximately 10 percent of our imported food contains illegal

pesticide residues. Imported coffee is the worst offender, with 43.7 percent containing residues of domestically banned pesticides. Also, residues from thirty-four pesticides have been found in imported sugar, and twenty-five have been detected in imported bananas. Tests of imported tomatoes, peppers, beans, and cabbages also have revealed concentrations of toxic substances (*Dollars and Sense*, 1981: 19).

The Politics of Cancer

Closely related to the deteriorating environment is the current epidemic of degenerative illnesses—cancer, cardiovascular diseases, rheumatism, arthritis—which modern medicine neither can prevent nor cure. A growing proportion of the population is struck by these illnesses even though more and more elaborate medical technology is available. Current American Cancer Society statistics, for instance, estimate that one out of four Americans will be diagnosed in their lifetimes as having cancer, compared to approximately one out of twenty-five at the turn of the century. The death rate from cancer has continued to rise in spite of statistical adjustments for an aging population and in contrast with the death rate from heart disease, which has begun to decline. Particularly dramatic has been the rapid rise in death rates from certain cancers thought to be chemically related, such as cancers of the lungs and pancreas. Overall, the government estimated that about 80 percent of cancers are "environmentally related," with possibly as many as 40 percent of cancers in the United States being related to work (Hayden, 1980: 126–27).

Actually, of all the factors that help maintain health, modern curative medicine may be one of the least effective. "There are more and more doctors and more and more sick people," stated Gorz (1980: 150). "For the last ten years or so, people in all industrialized countries have been dying younger and are more sickly. This is happening in spite of the expansion of medicine—but also because of it."[11] According to Gorz's statistics, during the last decade doctors have actually made more people sick than they have cured. The modern health care system thus contributes to the spread of diseases in several ways.

First, Illich estimated that there are more medical-induced deaths, for instance, than fatalities caused by both traffic accidents and war-related activities.[12] Similarly, a National Institute of Health study found that 1.5 million people were hospitalized following troubles brought on by medications prescribed by their doctors. Furthermore, Laventurier and Talley estimated that at least 30,000 people die every year in U.S. hospitals from medication poisoning.[13] Second, it is the primary duty of the modern physician to reduce the symptoms that make the sick unfit for their social roles, especially their occupations. By urging people to take their illnesses to the doctor, society keeps them from laying the blame on the fundamental and long-range reasons for their ill health. By treating illnesses as accidental and individual anomalies, the doctor masks the real structural reasons underlying these difficulties. Finally, doctors sometimes contribute to making people ill by encouraging medical dependency in the healthy as well as in the sick. They reinforce the idea that health can be bought, thereby lowering the threshold of illness and reducing the patient's resistance to the environmental poisons inherent in our industrial civilization.

> By claiming to patch up case by case those problems that are becoming more and more sickly, medicine masks the deeper causes of their diseases—which are social, economic, and cultural. While claiming to relieve all suffering and distress, it forgets that in the final analysis people are damaged in body and soul by our way of life. Medicine, in helping them put up with what is destroying them, ends up contributing to this damage. (Gorz, 1980: 152)

Effective or not, one unarguable fact is that modern curative medicine is increasingly expensive. Our soaring national health bill totaled $200 billion in 1980, which is more than 10 percent of the nation's total gross national product. More than three-quarters of all American health care expenditures are aimed not at taking care of disease but at examinations, medical tests, and other related types of preventive treatment in order to take care of the health that might be in danger. So expensive is this preventive health care that, according to the president of the Los Angeles County Medical Association, "we are now in a position to spend the entire national budget on medical tests and procedures" (Bosker, 1981: 16).

The professional organization of Western medicine has an elitist structure which ranks medical knowledge in a way that gives specialists of rare diseases the highest status and income. As a consequence, modern curative medicine favors the rare 5 percent of diseases that require very specialized care and expensive and complex equipment over the 95 percent of diseases that are most common. Medicine has become a technical ritual and a type of social control mechanism which, rather than attacking the deeper causes of illnesses, limits itself to keeping track of them and isolating their symptoms. Doctors offer to reduce discomfort and mask pain in an attempt to keep people's anguish from getting worse.

According to a government report cited by Doyal (1979: 179), almost 60 percent of all medications and perhaps 80 to 90 percent of all antibiotics are administered needlessly. Other studies estimate that in about 90 percent of all illnesses the person will get well without curative medicine, and that in three-quarters of all medical cases the advice of general practitioners, with their administered drugs, has a psychological or psychosomatic effect rather than curing any strictly medical problem. Thus, the effectiveness of medicalized health care is very limited at best, and "in nine cases out of ten, there is no point having a medical professional diagnose and treat a common illness," concluded Gorz (1980: 166). "The symptoms are clear, the remedies well-known and very cheap, and, if they promote healing, the medical professionals are not necessary for healing."

Good health is basically an achievement rather than a biological given, and consequently good health care is an extramedical matter. Polluted cities, scientifically managed work environments, authoritarian family interactions, loneliness, and isolation produce illness. Liking one's work, having friends, being comfortable in the neighborhood, and living in a nonpolluted environment, on the other hand, provide the real basis for health and longevity. Medical professionals have succeeded in creating dependency, whereas good health demands independence, democratic relations, self-reliance, and people who are increasingly capable of taking care of their own health needs. Individuals must learn to blame what really makes them sick—mortgaged homes, unemployment, or their teacher's or boss's unrealistic expectations—and thereby recover their own basic powers over their bodies, illnesses, and spirits.

Ecology and Human Development

All production is destructive. It disturbs the ongoing equilibrium of the earth's ecosystem and involves borrowing from the finite resources that will be available to our children. At least since the coming of agriculture, human beings have been in the business of interfering with nature and in determining, for instance, which plants and animal species will be domesticated and pampered and which species will be killed or poisoned. With the coming of industrialization, this interference with the natural order has escalated rapidly, and, especially in the forty years since World War II, there has been more destruction and pollution of the earth's natural reserves than has occurred in all of human history.

The increasingly paramount ecological concerns in our advanced industrial age, as Gorz (1980: 21) has argued, involve: 1) whether these exchanges with nature preserve or carefully manage the world's stock of nonrenewable resources, and 2) whether the obstructive effects of production do not exceed the productive ones by depleting renewable resources more quickly than they can regenerate themselves. The general problem is not to deify the past or to attempt to return to nature but rather to take into account the fact that both persons and societies find in the natural world their external limits. Furthermore, disregarding these natural limits is likely to cause increasing environmental resistance and ultimately a series of more severe crises as these external contradictions become more critical.

Replacing the Current Growth/Consumption Ethic with Stewardship

It would be unrealistic to assume that continued growth and increased consumption in American society could go on forever. Given the present level of environmental exploitation, even with zero growth the continued consumption of scarce resources would eventually result in soaring costs and the exhaustion of the earth. What is required, then, is not merely a pledge to refrain from new forms of waste and outside destruction but rather a new social ethic based on the careful stewardship of renewable resources and the decreasing consumption of energy and raw materials.

Suggested above is the idea that in modern society the connection between *more* and *better* has been broken. Given these increasingly severe environmental constraints, it may even be possible to live better by working and consuming less if we can make more efficient use of available resources, eliminate waste, and produce more durable goods. Better might come to mean the creation of as few needs as possible, satisfying them with the smallest possible expenditure of materials, energy, and work and imposing the least possible burden on the environment. It is increasingly irrational to measure the standard of living by the amount of annual consumption, for instance; a better goal would be a maximum of well-being with a minimum of consumption.[14]

Industrialization, as we have seen, reinforced in both workplaces and other institutional areas the hierarchical patterns of social organization which necessarily were accompanied by authoritarian forms of control. Power was consolidated in the hands of top managers, ensuring dependency, alienation, and underachievement by those below. In the present crisis, however, it appears unlikely that either government bureaucrats or corporate executives will be able to resolve most people's problems. This ineffectiveness of current institutions should encourage self-reliance by many individuals who will be compelled to fend for themselves. They will be forced to reevaluate their work, patterns of consumption, values, and life-styles in light of the changing realities of scarcity. "It is the prudent thing to do—to find a secure source of income, to get by with less, to protect children during their most vulnerable ages, and to avoid being trapped in a hazardous situation in old age," explained Johnson (1979: 26). "More and more individuals will develop cooperative arrangements with others to make life better and more satisfying."

Conservation and Renewable Energy

A rational energy policy would start with the fact that the nation must use significantly less oil. In the United States and the world in general, oil is headed for exhaustion. It is already too late to produce enough domestic oil to run the country, but importing $50 billion worth of crude oil each year transfers economic and political power to the dollar holders abroad and also fuels a disastrous inflation at home. One proposed solution to the energy problem is to convert to such conventional energy alternatives as nuclear power and coal, but both of these fuels present significant problems. The production of coal, for instance, uses huge amounts of water, which is also increasingly scarce; is dangerous to mine; ruins landscapes; and pollutes the environment. Although coal, along with natural gas, may serve an important role as transitional fuels in moving from oil to the renewable energy resources discussed below, they are both unlikely primary fuels for the twenty-first century.

The problems related to nuclear energy are much more severe. Uranium is one of the rarest elements on earth and, as a consequence, is becoming very expensive. Nuclear power plants are also becoming extremely costly to build and to date have had a poor record of reliability, especially the newer and larger ones. Safety requirements for nuclear power plants are necessarily complex and expensive; large breeder reactors produce weapons grade plutonium as a by-product which, as discussed below, will undoubtedly allow additional countries and terrorist groups access to nuclear weapons; nuclear plants produce thousands of tons of radioactive waste materials that cannot be properly disposed; and the plants require such extreme security measures to avoid theft and sabotage that they severely restrict workers' personal conduct and liberty. "No degree of prosperity could justify the accumulation of large amounts of highly toxic (nuclear wastes) which nobody knows how to make 'safe' and which remain an incalculable danger to the whole of creation for historical or even geological ages," declared Schumacher (1973: 137).

Through energy conservation and emphasis on renewable energy technologies, however, we might be able to achieve a stable balance between energy supply and demand without destroying the environment, altering the climate, invading Saudi Arabia, or risking nuclear war. The United States cannot continue to consume such a large proportion of the world's energy resources without incurring increasing conflicts with other countries. Any national energy plan, therefore, must include a serious conservation program involving, for instance, the redesign of buildings, the encouragement of home jobs, and the creation of subsidies and penalties to help ensure less wasteful industrial production processes.

Currently, the oil companies are able to profiteer from inflation in energy prices, create fuel shortages either by design or mismanagement, and invest in controlling power over competing energy sources such as uranium, coal, and centralized solar technologies. Emphasizing control over energy policy in the public interest, laws could be passed that would prohibit oil companies from buying alternative energy sources and diverting their energy profits into other nonenergy businesses, such as office equipment companies, department stores, and condominiums, rather than reinvesting these profits in the search for more energy.

Unfortunately, the present economic marketplace is rigged against soft energy companies. Oil and nuclear industries have received an estimated $100 billion during the past generation in direct and indirect government subsidies. Almost all government money for soft energy research is being given to global corporations, such as Exxon and Mobil, which have little incentive to find a decentralized alternative to the present energy crisis. Instead of mandating energy wastefulness, then, the federal government should require not only the use of solar and soft energy equipment where they are cost competitive in new construction and in current renovation projects but also provide research funds to organizations that are truly dedicated to seeking a soft energy future for the United States (Hayden, 1980: 114).

A decentralized way of life, based on conservation and the frugal use of renewable resources, is certainly a feasible alternative. This country has a well-trained work force, advanced technology, a good transportation and communications system, and a low population in relation to land and natural resources. A basic goal of this transition toward a conserving, renewable energy society should be community energy self-sufficiency which would involve local decisions about how best to achieve energy self-reliance.

> . . . homes well insulated and shaded, commercial buildings retrofitted with energy-saving devices, factories using solar for process heat and cogenerators for power; farms using solar for drying and wind for electricity; recycling programs harvesting paper, glass and metal; food production happening in backyards, greenhouses and community gardens; schools, stores, hospitals and services being located within reach of bus lines and bicycles. Capital will be recycled, like any other scarce resource, to those businesses and jobs within the community providing the energy services needed. The democracy of town meetings will become more meaningful in people's lives. And as Americans change from passive energy consumers to active energy producers, they will daily marvel at the possibilities concealed from them during the age of profitable waste. (Hayden, 1980: 123–24)

Every day enough sunlight falls on earth to meet the world's energy needs for fifteen years. An active program, stressing conservation and renewable energy, will lend itself to an attitude of stewardship toward the environment and a basic commitment to self-determination and personal self-reliance. Basing our lives on nonrenewable fuels is living parasitically, and, while possibly justifiable as a temporary expedient, this way of life can never have permanence. The struggle for the future will therefore involve the choice of an energy path, and this choice, in turn, will be an important expression of our basic attitudes and values.

Food Self-reliance

Nutrition is the most basic human right because without it other rights lose their meaning. A primary goal for U.S. and world food production, therefore, should be the maximum feasible food self-reliance by regions and local communities. Due to increasing transportation costs, federal policy should favor the consumption of food to the greatest possible extent in the regions where it is grown. This also will help in eliminating middle-person costs that have risen dramatically during the last decade. "Food prices are higher than they need to be because of concentration in the industry," observed Barnet (1980: 190). "The energy costs in the food system—transportation, petrochemical fertilizers, petrochemical packing—need to be radically reduced." This would involve changing federal policies that currently favor corporate farming at the expense of the smaller farm and that encourage energy-wasteful and inefficient global growing and marketing policies. Present agricultural patterns also promote the excessive use of chemical fertilizers and pesticides in the production of food as well as the heavy reliance on additives, colorings, and preservatives in the distribution and marketing of food products.

> Until it becomes more profitable to conserve energy and to produce moderately priced nutritious food than to market expensive processed food, the food system will continue to be biased against the consumer and the small farmer. . . . The national commitment to agribusiness should be reexamined. The concentration of the food industry into a highly capital-intensive, energy-guzzling system is producing declining returns for those who actually produce food, and skyrocketing prices for those who eat it. Federal policy should encourage smaller farms because they are more saving of both soil and energy and should discourage the takeover of strategic farmland by out-of-state and foreign corporations, particularly those primarily in other businesses. Land tilled by local people who make the basic decisions about it and are rewarded for it serves the interest of consumers better than land that functions primarily as a corporate asset. (Barnet, 1980: 190)

Self-reliance thus would make the central question not what crop might have an edge in the future world market but what can be grown on this land to help people most adequately feed themselves? Making the United States less dependent on imported food and on pushing our food on others also would be helpful, both to domestic agriculture and to other countries which are now becoming more food dependent. In the meantime, high food prices have spawned an alternative food system in this country, consisting of consumers' cooperatives (which did about $500 million worth of business in 1981 according to Evans [1983: 9]), farmers' markets, community gardens, food buying federations, and increased home food production and processing. In the future, working toward food self-reliance might take a multiplicity of approaches; for instance, one might:

> Organize a food cooperative and grow your own food so you can opt out of the 'food-as-a-profit-commodity' system that creates scarcity. Get behind a network to link directly farmers to consumers in your area. It is a sure way to learn about farmers' problems. Worker-managed food systems are evolving in cities as different as Minneapolis and San Francisco. Work for regional food self-reliance policies in the United States that will carry with it a message for all Americans: We do not have to import food from hungry countries or waste our fossil fuels transporting food thousands of miles. (Lappe and Collins, 1977: 407)

Deprofessionalizing Health Care

Americans need to rethink the role of professional medicine with regard to basic issues of health and illness. Particularly important is a reexamination of the current trends toward an enlarged and increasingly more expensive medical establishment, the growing monopoly of doctors over issues of health and illness, and the tendency toward using hospitals and doctors (for example, psychiatrists) as agents of social control and the further medicalization of life. According to Illich (1976: 3), "the disabling impact of professional control over medicine has reached the proportions of an epidemic," and the only healthy response to this crisis is a deprofessionalization of medicine and the recovery of ordinary people's autonomous ability to take care of themselves. This is not to deny the training and skill of health care experts, whom persons may need on certain particular occasions,

"but it means that recourse to professionals should be occasional
and kept to a minimum," emphasized Gorz (1980: 177). "The
society that offers its members optimal health is not the one that
hands them over to a giant conglomerate of professional therapists. On the contrary, it is the one that distributes among the
total population the means and the responsibility for protecting
health and coping with illness."

Healthy people are those engaged in self-directed and interesting work, living in supportive and caring homes, eating a well-
balanced diet, and generally controlling their own lives. Such
people do not need to be made dependent on experts or experience bureaucratic interference when they give birth, mate, and
die. On the other hand, people are unlikely to recover their health
until it stops being the exclusive responsibility of professional
technicians and becomes a natural part of a social and communal
way of life founded on fraternity and mutual help.

THE PERMANENT WAR MACHINE

A third basic area of authoritarian crisis in America today relates
to nuclear war. Society has gained a power to destroy which is
unprecedented in human history. This destructive potential is
dramatically evidenced in the natural world, as discussed above.
"In nearly every region, air is being befouled, waterways polluted, soil washed away, and land desiccated, and wildlife
destroyed," emphasized Bookchin (1980: 35). "Coastal areas and
even the depths of the sea are not immune to widespread
pollution."

The potential for human destruction, however, is most omi-
nously portrayed by the current nuclear arms buildup. Since
July 16, 1945, when the first atomic bomb was detonated in New
Mexico, each year has brought about a dramatic growth in the
number of nuclear weapons until now there are perhaps 50,000
nuclear bombs and warheads in the world. Their combined
destructive power is roughly that of 20 billion tons of dynamite,
or 1,600,000 times the yield of the bomb that was dropped by
the United States on Hiroshima (Schell, 1982: 47).

A growing number of nations are in possession of nuclear
weapons, with the number expected to grow from twenty to
twenty-five nations (and perhaps even some terrorist groups) by
the year 2000. According to the U.S. Arms Control and Disar-
mament Agency, there will be enough weapons grade nuclear

material moving about the earth in 1985, in addition to that controlled by the acknowledged nuclear powers, to make 20,000 Hiroshima-range nuclear weapons (Barnet, 1980: 92). There are also more nuclear accidents each year as the number of weapons increases: bombers crashing with nuclear weapons on board, silo explosions because of gas buildup, and an explosion in 1980 when a repairman dropped a ratchet wrench next to a Titan II missile (Gordon, 1982: 22). Moreover, on at least three occasions during the last few years, accidents caused American armed forces to be placed on a full-scale nuclear alert: twice because of the malfunctioning of a computer chip and once because of the loading of a test tape into the computer system, giving the appearance of a real Soviet attack. Whereas twenty years ago it took six hours for a manually operated bomber and its nuclear payload to travel from the Soviet Union to the United States, today it takes less than thirty minutes for a missile to reach an American target, and within a few years it will take only a few minutes (Gordon, 1982: 22).

The effects of various types of nuclear attacks on the United States have been calculated by the U.S. Office of Technology Assessment (1982: 514), although these researchers also warn that "the effects of a nuclear war that cannot be calculated are at least as important as those for which calculations are attempted." Below we will describe briefly some of the more obvious effects of a full-scale nuclear attack on the United States. While the details of this section are somewhat gruesome, it is important at this time, nearly forty years after the first nuclear explosion, for Americans to understand the destructive effects of these weapons upon which our national defense is built.[15]

Toward a Nation of Insects and Grass

Compared with most conventional bombs that produce only one destructive effect—a shock wave—nuclear weapons produce an explosive force, intense heat and blinding light, an electromagnetic impulse, and radioactive fallout, some of which can kill people many hundreds or even thousands of miles from the original explosion. "When we strain to picture what the scene would be like after a holocaust we tend to forget that for most people, and perhaps for us, it wouldn't be like anything, because they would be dead," declared Schell (1982: 65). One means of beginning to understand the destructive effects of modern nuclear weapons is to describe the consequences of a 20-megaton bomb (containing 1,600 times the explosive power of the Hiroshima bomb) which is dropped on a large urban area such as New York City. The Soviet Union already has tested a 60-megaton nuclear bomb and is thought to have at least 110 of the 20-megaton bombs, which can be delivered either as warheads on their SS-18 missiles or carried by their *Bear* bombers.

If a 20-megaton bomb were ground-burst in the vicinity of the Empire State Building, explained Schell (1982: 84), a fireball six miles in diameter would be produced, and the area of severe damage would cover Manhattan from Wall Street to northern Central Park as well as parts of Brooklyn, Queens, and New Jersey. Everyone in this area would be killed instantly, with most of them immediately disappearing as they were pulverized into dust. Besides local fallout, a radioactive cloud would be created that would shower radiation on several thousand square miles of the northeastern United States. It is estimated that this one bomb would probably kill about 20 million Americans, or almost 10 percent of the population. Even more destructive would be the nuclear fallout of a 20-megaton bomb if it were air-burst over the Empire State Building at an altitude of 30,000 feet. Schell described the destruction:

> . . . the zone gutted or flattened by the blast wave would
> have a radius of twelve miles and an area of more than four
> hundred and fifty square miles, reaching from the middle
> of Staten Island to the northern edge of the Bronx, the
> eastern edge of Queens, and well into New Jersey, and the
> zone of heavy damage from the blast wave (the zone hit by
> a minimum of two pounds of overpressure per square inch)
> would have a radius of twenty-one and a half miles, or an
> area of one thousand four hundred and fifty square miles,
> reaching to the southernmost tip of Staten Island, north as
> far as southern Rockland County, east into Nassau County,
> and west to Morris County, New Jersey. The fireball would
> be about four and a half miles in diameter and would radiate
> the thermal pulse for some twenty seconds. People caught
> in the open twenty-three miles away from ground zero, in
> Long Island, New Jersey, and southern New York State,
> would be burned to death. People hundreds of miles away
> who looked at the burst would be temporarily blinded and
> would risk permanent eye injury. . . . The mushroom cloud
> would be seventy miles in diameter. New York City and its
> suburbs would be transformed into a lifeless, flat, scorched
> desert in a few seconds. (1982: 83–84)

Even holding back weapons for a second and third strike capability, both the United States and the Soviet Union would have the capacity to launch 10,000-megaton nuclear attacks on the other nation. In the case of the Soviet Union, this would permit them to target every nuclear silo and military base in this country as well as every community with over 1,500 inhabitants. "The targeters would run out of targets and victims long before they ran out of bombs," stated Schell (1982: 85). "If you imagine that the bombs were distributed according to population, then, allowing for the fact that the attack on the military installations would have already killed about twenty million people, you would have about forty megatons to devote to each remaining million people in the country." This ratio of nuclear weapons, for instance, would allow 300 megatons of bombs to be dropped on New York City alone, with its nearly 8 million people, and would involve tremendous overkill.

In a 10,000-megaton nuclear attack, tens of millions of people would be disintegrated instantly, and millions of others would be irradiated, crushed, or burned to death in the following few minutes. Flashes of light would illuminate large areas of the country with a brightness equivalent to thousands of suns. As the attack proceeded, perhaps three-quarters of the United States could be subjected to incendiary levels of heat and most inflammable materials would be set ablaze. The blasts created from these weapons would level most of the urban areas, pulverizing and vaporizing out of existence almost everything that was humanmade. Fires would start in forests and cities and would burn much of the remaining flammable objects. Electromagnetic effects of the bombs would destroy all radio, television, computer, and related electrical signals. Moreover, the initial nuclear radiation would subject tens of thousands of square miles to lethal doses, and the U.S. Office of Technology Assessment (1982: 525) estimated conservatively that such a large nuclear attack would probably kill 70 to 160 million Americans during the first thirty days, with many more millions dying from the attack in the months that followed. Under these circumstances, a system of civil defense would be relatively useless, as Lila Garrett, a physician, observed:

At any moment, . . . 50 million people could be blown up, and in the following weeks, 100 million more would die. It's an outrage to talk about mobilizing doctors to help because doctors will die along with the rest of us. Besides,

> any one victim of a nuclear burn is so ghastly and requires
> so many hundreds of pints of blood that to say you could
> treat millions of these people is irresponsible beyond belief
> . . . what you have here are leaders with not just boyish
> mentalities, but infantile mentalities. I'm just stopping short
> of saying insane mentalities. But it's very difficult to stop
> short because what I'm beginning to believe is that what
> we're really dealing with here is madness, madness at the
> top. (Gordon, 1982: 22)

A 10,000-megaton attack also would produce an average
radiation level around the country of about ten thousand rads,
enough to kill most mammals and birds, and only selected species
of insects could be predicted to survive. Plants have higher tolerance levels for radioactivity, but trees and food crops would
be devastated by such an all-out nuclear attack. Any survivors
coming out of their shelters would predictably find dead forests
and vegetation, with perhaps only some of the grasslands being
able to survive the holocaust. "A full-scale nuclear attack on the
United States would devastate the natural environment on a
scale unknown since early geological times," declared Schell (1982:
90); "it appears that at the outset the United States would be a
republic of insects and grass."

Most of the survivors of a major nuclear attack would themselves be injured. Deciding who would get into the existing shelters would undoubtedly cause much chaos. There also would be
epidemics resulting from the decaying of millions of dead human
and animal corpses. Cholera and typhoid would be spread by
polluted water supplies and by fast-growing insect populations
whose natural enemies had been eradicated. The economy would
no longer function, and the struggle for food would become a
day-to-day matter. Furthermore, people's genetic endowment
would be contaminated, and sicknesses and deformities would
be widespread. It is estimated that a dose of 300 rems of nuclear
radiation, well below average radiation levels generated by a
large nuclear attack, would cause virtually everyone to incur
some type of cancer during their lifetime. Birth defects and genetic
abnormalities would increase dramatically, and it is uncertain
whether many human beings would survive very long under such
deteriorated circumstances.

Observers who speak of "winning," or even "surviving," a
nuclear war are dreaming about a military past that has been
swept away by nuclear weapons. In addition to dramatic climate

changes and all the other devastating effects of nuclear war, such an attack would most surely destroy much of the ozone layer in the earth's upper atmosphere. This ozone layer has a critical importance to life on earth because it protects the earth's surface from the harmful ultraviolet radiation in sunlight which otherwise would be lethal to unprotected humans and animals. Among other effects, ultraviolet radiation can cause blindness which could only be prevented if people wore goggles and stayed outdoors for short periods of time, perhaps only for ten- to fifteen-minute intervals. Hair would provide animals with some protection from these lethal sun rays, but most animals would become blinded and without sight could not usually survive in nature, further compounding the aftereffects of a nuclear war. All of this nuclear destruction combined would undoubtedly lead to the extinction of humankind.

Beginning with Directive 59, President Jimmy Carter announced the abandoning of the older nuclear strategy of mutual assured destruction and the development of a new "limited" war-fighting nuclear strategy for the United States. However, a limited nuclear war may be an unrealistic dream of military planners as such limited attacks would undoubtedly kill hundreds of thousands and perhaps even millions of people. Given such high levels of mass destruction, it is dubious that the "losing" side in such an engagement would observe the limits for very long. A more likely outcome of a nuclear holocaust, unpleasant as it is to contemplate, is a human race whose biological and social existence has ceased to be.

Achieving Basic Security

"The United States is still the largest economy, the most impressive military power, and the greatest cultural influence in the world," stated Barnet (1981: 108). Certainly this is true relative to the Soviet Union which survives as an aging, authoritarian regime and, even with its larger population, has a relatively stagnant economy one-half the size of the United States and remains in many respects an underdeveloped country. There are few places in the world where the Soviet model is admired or imitated, and, although their military interventionism has increased during the last few years, their influence in world politics has correspondingly decreased.[16]

As we have seen, however, the United States is not the dominant world power that it was twenty years ago. Events such as the decline of the dollar, a slow growing economy, inability to solve the twin economic problems of inflation and unemployment, kidnapped American ambassadors and military leaders, the Iranian hostage crisis, and the disastrous military defeat in Vietnam have all contributed to a growing American sense of powerlessness and insecurity. Modeled after nineteenth-century Great Britain, for a brief quarter century the United States played a traditional imperial role on the world scene, but, with the decline of colonialism and the emergence of more than one hundred newly independent nations, the ability of America to retain its traditional world dominance has declined. Billions of people have come into consciousness during the last couple of generations, and it is no longer possible to settle the fates of millions of Asians, Africans, and Latin Americans with agreements among a handful of American and European leaders (Barnet, 1981: 91).

Coping with Declining Power

We seem fated to live in a Balkanized world where power is more diffused and where the world order is less dominated by any single nation. This decline in U.S. power has sparked a national debate on military security between those who believe that America must now escalate the arms race and restore this nation's former military dominance and those who believe that basic security cannot be achieved in this country with increased numbers of tanks, guns, and nuclear bombs.

The world is unstable and dangerous, but the problem with former U.S. domination strategy is that the world is now a much more complex place with more nations and groups within nations competing for power. Furthermore, an uncontrolled arms race tends to make the world much less safe rather than more secure, and it is this nuclear arms race itself that becomes the biggest threat to basic security and human survival. "Anyone who ponders the elaborate system of war prevention we have erected," declared Barnet (1981: 102), "can understand why a growing number of scientists state flatly that if the arms race continues nuclear war is now inevitable."

The increasingly unmanageable world reinforces the basic impulse to assert American dominance. Since World War II the

United States has spent more money on armaments than any other nation—almost $3 trillion—and over the next five years the Reagan administration proposes even greater defense expenditures. Currently, this country is the only global power with hundreds of military bases around the world, thereby having more destructive ability than any nation has ever possessed (Barnet, 1983: 4).

The important question, however, is whether or not these costly military expenditures have actually increased our basic security. Do we feel safer than we did a quarter century ago, and will we feel more secure five years from now than we do today? The military problem in the United States and the Soviet Union is to maintain the readiness of armies that are designed not to be used and which have no hope of victory. To build a military force on the prospects of either permanent inaction or annihilation is a difficult task. This reality leads military leadership on both sides to develop war-winning fantasies and consequently to alarm each other.[17] The vicious circle escalates, and we move even closer to a nation—and a world—populated solely with insects and grass.

Peace in an Age of Limits

Given the low level of knowledge about foreign affairs among the general population, most debates about arms and warmaking are conducted at a very simplistic and unreal level, usually affirming primarily that America is good and the Soviet Union is evil. This leaves military policymakers largely unaccountable to the rest of society in their planning for the greater glory of the country and themselves. This excessive military buildup, however, leads to a deterioration of the dollar, contributes to inflation, and stifles economic growth. At the present time, for instance, over one-half of the nation's scientists and engineers work directly or indirectly for the Pentagon. The civilian economy is starved of innovative technical and managerial talent, and the United States now lags behind other industrial nations in the percentage of its gross national product devoted to nonmilitary research and development. A giant tax-supported military bureaucracy of more than one-quarter million persons has been created which produces no energy or other useful civilian goods. This public tax drain gives a tremendous competitive advantage to Japan, Germany, and other smaller nations which have less wasted tax revenues and can produce consumer goods for export more cheaply and efficiently than the United States (Barnet, 1981: 96).[18]

Survival and freedom dictate that a comprehensive arms limitation agreement, which would be verifiable and retain the principle of "rough equivalence" for both sides, be negotiated with the Soviets. In spite of military fantasies to the contrary, nuclear wars are not winnable, and only through arms limitation agreements is it possible to increase the amount of basic security in our lives and country. In this regard, Barnet (1981: 103) suggests an agreement that would include a three-year moratorium on the testing and deployment of all bombers, missiles, and warheads. Such a moratorium would be verifiable by existing intelligence capabilities on both sides, and, during that period, both countries could undertake to negotiate a formula for making across-the-board reductions in their strategic nuclear arsenals. Like the successfully negotiated atmospheric test ban, this arms moratorium would enable the negotiators to keep ahead of military technological developments and to create a more favorable climate for the ratification of long-term arms limitation agreements. Choosing the alternative, an escalating arms race most inevitably will lead to an increasingly unmanageable and chaotic world and one in which human annihilation is ever more likely.

THE INTENSIFYING POLITICAL CRISIS: CAN WE ANY LONGER AFFORD DEMOCRACY?

A remarkable meeting took place during May 1975 in Kyoto, Japan. A blue-ribbon group of influential leaders from Western Europe, Japan, and the United States were invited by David Rockefeller, chairman of the Chase Manhattan Bank, to consider the "excesses of democracy" afflicting many of the world's advanced industrial nations. Financed by Rockefeller, this meeting was attended by executives from many of the world's most important banks, top officers from major global corporations, government leaders, selected senators and representatives, and a few of the more dependable and conservative labor leaders.

These guests were all members of the 300-person Trilateral Commission founded by Rockefeller in 1973, and the conference report, *The Crisis of Democracy* (1975), was also remarkable for its pessimism about the present world condition and for its generally authoritarian tone. The commission's report recommended a "moderation of democracy" in America and other advanced industrial nations to make these countries more easily governable. According to the commission, a central problem in the United States was a "democratic surge of the 1960s" which had challenged the existing authority systems in society and which had created a generation of people no longer deferential or automatically willing to accept the orders of established authorities. Values had changed during the last two decades, and, as people became more active and politicized, their disappointment was inevitable because democratic societies cannot work when much of their citizenry is not passive. The result was a substantial withering away of confidence in government and a generation of people incapable of realizing that the "arenas where democratic pressures are appropriate are limited."

The news media were also partly to blame, according to the commission, because they were too often "inclined to side with *humanity* rather than with authority and institutions." The report thus recommended increasing regulation of the press and a number of other curbs on the present excesses of democracy in industrialized nations. Also recommended were centralized economic planning, stronger political leadership by the president, and a more limited and expensive higher educational system that would lower people's career aspirations and ambitions.

Therefore, in addition to the economic, ecological, and military aspects of the current authoritarian crisis, there exists the political struggles relating to the proper role and scope of democracy in the modern world. By attacking presumed democratic excesses, this report is a symbol of the intensifying ideological struggle over people's authority and rights to control their own lives. To better understand why such a prestigious upper-class body as the Trilateral Commission would mount such an open and visible attack on our fundamental democratic institutions, we must consider certain recent developments in America and on the world scene.

Democracy's Rebirth

Traditionally, business and other dominant elites have generally benefited from the limited political democracy in American society for at least two reasons. First, American democracy made a sharp separation between the economy and the political system, in which the formal equality promised in political life (one person, one vote) helped to counteract and make bearable the blatant inequalities and types of unfairness fostered by the economic system. Second, American democracy "seemed to offer just enough hint of fairness to be seen as legitimate by the majority, yet also provided dominant groups with enough control to serve their needs as well." People thus accepted certain political rights in return for their economic servitude and willingness to let the experts run most of the major institutions in society (Wolfe, 1980: 295).

The economy is in trouble at the present time, however, and is increasingly unable to deliver on its promises of abundance and prosperity. As O'Connor (1973) so perceptively argued, this also has made businesses more dependent on the government which must now directly or indirectly supply the capital, tax incentives, regulations, and investment credits that are necessary to keep the whole system afloat. Rather than being a neutral arbitrator of rival claims, the government has been forced more and more to become an active participant in the economy on behalf of private capital, and control of governmental policy thus has become an important aspect of normal modern business procedures.

However, while governmental control by dominant groups has become more important, at the same time, it also has become less possible. In the 1940s "Truman had been able to govern the country with the cooperation of a relatively small number of Wall Street lawyers and bankers," emphasized the Trilateral Commission's report (Sklar, 1980: 37). Unfortunately, according to the commission, this is no longer feasible in the 1980s because so many individuals and diverse lobbying groups have become involved in the governmental process. During the last few decades, for instance, modern social movements, such as the civil rights movement, the Vietnam antiwar movement, the antinuclear and environmental movements, and the women's movement, have politicized and made active in the legislative process thousands of separate groups and millions of individuals. "Large numbers of people appear to be taking democracy far more seriously than they ever had before," observed Wolfe (1980: 296). This increased popular participation has been responsible for stopping one major war and for forcing two incumbent presidents—Lyndon Johnson and Richard Nixon—to leave office.

Myriads of local grass-roots groups devoted to self-help, protest, special interests, and mutual aid have developed in the last decade. A clearinghouse for information about neighborhood activities in New York City also found that since the mid-1970s several thousand block clubs have formed, addressing issues ranging from rent and crime control to health care and urban gardening. Community organizations and coalitions, such as the Citizens Action Program in Chicago, the Communities Organized for Public Service in San Antonio, United Neighborhoods Organization in East Los Angeles, and the Oakland Community Organization, are only the largest and most visible representatives of the neighborhood organizations now existing across the country (Boyte, 1980: 2–4).

Cooperatives also have grown at a rate of over 1 million members per year during the 1970s, and women's health clinics, art fairs, neighborhood newspapers, housing rehabilitation projects, and cooperative athletic programs all testify to the expansion of an American democratic culture. In a 1978 *Christian Science Monitor* poll, about one-third of the community residents claimed to have already taken part in some kind of neighborhood improvement effort or protest, and a majority declared their future willingness to take some sort of direct action in defense of their neighborhood (Boyte, 1980: 2–4).

The Antidemocratic Backlash

For ruling class groups in recent years, controlling the government has become both more essential and, at the same time, more difficult. It is understandable, then, why the Trilateral Commission should search for ways to restrict the democratic context of politics. One result has been the general decline of legislative power, both at the state and federal levels. "The basic process at work here is the substitution of administrative power for power derived from the electorate," explained Edwards (1979: 211). "As a result, party politics, citizen voting, and the entire electoral process have come to have less and less effect on government policy." This growth of administrative power also has been reflected in the rapidly growing power of such bureaucracies as public authorities, expert or professional regulatory bodies, permanent commissions, and courts.

As the Federal Reserve Board, National Security Council, and the various great federal departments impose their will, they erode democratic power by replacing it with

administrative power. Choices are removed from the political sphere, where they can be seen as products of clashing
material interests and instead are placed in the hands of
administrators and technocrats, who can make decisions on
the basis of technical or administrative criteria. The distinction is apparent even in their manner of selection: the
Congress is popularly elected, of course, while the bureaucracy and court positions are appointive. Moreover, while
officials in popularly accountable bodies tend to serve fairly
shor terms (two, four, or six years), the nonaccountable
agencies are run by officials enjoying, as an additional protection from popular will, extremely long terms (five, seven,
or ten years, or even life). (Edwards, 1979: 212)

As the Trilateral Commission recommended, the power of
the president has been considerably extended in recent years.
Although this position is elected, executive power has been
increasingly institutionalized and insulated from popular influence through the creation and expansion of executive offices, the
establishment of the national security apparatus, and the executive branch's capture of the process of drafting legislation. These
changes all require experts and bureaucrats to be in charge, with
little or no provision for popular participation. The effect of these
changes has been to gut much of the *substance* of democratic
government, even while still retaining the esssential *form* and
rhetoric of democracy (Edwards, 1979: 212).

The Restoration of Self-government

Democracy is a group process that allows opportunities for
both opponents and supporters of various measures to make
themselves heard. With most complex issues there are legitimate
differences of perception and interest. Spokespersons from various regions, industries, labor groups, communities, and other
special interest groups will undoubtedly see issues from different
and often conflicting perspectives. However, the genius of a democratic system "is that it provides an arena for the controlled
conflict of competing values and ideas," stated Johnson (1978:
149), and, in most cases, "it permits the resolution of conflicts
without civil war."

Democratic processes become even more important in times
of great challenge and change such as the present. Far from
being an inefficient way of resolving problems, democracy becomes

increasingly necessary when there are fundamental issues at stake. Democratic processes, while often halting and leading to only modest and incremental steps forward, help people to avoid fundamental mistakes. As we have seen, such processes also prevent basic types of alienation and resentments which are a product of other forms of authoritarian decision making. It is a down-to-earth and courageous process which leads to communications and negotiations with other people. As Ralph Waldo Emerson once perceptively commented, "democracy is a raft which will not sink, but then your feet are always in the water."

BEYOND AUTHORITARIANISM

Since World War II both the Democrats and Republicans have been dedicated to policies that would guarantee growth in the American economy. This has allowed policymakers to postpone consideration of many problems of authoritarianism during the last three generations. Growth has become a fetish and a substitute for interest politics, a promise of a cornucopia that would keep everyone happy and thus disintegrate classes and ideologies with the magic solvent of money. This new growth politics has produced an alliance of business, organized labor, and the military. For its part, labor has abandoned militant mobilization from below in exchange for a piece of growing economic pie. Moreover, Democrats and Republicans have increasingly converged, both accepting growth as a given in American life and arguing mainly over the speed and costs of inducing such growth. Freedom itself has come to be identified with the promotion and maintenance of these policies which advance economic growth (Moberg, 1982: 2).[19]

In the present ambiguous period, as the obstacles to growth begin to mount, policymakers and the rest of us will be forced to begin to deal with these issues related to authoritarianism. We will increasingly be compelled to confront questions of self-regulation, as opposed to regulation by experts, and of self-control as opposed to control by bureaucratic institutions.

7

Growing Up Human

I have no fear but that the result of our experiment will be
that men may be trusted to govern themselves without a
master. Could the contrary of this be proved, I should conclude either there is no God or that he is a malevolent being.
—THOMAS JEFFERSON

Apologists for the status quo in authoritarian societies have always
argued that persons cannot be relied upon to govern their own
lives. During the past century advocates of the desirability, or
at least the inevitability, of domination have argued that general
reliance in society upon democratic social relations is impossible
because these relations are fundamentally incompatible with
modern civilization, advanced industrial technology, and/or, more
basically, with human nature itself. At this point, however, it is
possible to examine carefully instances of democratic social relations that currently exist and to provide an analysis of the relationship between these democratic social processes and the
achievement of freedom.

"If we want individuals to be free," observed John Dewey
(1939: 34), "we must see to it that suitable conditions exist."
Our task is to understand the immediate positive conditions that
nourish freedom and to engage ourselves in the struggle to realize
these conditions in our own lives and in the lives of those around
us. Therefore, what is the essential nature of democratic social
environments and how do these environments promote full human
development? Since our consciousness of freedom in this society
is often submerged in the overriding experience of authoritarian
socialization and power relations, we will analyze first in this
chapter a number of case studies illustrating the dynamics of

democratic social relations in various social contexts. These studies provide a basis for the subsequent analysis of the social processes that facilitate the growth of individuals' essential human capacities and potentials.

STUDIES IN SELF-REGULATION

The focal point of internalized social control, guilt, and repression in Western societies traditionally has been in the area of human sexuality, but are all of these guilts and neuroses resulting from outside domination of our sex lives really necessary? Examined below is English anthropologist Bronislaw Malinowski's classic 1929 study of the self-regulation of childhood sexuality among the Trobriand islanders in British New Guinea and, considered in subsequent sections, are case studies of democratic environments in two more contemporary social settings. Before proceeding with an analysis of the general disalienation process, the purpose of these studies is to provide some initial glimpses into the types of possible comutual relations that have already been established in various historical situations.

Sexuality Among "Savages"

Trobriand children, observed Malinowski (1929: 52), enjoyed much freedom and independence. Some were more respectful and obedient than others, but this was entirely a matter of personal preference; there was "no idea of regular discipline, no system of domestic coercion." In these unfettered circumstances, children formed their own little community in which they remained from about age four or five until puberty. "This community within a community acts very much as its own members determine," noted Malinowski (1929: 53), "standing often in a sort of collective opposition to its elders." If the children wanted to go for a day's expedition, for instance, "the grownups and even the chief himself, as I often observed, will not be able to stop them."

The children's autonomy also extended to the control of their own sexuality. They heard and witnessed much of the sexual life of their elders since, within the one-room houses, the parents had little possibility of finding privacy. If children were observed watching their parents' sexual enjoyment, for instance, they "would merely be scolded to cover their heads with mats." Nakedness in this tropical society was also regarded as natural since it was often necessary.

In addition, there were numerous opportunities for very young children to receive erotic instruction from their friends. Malinowski (1929: 57) estimated that the active sexual life of Trobriand girls typically began at about age six to eight and the sexual life of boys at age ten to twelve.

> A premature amorous existence begins among them long before they are able really to carry out the act of sex. They indulge in plays and pastimes in which they satisfy their curiosity concerning the appearance and function of the organs of generation, and incidentally receive, it would seem, a certain amount of positive pleasure. Genital manipulation and . . . oral stimulation of the organs are typical forms of this amusement. Small boys and girls are said to be frequently initiated by their somewhat older companions, who allow them to witness their own amorous dalliance. As they are untrammelled by the authority of their elders and unrestrained by any moral code, . . . there is nothing but their degree of curiosity, of ripeness, and of 'temperament' or sensuality, to determine how much or how little they shall indulge in sexual pastimes. (1929: 55–56)

In this regard, the attitude of Trobriand adults toward their youngsters' sexual activities ranged from complete indifference to tolerant amusement.

As the children entered adolescence the nature of their love-making became more serious. Now sexual activities ceased to be mere child's play and assumed a prominent place in the young people's lives. This stage also differed from the previous one because personal preference was now more important and there was a greater tenderness and permanence in the relationships. As Malinowski (1929: 63) observed, "the boy develops a desire to retain the fidelity and exclusive affection of the loved one, at least for a time." This tendency toward more enduring relationships, however, was not associated at this stage with any definite idea of marriage or of single exclusive relationships. The adolescents still wished to have other sexual experiences and to enjoy "the prospect of complete freedom"; they had "no desire to accept obligations."

These youthful attachments of adolescence grow out of earlier childish games and intimacies, and this intermediate adolescent period, in turn, forms a natural basis for the more intimate
relations that precede marriage. Malinowski thus has described
a society in which sexuality developed, in its normal course, from
the spontaneous pleasurable indulgences of children to the mature
love relationships of young adults based upon a high degree of
mutual understanding and intimacy. This growth of sexual
capacities and potentials was accomplished primarily as a matter
of self-expression and self-regulation, with a minimum of direct
control by adult authorities or internalized social controls based
upon the growth of a compulsive morality. This natural self-
regulation seems to have created little need for expressions of
inauthenticity, repression, or resentments which are inevitable
by-products of these authoritarian controls. Since there was little
need for the splitting of public from private selves, Malinowski
noted that virtually no sexual perversions or neuroses developed
among the young Trobrianders.

Educating the Semifree Child

Perhaps the best known attempt to create a community
formed on democratic social relations has been the private English boarding school, Summerhill.[1] This free school was founded
in 1921 by A. S. Neill in a small rural village about one hundred
miles from London. Against intense financial and social pressures, this school has now maintained itself for more than a half
century, with average enrollments of fifty to seventy-five students
usually between the ages of five and seventeen. "Some may say
I have said too damn much [about education]," commented Neill
(1953: 7), "yet I have something in my favor: I have not spent
the last forty years writing down theories about children; most
of what I have written has been based on observing children,
living with them."

Because the idea of a free school was not widely accepted,
few parents in the early years of the school were willing to risk
placing their children at Summerhill. Therefore, uncontrollable
children and those with severe emotional or behavioral problems
often were sent to the school as a last resort. The problems of
establishing a free community, based on democratic social relations, were thus made more difficult by the children's early
authoritarian backgrounds. As Neill observed (1953: 30), since

the devastating effects of this early domination could never be entirely eliminated, the real task at Summerhill was to provide the necessary social conditions for developing semifree children. "I am calling [Summerhill's] pupils semi-free because most of them were conditioned before they came to school. Some had been spanked; most had been trained in the nursery to feed at scheduled times and to be house clean; some had problem parents; a few had had religion taught to them, and a goodly number knew the discipline of a State or Prep or Public School."

It is children's intrinsic vocation to live their own lives, Neill believed, and not the lives that anxious parents or other adult authorities think they should live. He thus set out to establish a school that was fit for children instead of making children fit the school. "To impose anything by authority is wrong," stated Neill (1960: 114); "the curse of humanity is the external compulsion, whether it comes from the Pope or the state or the teacher or the parent." A guiding principle of the school is adult noninterference in the natural growth of its students. Summerhill therefore is a democratic, self-governing school. Everything connected with community life, including punishment of social offenses, is settled by vote at the weekly general school meetings. Each member of the teaching staff and each child, regardless of age, has one vote. This does not mean an absence of rules governing social life, only that these rules are self-made and self-enforced. As Bernstein (1968: 38) recalled of his visit to Summerhill, "I was shocked to find a series of bulletin boards filled with page after page of single-spaced, typed rules—with accompanying penalties. One 15-year-old boy told me: 'There are more rules in a free school than anywhere else, even though we make them all for ourselves.'"

Neill believed that it was the broad outlook that free children acquire that made self-government so important. "The educational benefit of practical civics cannot be overemphasized," he concluded (1960: 55). "In my opinion, one weekly General School Meeting is of more value than a week's curriculum of school subjects. It is an excellent theater for practicing public speaking, and most of the children speak well and without self-consciousness. I have often heard sensible speeches from children who could neither read nor write."

Classes are optional at Summerhill, and students can stay away from them as long as they care to do so. Everyone has equal rights; both staff and students eat the same food, for instance, and both must obey identical community laws. "No one is allowed to walk on my grand piano," explained Neill (1960: 9), "and I am not allowed to borrow a boy's cycle without his permission." This general equality and lack of domination also seems to reduce the children's natural fears of adults, but it does not entirely eliminate conflicts.

> I spent weeks planting potatoes one spring, and when I found eight plants pulled up in June, I made a big fuss. Yet there was a difference between my fuss and that of an authoritarian. My fuss was about potatoes, but the fuss an authoritarian would have made would have dragged in the question of morality—right and wrong. . . . To the children, I am no authority to be feared. I am their equal, and the row I kick up about my spuds has no more significance to them than the row a boy may kick up about his punctured bicycle tire. It is quite safe to have a row with a child when you are equals. (1960: 8)

To Neill, controlling children's conduct through moral prohibitions was psychologically wrong. Children only grow through experiencing the consequences of their own free activities.

Reactions to Freedom

How do these unfree children from authoritarian homes and schools react to Summerhill's democratic conditions? According to Neill, the major observable changes were general increases in tolerance, sincerity, and self-confidence accompanied by a progressive lessening of destructiveness and aggression. However, it took time for these dominated children to discover their real feelings and needs beneath the layers of pretenses and deceptions that had accumulated as a result of their previous encounters with adult authorities.

> For the first week or two, they open doors for the teachers, call me 'Sir,' and wash carefully. They glance at me with 'respect,' which is easily recognized as fear. After a few weeks of freedom, they show what they really are. They become impudent, unmannerly, unwashed. They do all the things they have been forbidden to do in the past; they swear, they smoke, they break things. And all the time, they have a polite and insincere expression in their eyes and in their voices. It takes at least six months for them to lose their insincerity. After that, they also lose their deference

> to what they regarded as authority. In just about six months,
> they are natural, healthy kids who say what they think
> without fluster or hate. (1960: 110–11)

Since there are no artificial standards of behavior imposed on students, they have little necessity for pretenses. This sincerity of free school children is further accompanied by a natural self-confidence. There is no such thing as stage fright at Summerhill, explained Neill (1960: 67); the little children live "their parts with complete sincerity."

Free, happy children also are not likely to be cruel. As we saw in Chapter 2, much of the destructiveness in persons is a result of the outside discipline and imposed morality that accompany authoritarian socialization. "You cannot be beaten without wishing to beat someone else," commented Neill (1960: 269); children "in strict schools are more cruel to each other than are the children at Summerhill."

> The proverbial revolt against the parents, taking place
> at any time between the ages of 14 and 19, is surely an
> artificial product of parental authority and possessive love.
> I prophesy that self-regulated children will not go through
> that unpleasant phase; I cannot see why they will ever need
> to, for if they have no feeling of being tied and absorbed by
> parents when they are in the nursery, I cannot see any
> reason why rebellion against parents should arise later. Even
> in semi-free homes the equality between parents and chil-
> dren is often so good that the rebellious striving to get free
> from the parents does not arise. (1953: 48–49)

Learning To Be Free

Despite persistent lack of funds and inadequate facilities, Summerhill provides an instructive example of the potential benefits of democratic social environments.[2] In a survey of fifty graduates, for instance, Bernstein (1968) concluded: "Upon completing the five weeks of interviews, my feelings were mainly positive. Almost all the former students were working, raising responsive children, enjoying life." Thus, he (1968: 41) found that most of the former students interviewed "seemed able to cope with authority effectively" in their later careers, and almost all did well in public schools after attending Summerhill. "Without exception, former Summerhillians were raising their own children in a self-directive way. Their interrelationship was warm; the children appeared happy and spontaneous." The occupations of the former students varied widely including teachers, artists, truck drivers, secretaries, housewives, physicians, and lawyers.

Neill has created Summerhill to demonstrate the beneficial results of freedom. Whereas words can often be refuted by other words, real life deeds such as this can only be negated by superior demonstration projects. It is thus incumbent upon the believers in domination to prove that authoritarian environments can do as well. In his words, "how can happiness be bestowed? My own answer is: Abolish authority. Let the child be himself. Don't push him around. Don't teach him. Don't lecture him. Don't evaluate him. Don't force him to do anything. It may not be your answer. But if you reject my answer, it is incumbent on you to find a better one" (Neill, 1960: 297).

Workplace Democracy

Can American adults also develop the types of freedom and self-regulation that we witnessed among Trobriand and Summerhill children? Two centuries ago the United States pioneered the concept of political democracy, but as yet there is little workplace democracy in this country. Corporate employees still do not possess the political rights of free speech and due process that are guaranteed to American citizens in the Constitution, for instance, and they typically have little control over company decision making or the distribution of profits. Hunnius, Garson, and Case emphasized that such worker self-regulation

> . . . means democratizing the workplace: the office, the factory, the shop, the company or institution. It means that a firm's management should be accountable to its employees. And it means, conversely, that the workers—blue and white-collar alike—should bear the responsibility for running the enterprise's operations. Workers' control suggests both an ultimate goal—of a self-managing, publicly responsible economy—and a strategy for reaching that goal. (1973: ix)

Perhaps the most important contemporary North American experiment in workplace democracy is an employee-managed and owned insurance corporation, International Group Plans (IGP), located in Washington, DC.[3] Between 1953 and 1977 this highly successful company grew from 4 to 340 employees, with gross assets eventually in excess of $60 million and yearly profits of almost $1 million. Self-management has not been pursued at IGP as a goal in itself. Instead, "the end objective is maximizing humanness," exclaimed IGP President James Gibbons. What is of importance is "creating an environment of justice, equity, equality, beauty, truth—an environment where each member of the community has the opportunity to grow and develop in his or her own unique way, to self-actualize."

In this environment though do workers really make decisions any differently than do traditional managers? Zwerdling (1978: 121) compared the working conditions at IGP and a traditionally managed corporation, Geico, a major insurance company with headquarters also in Washington, DC. A claims examiner at Geico described the conditions in her office:

> 'A bell rings at 8:30 and if you're five minutes late they reprimand you,' she says. She is speaking at home because, 'I'd get fired if I talked to you at the office.' Clerks aren't supposed to drink coffee at their desks and they're not supposed to talk, unless it's about business. Supervisors assign us our work each day, and if we ask questions they tell us 'It's not ours to wonder why, just do as you're told.' I ask questions anyway and they've classified me in my personnel file as 'insubordinate.'

The working atmosphere, however, is somewhat different at IGP, as Zwerdling explained:

> At IGP, clumps of workers sit on their desks, drinking coffee and chatting about a recent CRA [IGP workers' congress] vote to reimburse workers for meals, transportation, and even babysitting fees if they work after hours or on the weekends. . . . There's no morning bell at IGP. 'I've been coming to work at noon lately because I'm training some horses every morning at a stable,' a researcher in the life insurance department says, 'I stay and work until 8 o'clock.' The Geico employee has 'never even met the company president' but Gibbons and three top managers take 45 minutes one morning simply to meet with an angry IGP employee who has questions about disciplinary procedures 'which just can't wait.' (1978: 121)

The worker-owners at IGP enjoy far greater benefits than most American workers. In a city where the starting pay of many clerks and secretaries was about $6,000 per year in 1977, IGP employees received a minimum annual salary of $10,600 plus an equal share of the corporate profits. They also are free to set their own working hours between 7:00 A.M. and 7:00 P.M., with many employees working only four days. There are no attendance records, and persons can leave a few hours early or take an entire day off from time to time as long as their work is done. Vacations range from no less than two weeks per year and "no more than the job responsibilities, team, and team leader will agree to," with many clerical workers taking a month off each year. There is unlimited sick leave and three months' maternity leave with full pay. Moreover, employees are reimbursed by the company for courses they take which relate somehow to their work.[4]

IGP Self-government

Self-government at IGP is an ongoing experiment rather than a perfected system, and consequently workers must continue to struggle to improve their democratic procedures. Currently, worker teams of six to twelve employees who perform the same job have effective responsibility for organizing and managing most of the company's day-to-day work and making personnel decisions relating to hiring and firing. One claims clerk explained that "individuals like myself, making close to [IGP's] minimum wage, make decisions on our own that could affect the whole insurance plan, such as whether certain people are eligible to receive claims or not—decisions which only a manager could make at any traditional insurance company."

Departments, composed of several worker teams, are administered by department operating committees that include team leaders (worker representatives elected from each team) and department coordinators whom the team leaders, in turn, help select. The department coordinators have less power than traditional corporate department heads and are supposed to be democratic leaders who guide the staff and carry out the decisions of the operating committees. In a like manner, the policies of the major divisions in the corporation are made by democratically elected division operating committees that are accountable to an overall corporate operating committee and ultimately to the board of directors.

Two other important committees are the Personal Justice Committee, a seven-member worker-elected court that makes final decisions on disputes over such issues as salaries, promotions, or job transfers, and the Community Relations Assembly that is a company-wide worker legislative body. This workers' congress is composed of twenty representatives elected by popular vote, each by constituencies of about fifteen employees. The assembly formulates personnel and workplace policies including wages, fringe benefits, and hiring and retirement policies. "If I were at a traditional company I'd still be just a clerk," observed a college dropout, "but here I've been elected to committees where I've learned skills I never could have learned in school— how to work with people and how to run a multimillion dollar business."

The Struggle Ahead

In the United States there are many legal obstacles to workplace democracy, and it took Gibbons almost two years just to work out an arrangement for giving away corporate stock to the employees without paying astronomical gift taxes. Major human obstacles also exist in this society since neither managers nor workers have been adequately educated in self-management techniques. Only about one-third of the IGP employees have college degrees, and most bring into the company a traditional domesticated employee mentality. "How many of us have ever been on a company committee like this before and been asked to make corporate policies?" asked a CRA representative. Another employee wrote in the IGP newspaper: "Lots of us come from such uptight work or school environments that it's hard to eye a less structured situation without suspicion. Knowing only gross manipulation by employers or instructors, we expect it. . . . At least the old system clearly defines the enemy. Are we strong enough to risk a system where there may not be an enemy, other than our own cynicism?"

At IGP employees must master the art of listening to others, sharing feelings and opinions openly, and negotiating daily decisions in an honest, frank, but efficient manner. However, too often, as Zwerdling (1978: 123) emphasized, several committee members talk at once and cannot hear what each other is saying, or they shrink from saying anything at all and let one or two members dominate. There is also the problem of employee exhaustion from becoming too involved in the endless committee work and negotiated decision-making processes. "After six months here, you just burn yourself out," explained a researcher who had participated in many IGP committees, "and you still have your normal work to put out."

If workers often feel overwhelmed and confused by their increased responsibilities, managers also find it difficult at times to master the techniques of democratic leadership. More than eighteen top managers have come and left IGP since 1974. "Self-management advocates," observed Zwerdling (1978: 124), "emphasize that a good leader shares information with the rank and file employees, delegates power as much as possible, inspires and motivates workers rather than gives orders, and, most important, sees his or her role as working on behalf of the workers, not over them." However, democratic processes take time and require well-developed leadership skills. "At my last job if a secretary so much as talked back to me I could have said, 'you're fired, finished,'" a department head stressed, "but now at IGP if I try to boss someone around I could be fired, or at least deposed . . . it's hard suddenly having to accept a secretary or mailroom clerk as equals."

Like workers elsewhere, IGP owner-employees are facing problems, but, despite ongoing struggles, the system does work. It is not easy to experiment with work democracy in a society dedicated to hierarchical decision making and profitability. "The difference is that workers at IGP can shout their complaints and problems if they want, without fear of getting fired," concluded Zwerdling (1978: 130); "more important, they've got the power to change their corporation."

ANATOMY OF THE GROWTH PROCESS

Growth involves changes or transformations in persons that bring about the realization of essential human capacities and potentials. These transformations are dialectical because they inevitably involve mutual interactions and reciprocal relations between persons and their outside environments. They are also the result of dynamic tensions between opposing forces within persons that directly or indirectly have been generated in their dealings with the outside world. Change can be destructive as well as constructive, and we saw in Chapter 2 how authoritarian environments produce forces that tend to reduce the natural two-way communication and honest interaction with the outside world and ultimately, therefore, to reduce the direct communication between opposing forces within individuals as well. Over time these internal contradictions magnify and grow more absolute and dealing with them requires the utilization of increasing amounts of people's vital energies and resources.

As we have seen, authoritarian relations produce deep ambivalences within persons that can be dealt with but only temporarily resolved through growth-inhibiting techniques such as identification with authority, compulsive rebellion, and general resignation. The devastating effects of domination extend beyond the mere severance of vital interpersonal ties. The basic insecurity and pervasive feelings of unworthiness produced in these autocratic environments lead to a general reliance on destructive, adaptative techniques like repression of unwanted thoughts and emotions and the frequent presentation of false selves. The end result of these mutually reinforcing types of separation is a growing alienation that progressively weakens people's essential ties with themselves and their outside worlds.

The above case studies, however, demonstrate a different set of dialectical relations between persons and their outside environments. In these situations, outside power is not generally relied upon as a basic mechanism for separating persons from their own spontaneous thoughts and activities. Individuals thus do not experience the basic feelings of powerlessness and insecurity that are the intrinsic features of authoritarian environments. They have general responsibility for their own conduct and, rather than being forced to misdirect their vital energies in efforts to appear worthy to authorities, they are more often in situations where they can now experience the direct consequences of their own voluntary actions.

The outcome of democratic relations is the growth of individuals' capacities for self-regulation and self-direction. Since less energy is required in self-defeating behaviors, persons are more productive. Their real life accomplishments become the basis for increased self-confidence and sincerity which, in turn, serves to reinforce the development of new human potentialities. Given power equality and the general absence of domination, conflicts with others can be satisfied more often on a negotiated basis which produces less unresolved resentments and repressed anger. Instead of being measured in terms of absence of constraint, freedom now becomes the joint struggle with others to confront mutual obstacles and problems.

In the Trobriand islands, Summerhill, and IGP are portrayed environments in which general social order is established and maintained through democratic social relations. Although there still exists contradictions and unresolved conflicts in each of these situations, they nevertheless provide us with an initial picture of the structure and functioning of growth-producing social environments. Below we will consider in more detail the nature of these democratic social relations, and a more intensive analysis will be made of the dynamics of the growth process itself.

Democratic Versus Permissive Relations

As described in Chapter 2, democratic relations are characterized by mutual decision making and power equality. Advocates of domination often confuse these comutual relations with "permissive social relations" which involve letting others do whatever they want to do. Since permissiveness implies an inverted type of domination that can also be destructive of human growth, it becomes necessary to distinguish carefully this latter type of social relations from the democratic relations illustrated in the above case studies.

Figure 2 presents a symbolic representation of the essential types of social relations referred to in this analysis. Thus, as mentioned previously, in authoritarian relations it is the authority figures themselves who have the general responsibility for making and enforcing decisions in their dealings with other persons. By contrast, in permissive relations the power relationship is reversed and now the other persons are allowed to make decisions without taking the authority figures into account. Since these permissive relations are also power relationships, they too produce the types of inauthenticity, repression, and resentments that characterize authoritarian environments, although the tables are now reversed and it is the authority figures who exhibit many of the debilitating actions and feelings. Strictly speaking, democratic relations do not involve authority figures; rather, persons form relationships on the basis of equality in instances where it is possible for them to construct mutually acceptable plans of action.

Gordon (1970) characterized the difference between the democratic and permissive relations that may arise in home environments. In permissive relations, the parent and child encounter a conflict-of-needs situation, the solution to which inevitably involves surrender by the parent. What does it do though to

Figure 2. Power Versus Nonpower Relations

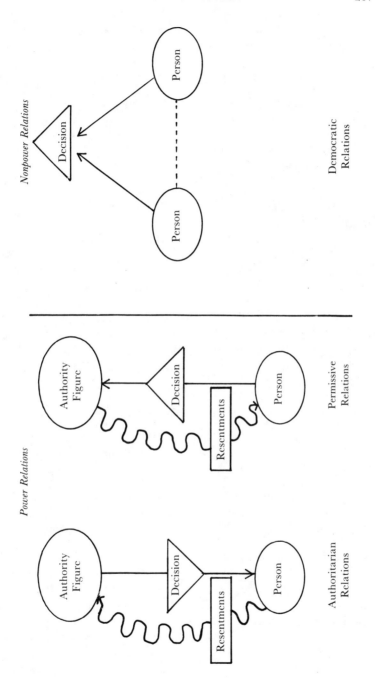

children to grow up in homes where they usually win and their parents lose?

> These children learn how to throw temper tantrums to control the parent; how to make the parent feel guilty; how to say nasty, deprecating things to their parents. Such children are often wild, uncontrolled, unmanageable, impulsive. They have learned that their needs are more important than anyone else's. They, too, often lack inner controls of their behavior and become very self-centered, selfish, demanding. (1970: 159)

Perhaps the most serious outcome for children raised in permissive homes, however, are the deep anxieties about being unloved that are generated. In authoritarian homes resentment radiates from children to their parents, but in permissive homes this flow of resentments is reversed. In this latter situation children may sense that their parents are frequently angry and resentful toward them, and, when similar messages are received from others in their environments, the children quite naturally begin to feel unloved because they do produce much irritation and hostility in others. In contrast to permissiveness, Gordon (1970: 196) described decision making in democratic parent-child relations:

> Parent and child encounter a conflict-of-needs situation. The parent asks the child to participate with him in a joint search for some solution acceptable to both. One or both may offer possible solutions. They critically evaluate them and eventually make a decision on a final solution acceptable to both. No selling of the other is required after the solution has been selected, because both have already accepted it. No power is required to force compliance, because neither is resisting the decision.

The advantages of democratic decision making are thus obvious. The analytical skills of both persons are more fully utilized in making the decisions. Less resentment and repressed anger is produced in the process, and both persons are more motivated to carry out the solutions. The efforts required in enforcement are reduced, as are the needs for power in maintaining future relations. The decision-making process is based on mutual regard and joint cooperation, and the resolution of conflicts strengthens rather than weakens the basic relationship between persons.

Neill continually emphasized the distinction between democratic and permissive social relations. "It is this distinction
between freedom and license that many parents cannot grasp,"
he explained (1966: 107). "In the disciplined home, the children
have no rights. In the spoiled home, they have all the rights."
The proper home is one in which children and adults have equal
rights. And the same applies to school."

Summerhill is often misunderstood because persons reared
in authoritarian environments do not comprehend the essential
difference between these two types of social relations. Neill (1966:
14–15) described such an instance of permissiveness by a well-
intentioned parent:

> I was talking with an American business man. His son
> of thirteen was bored by our conversation. He jumped up,
> interrupted, and cried, 'Daddy, give me the car key. I'll
> take a ride.' 'Okay, son,' said the father, and he handed the
> boy the key to his new Cadillac. That to me was just fool-
> ishness and license—not to mention the criminality of put-
> ting a death machine into the hands of a young boy.

Democratic social relations, on the other hand, are disciplined
relationships that demand greater efforts at active listening and
empathy and also greater skills in the honest expression of needs
and feelings. "Freedom must come from both sides," concluded
Neill (1966: 15). "The child should be able to refuse interference
by the parent with his personal life and his personal things, and
the parent should be free to refuse his son . . . his golf clubs, or
his necktie, or the peace of his study room, or the interruption
of his afternoon nap."

> At Summerhill we treat children as equals. We respect
> the individuality and personality of a child just as we would
> respect the individuality and personality of an adult, know-
> ing that the child is different from an adult. We adults do
> not demand that adult Uncle Bill must clear his plate when
> he dislikes carrots, or that father must wash his hands before
> he sits down to a meal. By continually correcting children,
> we make them feel inferior and we injure their natural dig-
> nity. (1960: 160–61)

As mentioned above, these distinctions between essential
types of social relations are somewhat oversimplified for purposes
of the present analysis. Individual parents, for instance, are not

typically authoritarian or permissive in all situations. "I am
permissive with my children until I can't stand them," explained
one vacillating parent, "then I become strongly authoritarian
until I can't stand myself" (Gordon, 1970: 162). In real life there
is also much overlap between permissive and democratic relationships, but for this analysis the general distinction between
these basic types of social relations is of fundamental importance.

Democratic Relations and Progressive Disalienation

The fundamental dilemma in authoritarian environments
revolves around the impossibility of reconciling personal feelings
and needs with the external requirements of the autocratic social
order without sacrificing the basic integrity of the individual in
the process. Persons are thus placed in a double-bind situation
of reconciling the conflict between their two antagonistic selves—
the real self that nature has created and the public self that moral
education has fashioned. When, as a part of their moral education, parents spank children or offer them money to stop suck-
ing their thumbs or wetting their beds, for instance, they are
creating an unfair conflict because both of these behaviors are
beyond the control of the will. This dual nature dilemma becomes
a basic source of insecurity and motivation for the diversion of
increasing amounts of vital energy into the creation and maintenance of alienated public selves.

In democratic environments, however, decisions and mutual
plans must be negotiated rather than being imposed unilaterally.
This creates pressures on persons to become skilled at articu-
lating their underlying concerns and interests and in developing
their powers of persuasion and reasoning. If social patterns are
to be established through consensus and bargaining, then individuals often find it to their advantage to be able to understand
the requirements of others and to express their own essential
wants and needs. These democratic problem-solving skills do not
develop immediately, but over time the basic structure of comutual environments does establish the general conditions for progressive disalienation and growth. Therefore, given the framework
developed in Chapter 2, we will discuss below this disalienation
process as it is characterized in the strengthening of basic relations between persons and themselves, other persons, and the
outside world.

Integration with Activities

Human behavior can be regulated in two ways: externally or internally. As we have seen, external regulation can be accomplished either as a direct result of rewards and punishments administered by outside authorities, or as a somewhat less direct result of the incorporation of the standards and expectations of these powerful others that, in turn, become the basis for a person's conscience and compulsive morality.[5] Self-regulation, on the other hand, springs not from external authority but from the immediately perceived needs and interests of persons cooperatively involved in given situations. It is the result of voluntary social processes in which persons relate to one another on the basis of equality and make decisions and construct plans of action mutually agreeable to all. In instances where individuals' actions do not affect the lives of others, self-regulation springs directly from persons' selves and their assessments of their own personal needs and interests. Sexuality among Trobriand children can thus be said to be mostly self-regulating because it was controlled primarily by agreements reached voluntarily by those youngsters participating in the sexual encounters rather than being a fixed result of external rules or parental expectations. Similarly, the activities at Summerhill and IGP also showed a high degree of self-regulation by the persons directly implemented in them instead of being the result of externally imposed authority.

As opposed to the externally conditioned persons, whose behaviors and consciousness have been shaped by the continuing application of outside forces, self-regulated persons are both the product and the purveyors of democratic social relations. In these democratic environments they have been allowed general responsibility for their own lives and the opportunity to experience and learn directly from the consequences of their own actions. As described above, the result, instead of progressive alienation, is an increasing integration of persons and their behaviors.

Reliance upon social conditioning as a basis for social order and human development has other serious defects when compared with self-regulation. First, such external conditioning is time-consuming and often ineffective in molding more complex behavior patterns. The reinforcements must be available immediately if they are to be effective. Promising a child a candy bar when the parent goes to the store, for instance, may fail to produce immediate effects on the behavior of a six-year-old. Second, there must be considerable consistency in the administration of the rewards and punishments. Thus, despite the situation or the present mood of the authority figures themselves, to be effective in the domination process they must consistently dispense with the proper reinforcements on the appropriate occasions.

Finally, authority figures must possess the types of resources that highly motivate persons in given circumstances. In raising children, for example, this is a continuing problem, and the types of reinforcements that are effective with a small child may not fulfill strong needs in older children. Consequently, at about the time of adolescence many parents "run out of power" as they no longer have the types of threats and positive reinforcers that will sustain their external domination over their children. The result, then, is that social conditioning is most effective in molding rather simple behaviors but much less effective in molding more complex behavior patterns.

> Reward and punishment can work to teach a child to avoid touching things on the coffee table or to say 'please' when asking for things at the dinner table, but parents will not find this effective to produce good study habits, to be honest, to be kind to other children, or to be cooperative as a member of the family. Such complex behavior patterns are really not *taught* children; children learn them from their own experience in many situations (Gordon, 1970: 174).

As we have seen, socially conditioned children live with much inauthenticity. They have been taught to obey external compulsion rather than to dare being themselves. Self-regulating children, however, have less need to protect themselves through dishonesty and the presentation of false selves. They have more responsibility for their actions and experience more direct feedback from the environment as to the nature and limits of their own abilities. Thus, children who draw pictures just to please their art teachers or to receive favorable grades may receive little information on the nature of the real feelings and contradictions that are inside themselves. In free environments, on the other hand, voluntary activities become a truer expression of persons' real feelings and impulses, and the products and outcomes of these activities provide a more useful gauge for the self-evaluation of personal growth. As Neill (1960: 108) commented, "my wife let [my daughter Zoe] play with breakable ornaments. The child handled them very carefully and seldom broke anything. She found things out for herself." In contrast, authoritarian parents do not give their offsprings enough personal responsibilities and the children are kept as perpetual infants. Only by allowing children the opportunities to select their own clothes, reading materials, friends, and movies, for instance, do they learn to regulate their own lives.

Experience in democratic environments further reduces the need for external discipline. Self-regulating children can be relied on more often to know their own interests and needs in various situations and to refrain from activities that would harm themselves and others. They do not experience the hate cycle toward authority since their behavior has not been molded through external fear and guilt. As we have seen, children are ambivalent and resentful toward those who have power over them, and they often cope with their feelings of unfairness through rebellion against these adult authorities. Just as hate breeds hate so, too, does trust breed trust, and self-regulating persons in comutual environments grow in sincerity, self-confidence, and the ability to govern their own lives.

The Withering Away of Compulsive Morality

Human infants are born with a life force that prompts them to eat, explore their bodies and surrounding environments, and gratify their various wishes. Authoritarian parents, however, believe that the nature of the child must be improved, and they proceed to teach the child how to live. They erect a whole system of moral prohibitions in which certain activities are labeled as either selfish, naughty, or profane. The result, as we have seen, is the child's increased reliance upon repression and the disowning of major parts of self. This leads to a tremendous growth in the unconscious and a deeper alienation as people's behaviors increasingly come under the direction of secondary social compulsions and needs. Since socially conditioned persons are no longer in contact with their primary needs and feelings, they find that they are incapable of regulating their own lives. Whereas self-regulating persons are naturally moral, these dominated persons are crippled by a compulsive morality. In the former case the sources of action arose spontaneously from within as personal desires and wishes, but, in this latter instance, the real inclinations of the persons have been smothered under so that the sources of action now lie outside in the form of compliance with certain standards, principles, or codes laid down by external authorities.

In democratic environments, persons must make decisions, take responsibilities for themselves, and become generally self-regulating. The emphasis is upon observing and understanding the real consequences of their activities. As Allport (1955: 73) emphasized, "specific habits of obedience give way to generic self-guidance, that is to say, to broad schemata of values that confer direction upon conduct." Conscience develops but judgments of right and wrong are made more often in terms of objective calculation of the real tangible effects of one's actions rather than on the basis of cultural tradition. Because of free persons' greater self-confidence and lack of guilt, there develops a new openness to experience and a general absence of repression and other forms of defensiveness.

We have seen, therefore, that character formation in authoritarian environments is the product of a collision between the natural impulses of persons and the frustrations imposed on them by outside domination. The authoritarian character structure thus arises as an attempt to defend the person in conflict situations with parents and other outside authorities. Because of the inauthenticity, repression, and resentments, such environments tend to lead to fragmented personalities and divided selves. Persons must live with many secret fears and guilty feelings, and they are often compelled to compartmentalize their lives, walling off important parts of themselves. They have developed an intermediate level of personality that in most situations effectively separates their public behaviors and conscious attitudes from their own inner core of feelings and needs.

A basic characteristic of democratic character, on the other hand, as Lasswell (1951: 495) emphasized, is "the maintenance of an open as against a closed ego. . . . The democratic attitude toward other human beings is warm rather than frigid, inclusive and expanding rather than exclusive and constricting." Democratic environments, in other words, encourage integrated personalities in which persons are unafraid to relate experiences of reality to their own standards of conduct and their different thoughts and desires with one another. Since persons have veto powers over decisions that affect their own lives, there develops a basic security and comfortableness in dealing with others. Furthermore, since decisions are usually negotiated, people's power to control the forces that shape their lives are directly related to their abilities to know and understand their real feelings, needs, and impulses in given situations. For instance, in democratic classrooms where readings and course procedures are negotiated between teacher and students, the ability of students to appropriate these experiences is directly related to their abilities to understand their true needs and interests in the situation.

As Reich (1972) has emphasized, the normal state of the democratic character structure that develops in free environments can best be represented by a two-tier personality model of the type presented in Figure 3. With the absence of the intermediate character layer of repressions and resentments, there is now much greater contact between the public behaviors and conscious attitudes of persons and their innermost feelings and desires. Such democratic persons will be forced to armor themselves when they are in clearly hostile situations, but the defenses that develop are much more closely tied to the immediate external threats themselves. Thus, once past the crisis, the character structures of these democratic persons tend to be open again to a wide variety of experiences and perceptions.

Social Solidarity

As described in Chapter 2, authoritarian environments produce deep social ambivalences that can never be resolved fully through techniques such as identification with authority,

Figure 3. Character Structures of Self-Regulating Persons

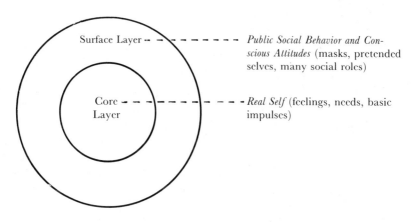

Democratic Character Structure
(in nonthreatening situations)

compulsive rebelliousness, or resignation. Democratic environments, by contrast, more often produce mutual fate situations in which persons are invested in one another's development. Since the quality of decisions is more closely tied to the skills and abilities of the individual persons who must jointly agree with whatever decisions are ultimately made, the structure of democratic situations promotes this mutual concern. The deficiencies and guilts that reside in other persons are thus limiting factors in our own personal development as well, and in these situations the freedom of one is more closely linked with the freedom of all. In this section it will be proposed that the growth potential of social relationships can be analyzed in terms of four basic dimensions: modeling, leveling, disclosure, and social support. The importance of democratic relations in strengthening interpersonal ties can thus be demonstrated by an analysis of each of these four social dimensions.

1) MODELING. Children learn much about what it means to be human from observing and imitating others who are more experienced, particularly their parents.[6] Thus, they develop such traits as honesty, discipline, and gender identities, not so much through explicit verbal instruction as through repeated observation and example. Because of the complexity of these activities, adults also are dependent on modeling in developing many types of higher skills. It would be difficult, for example, from verbal instruction alone, to perfect the finer points of advanced ice-skating or golf. In these instances, it is a virtual necessity that persons be able to observe the performances of other accomplished athletes who have more fully perfected these skills. Therefore, persons need association with others to see who they are and, by extension, who they might be. They acquire from other persons a conception of the range of human behavior, a kaleidoscopic view of the possibilities of existence as it is being lived today. Consciously or not, persons tend to imitate those characteristics and behavior patterns of others that appeal to them, often times discovering in the process new capacities and potentials within themselves.

Persons are continuously modeling for others, demonstrating by their actions, even louder than by their words, what they feel, value, and believe. Since the possibilities for greater human development are closely associated with the general achievement of democratic social relations in society, the growth potentials through modeling of these social relationships are consequently enormous. Democratic homes and schools become demonstration projects and laboratories for experiments in further human growth, and persons who have perfected nonpower interpersonal skills become invaluable resources in the common struggle for freedom. As is the case with other complex skills, to break out of the trap of domination individuals must be able to witness in their lives the successful efforts of parents, teachers, and community leaders who have committed themselves to the task of creating and perfecting democratic life-styles for themselves.

2) LEVELING. In addition to the influence of other persons as models, the growth potential of social relationships can also be measured in terms of the quality of the direct verbal feedback that these relationships provide.[7] To expand consciousness, persons need informed, honest, and trustworthy feedback about their thoughts and actions. Verifying their conceptions of themselves and knowledge about the world through the responses they elicit from other people remains throughout their lives an invaluable means of self-knowledge. Others provide an outside vantage point in observing their actions, and these outside views and opinions are important in validating and expanding people's consciousness. Individuals thus remain dependent on the reactions of others to give them feedback about what they are like as persons, and this "looking glass process" is a basic way by which they can develop and maintain their awareness of themselves and of the outside world.[8]

Festinger (1963) discussed the importance of leveling for human growth by contrasting beliefs and opinions that are dependent on "physical reality" for their validity and those, at the other end of the continuum, whose truth-value is almost completely dependent upon available "social confirmation." Individuals observing a surface they think is fragile, for instance, might easily receive confirmation of this belief by hitting the surface with a hammer. In areas such as politics, religion, or ethics, persons are much more dependent upon the feedback of others for confirmation of their consciously held opinions and beliefs.

Authoritarian relations establish the context for external domination, and, consequently, the feedback that persons receive about their opinions and activities is often subject to manipulation by these powerful others. Authoritarian parents, observed Gordon (1970: 276), often "lecture, cajole, threaten, warn, persuade, implore, preach, moralize, and shame their kids, all in an effort to force them to do what they feel is right." By means of threats or the active exercise of force, these authority figures are able to make their children take seriously their arbitrary external evaluations of the situation. Interpersonal feedback in these instances is thus distorted in the service of social control.

More trustworthy and honest feedback is often available in democratic environments, however, since no one class of persons in these latter situations is invested with unilateral power. Since the dynamic of influence in comutual environments is based on discussion and negotiation, those who would influence others are cast into the role of consultants. To be successful they must learn to share with other persons their knowledge and experience, much as consultants do when their services are requested by clients. In this regard, Gordon explained how parents in democratic circumstances might nevertheless be able to influence the values of their offsprings:

> The successful consultant *shares* rather than preaches, *offers* rather than imposes, *suggests* rather than demands. Even more critical, the successful consultant shares, offers, and suggests usually no more than *once*. The effective consultant offers his clients the benefit of his knowledge and experience, yes, but does not hassle them week after week, does not shame them if they don't buy his ideas, does not keep pushing his point of view when he detects resistance on the part of his client. The successful consultant offers his ideas, then leaves responsibility with his client for buying or rejecting them. If a consultant behaved as most [authoritarian] parents do, his client would inform him that his services were no longer desired. (1970: 275)

The structure of democratic decision making and conflict resolution facilitates the employment of the honest, informed, trustworthy feedback that is so essential for human growth and freedom. Persons who would be influential at the weekly general school meetings at Summerhill, for instance, must present generally valid information and cogent arguments to support their positions. The role of consultant is one that is best performed by those accomplished in facilitating the processes of mutual growth, and democratic environments promote the development of such growth-facilitating persons.

3) DISCLOSURE. Unless persons can verbally express to others on a fairly regular basis what is important to them, they tend to lose touch with these self-potentials.[9] With regard to positive human development, personal change and growth usually involve some degree of self-disclosure to other people. As

Jourard (1964: v) postulated, a person "can attain to health and fuller functioning only insofar as he gains in courage to be himself among others." Therefore, another measure of the growth potential of social relationships is the degree to which they provide opportunities and encourage individuals to talk with other persons about what is worthwhile.

> Authentic being means being oneself, honestly, in one's relations with his fellows. It means taking the first step at dropping pretence, defenses, and duplicity. It means an end to 'playing it cool,' an end to using one's behavior as a gambit designed to disarm the other fellow, to get him to reveal himself *before* you disclose yourself to him. This invitation is fraught with risk, indeed, it may inspire terror in some. Yet, the hypothesis . . . [is] that, while simple honesty with others (and thus to oneself) may yield scars, it is likely to be an effective preventive both of mental illness and of certain kinds of physical sickness. (Jourard, 1964: 153)

To deal with conflicts created by outside domination, as we have seen in Chapter 2, persons learn to present inauthentic selves that often do not portray accurately their real feelings and beliefs. This personal alienation compounds itself as the initial pretenses often must be bolstered by further pretenses until persons find themselves caught up in a web of inauthentic existence. The heart of the problem is that those in authoritarian environments are often afraid to be transparent in the presence of powerful others. The structure of democratic environments, on the other hand, encourages this type of honesty and openness because persons in these comutual environments often find it to their advantage to express their real beliefs and opinions. Such environments, based on negotiation and joint consensus, promote the elimination of pretenses and the articulation of real needs and interests. Democratic decision-making and problem resolution processes thus promote the types of dialogue and two-way communication that help persons grow and develop their capabilities.

4) SOCIAL SUPPORT. Very much related to the disclosure dimension is the importance in growth-oriented relationships of social support. As a dialectical process, human growth involves the courage to tear down comfortable existing belief and value structures and tolerate, at least for a time, a certain degree of discomfort and ambiguity until these old systems can finally be replaced by new structures that are more congruent with reality.

A final measure of the growth potential of social relationships, then, is the degree to which persons can provide safety for one another to take risks, learn tolerance for the mistakes and excesses that will inevitably result from honest struggle in this regard, and willingly encourage persons to trust their own basic impulses. From the foregoing analysis, it is apparent that the extreme power differentials involved in authoritarian environments reduce the potentials of these relations to provide this social support in major areas of people's lives. Democratic environments, on the other hand, provide conditions much more facilitative and congenial to this risk-taking that is such an intrinsic feature of the human growth process.

Integration with Reality

Just as the various types of alienation discussed in Chapter 2 compound and reinforce one another so, too, is the disalienation process discussed in this chapter a progressive one. Being encouraged more often to act spontaneously, persons in democratic environments consequently receive more honest and direct feedback concerning their abilities and limitations. Their integrated personalities allow them to utilize effectively more of their energies in life-affirming activities and to waste less of their efforts in the types of self-defeating behaviors so characteristic of authoritarian environments. Moreover, the social relationships in democratic environments are more growth facilitating as was described in the above analysis of modeling, leveling, disclosure, and social support. The result over time is persons whose overall ties with reality are progressively strengthened which, in turn, allows them to become even more effective participants in their democratic social environments. Thus, the vision that has been presented here of free individuals and a free society is one of institutions and life-styles in which persons are integrated with, rather than separated from, their own activities, thoughts and emotions, other persons, and the outside world.

Notes

INTRODUCTION

1. As Freire (1970: 57) declared, "a careful analysis of the teacher-student relationship at any level, inside or outside the school, reveals its fundamentally narrative character. This relationship involves a narrating Subject (the teacher) and patient, listening Objects (the students). The contents, whether values or empirical dimensions of reality, tend in the process of being narrated to become lifeless and petrified. Education is suffering from narration sickness."
2. This information is presented in Barnet and Müller (1974: 15, 26).
3. This information is presented in Bowles (1977: 22); and Brecher and Costello (1979: i).
4. Quoted by Bowles (1977: 21) from the Trilateral Commission's report, *The Crisis of Democracy* (New York: New York University Press, 1975).

CHAPTER ONE
WHAT IT MEANS TO BE FREE

1. How do we go about answering these essential freedom questions? Historically, questions involving the nature of freedom and full human development have been categorized generally as value questions and as matters of ethics to be settled by dogmatic authority. This surrender of moral authority to outside prophets and law-givers, however, has meant the consequent fostering of weakness and dependency on the part of individuals and perpetual conflicts among the believers in different authoritarian traditions as they fought each other to achieve predominance for their particular

moral systems. For a description of some of the problems of relying on authoritarian ethics, see Fromm (1947: 10).

It often has been noted that our approach to understanding health and sickness is very different. In contrast to our reliance upon outside evaluative standards in matters of health, when we declare someone ill we generally consider this a statement of "fact" and not an evaluation based on moral precepts. We also usually concede that the art of medicine requires an extensive body of theoretical knowledge and practical technique that has been painstakenly derived from a rational and systematic investigation of the real world.

Is it therefore possible to create such a body of rational knowledge concerning freedom? Could we develop rational ethics that did not derive from the arbitrary pronouncements and magical powers of outside authorities? Such a conception would involve a more or less complete integration of "facts" and "values," since the attempt would be to ground our understanding of the goals and possibilities of human life in the rational and empirical investigation of the human development process itself as an object of scientific study.

This separation between facts and values at present is undoubtedly a symptom of the general alienation of our times. Reflecting this general alienation, most social scientists have implicitly accepted the assumption that there are two exclusive worlds, facts and values, and then proceeded to consider how these separate halves of reality should be linked. An argument for the position taken here that descriptions of the world typically include both "factual" and "evaluative" elements is provided by Ollman (1971: 160–61).

2. In addition to deficiency studies, knowledge concerning freedom has been obtained from a number of other sources. Some of these include studies of personality change as a result of the therapy process (Rogers and Dymond, 1954) and of the effects of formal education (Holt, 1967); studies of creativity and outstanding achievement (Moustakas, 1967); studies of perceived maturity and "self-actualization" (Maslow, 1970); and cross-cultural studies of child training and personality development (Whiting and Child, 1953).

3. As a matter of linguistic convenience, several comparisons of "free" and "unfree" persons are made in this section. These terms are meant merely as a shorthand expression for contrasting differing degrees of human development. The English language is an imprecise tool for describing unfolding processes so words such as "developing" or "becoming" are used to indicate the general process of unfolding human capacities, and the words "more fully developed" or "free" to indicate a slightly more advanced stage or place on the continuing and perhaps never-ending road of human development.

4. Generally speaking, people's belief systems serve powerful and often conflicting needs to know and understand reality and, at the same

time, to ward off environmental threats. Rokeach (1960: 57, 68) proposed that, "for most persons in most situations, both sets of needs operate together to one degree or another. A person will be open to information insofar as possible, and will reject it, screen it out, or alter it insofar as necessary." Thus, both developing and less developed persons become more closed-minded and rigid in clearly dangerous situations. The essential difference is that in other nondangerous situations these less developed persons nevertheless are under fairly constant internal threat and have erected a some-what permanent defensive character armor as a means of protection. On the other hand, when the external danger has passed, developing persons may once more open themselves up to a wide range of direct experience. Again, they "can receive, evaluate, and act on relevant information received from the outside on its own intrinsic merits, unencumbered by irrelevant factors in the situation arising from within the person or from the outside" (Rokeach, 1960: 57).

This defensive armor is formed as a result of the chronic clash between instinctual demands and arbitrary authoritarian social restrictions that routinely frustrate these demands (see Chapter 2). As Reich (1972: 80–81) emphasized, the developing person's "ego also has an armor, but it is in control of the armor, not at its mercy. The armor is flexible enough to adapt itself to the most diverse experiences."

5. See also Erickson (1963: 265).

CHAPTER TWO
BECOMING SEPARATED FROM OURSELVES

1. Available archaeological evidence also supports the belief that humans never lived in isolation. The physical and mental structure of persons makes society possible, Washburn (1960) explained, because these individuals are themselves a result of past collective human existence. In the 1 million years or so of human evolution, the individual abilities—for example, large brain, precise eye-hand coordination, and bipedal locomotion—and tool-making skills that developed were precisely those that were favored by social living. The mental and physical abilities of persons are thus the products, not the creators, of society. Instead of antedating society, individual mental abilities arose through the processes of social interaction and community living.

2. Surveys of the vast social isolation literature are provided by such sources as Lindesmith, Strauss, and Denzin (1975: 237–59); Brown-field (1966); Montagu (1950: 53–67); and Malson (1972).

Media reports of neglected and partially isolated children also yield insights concerning the importance of routine social relations with regard to normal human development, but these accounts are usually incomplete. Moreover, after the initial excitement dies down, the media usually drop these cases and one is unable to find out what finally happens to the children.

3. As Freire explained, in democratic schools "the teacher presents the material to the students for their consideration, and re-considers his earlier considerations as the students express their own. . . . Students, as they are increasingly posed with problems relating to themselves in the world and with the world, will feel increasingly challenged and obliged to respond to that challenge." He further observed that students' "response to the challenge evokes new challenges, followed by new understanding; and gradually the students come to regard themselves as committed" (Freire, 1970: 69).

Problem-posing education thus affirms that reality is unfinished and that individuals are always in the process of becoming. This deepening consciousness of their situation leads persons to understand that present historical realities are susceptible to transformation. Resignation gives way to the drive for critical inquiry, over which persons feel themselves to be in control. They are encouraged to pursue their full humanity and the complete development of their potentials. Teachers and students become the Subjects of the educational process by overcoming the prevailing authoritarian conditions, and education becomes the practice of freedom as opposed to the practice of domination.

4. As incomplete creatures continuously in a state of becoming, human beings naturally experience many types of tensions and discontents. Some of these tensions, which Fromm (1947: 40–45) has called "existential contradictions," are an unalterable part of our existence. Crucial in this regard are persons' awareness of their own finite existence—the inevitability of their own deaths—and the fact that in the short span of their lives they will never be able to realize fully all of their potentials.

Other human tensions, however, are of a historical origin. The primary sources of these latter "historical contradictions" are material scarcity and authoritarian social relations. Such scarcity is the result of underdeveloped productive forces, and only with the coming of modern industrialization has there been the realistic possibility of relieving many of these sources of contradictions within people's lives.

5. Examples often given of persons engaging in spontaneous activities are those of artists and small children. See From (1941: 286).

6. The dynamics of this social conditioning process are most clearly presented by B. F. Skinner (1953). As summarized by Platt (1972), to understand how this successful external social conditioning is accomplished, one must consider three terms: "social situation,"

"activity," and "social reinforcement." Their relationship can be symbolized as follows:

$S^\wedge R$, thought of as repeated: $S^\wedge_{(1)}R \ldots S^\wedge_{(2)}R \ldots S^\wedge_{(3)}R$.

In this diagram the upper line represents the person's actions on the environment and the lower line the environment's reciprocal effects on the person: S is a social situation in which a person finds himself; A is some activity which that person performs in the situation; and R is the social reinforcement by authority figures present in the situation that affect the likelihood of the person acting in an identical or similar way in the future.

7. Gordon (1970: 167–74) and others have argued that rewards and praise often may be more destructive than punishments to people's development. Some of these negative effects of praise are summarized by Farson, as quoted in Gordon (1972: 15–16).

8. John Watson, founder of behaviorism in American psychology, was an early advocate of social conditioning techniques in the managing of human behavior. In one of his oft-quoted statements, Watson bragged: "Give me a dozen healthy infants, well formed, and my own specified world to bring them up in and I'll guarantee to take any one at random and train him to become any type of specialist I might select . . . regardless of his talents, penchants, tendencies, abilities, vocations, and race of his ancestors" (1924: 104).

Social conditioning techniques are being relied upon increasingly to "manage" human behavior. Hamblin et al. (1969), for instance, reported a successful study in modifying aggressive school behavior. These researchers assembled a group of four-year-old boys who were so aggressive that previously psychiatrists and social workers had been unable to handle them. An experienced teacher was then asked to employ traditional teaching techniques in an attempt to get the five boys to learn. After eight unsuccessful days of trying to control these aggressive youngsters, the teacher was given instruction in social conditioning principles and told to implement a "token-exchange system" in which, by exhibiting nonaggressive and cooperative behaviors, the boys could earn tokens that in turn could be exchanged for such things as movie admissions, snacks, or Playdoh. The strategy was to ignore aggression when possible and to reward, with tokens, any child who performed an act of cooperation.

The results from employing these social conditioning techniques were dramatic. By the end of the experiment the boys had increased their cooperative acts from approximately 55 to 180 per day, while aggressive acts had dropped dramatically from roughly 150 to 10 per day. The authors thus concluded that "in 'normal' nursery schools, our observations have shown that five boys can be expected to have 15 aggression sequences and 60 cooperation sequences per day. Thus, from extremely aggressive and uncooperative, our boys had become less aggressive and far more cooperative than 'normal' boys."

Although sometimes effective from a social control or management perspective, these social conditioning techniques reduce still further persons' spontaneous expressions and, at the same time, intensify the dual nature contradictions within them. Chapter 7 deals with some alternative techniques that the author believes are often more effective, especially with complex behavior patterns, and which also strengthen, rather than weaken, the person's own self-regulation and thus reduce the destructive internal contradictions within the individual.

9. The degree to which authorities choose to rely on guilt and internalized controls, as opposed to external controls, seems to vary widely among persons and cultures. Benedict (1946) has argued, for example, that in "shame cultures" internalized guilt is seldom relied on to control behavior. The argument here is not that internalized controls are an intrinsic part of all authoritarian environments. Rather, these controls become an effective option that can be exploited by power figures in instances where such controls are congruent with cultural traditions and personal preferences. Since our own culture has relied so heavily upon such guilt mechanisms as a basis for establishing authoritarian controls within persons, and since these internalized controls are often mistakenly labeled as "self controls" by apologists for the prevailing authoritarian order, the author has chosen to elaborate on the nature of guilt and conscience at this point in the analysis.

10. Fromm (1973: 482) amplified this thesis in his later work, which was dedicated explicitly to an understanding of the origins and development of human destructiveness.

11. This research and theorizing was stimulated by the publication of *The Authoritarian Personality* (Adorno et al., 1950), which led to perhaps as many as 1,000 journal articles and research studies concerning these deep-seated psychological dispositions toward authority. See summary by Greenstein (1973) of this research tradition.

CHAPTER THREE
WOMEN, MEN, AND THE MODERN ORIGINS
OF DOMINATION

1. As Cooley (1956: 202) emphasized, "we live in a system, and to achieve right ends, or any rational ends whatever, we must learn to understand that system." In a similar vein, see also Mills (1959: 1).

2. Social philosophers like Herbert Marcuse have proposed that historically the pervasiveness of authoritarian institutions may have

been linked to the existence of scarcity and low levels of production in society. In such underdeveloped societies, the "struggle for existence" becomes a predominant fact of life since there are not enough essential goods and services to meet the basic human needs of the entire population. Under these impoverished conditions, therefore, people become preoccupied with obtaining the basic necessities of life for themselves and their loved ones, and the relations of domination come to characterize most existing human institutions (Marcuse, 1955: 129–39).

By the same token, with the elimination of scarcity in society, this former dependence on authoritarian institutions is lessened. With the development of modern science and technology, and with the creation of a general level of abundance, there emerges the historical possibility of a truly democratic society. It becomes possible for the first time to imagine realistically a world in which major institutions and areas of living are characterized by general relations of power, equality, and negotiated decision making.

3. The argument here is a bit oversimplified. There were individual families in which the wife was dominant and had power, but this did not alter the basic relations of domination that have changed and grown more subtle over time.

4. It also should be noted that men were often coerced in this patriarchal system to behave in socially acceptable ways. To become a father was to accept the breadwinner role and to take major responsibilities to discipline the children.

5. About two-thirds of men still owned and worked on their own private family farms, but that percentage declined rapidly during the nineteenth century.

6. Most early historians reacted quite favorably to the implementation of this family wage system, generally ignoring its implications for the perpetuation of patriarchy and female dependence. For instance, see Pinchbeck's interpretation of the incomes of the family wage struggle (1930: 312–13).

7. Current estimates concerning the costs of children range up to $135,000. See, for example, *In These Times* 7 (February 9–15, 1983): 6–7.

8. The influence here was reciprocal, with sexism and race mutually influencing each other. For brevity, the effects of patriarchy on the racial climate have not been emphasized here. Important in this movement were black women like Ida B. Wells, a newspaper publisher who in 1883 charged segregated public accommodations and won the case; Lelia Smith Foley, first woman black mayor of Taft, Oklahoma; Maggie L. Walker, first female bank president; and Nina Mae McKinney, first black actress to play a major role in the movies (Davis, 1983).

9. This data was compiled from the U.S. Bureau of the Census, *Household and Family Characteristics: March 1980*, Current Population Reports

Series P-20, No. 366; U.S. Bureau of the Census, *Money Income and Poverty Status of Families and Persons in the United States: 1980,* Current Population Reports Series P-60, No. 127; and U.S. Bureau of the Census, *Marital Status and Living Arrangements: March 1980,* Series P-20, No. 365.

10. A list of these studies is provided in Howe (1977: 6).
11. Cited in Farley (1978: 74–75).
12. A summary of many of these studies is provided by Farley (1978: 37–41).
13. Material in this section has been drawn heavily from the excellent analysis provided by Easton (1978).
14. Also see readings such as Datesman and Scarpitti (1980) and Thorne and Yalom (1981).
15. This information is from Wessendorf (1983: 5).
16. Morgan is quoted in Cluster and Rutter (1980: 59).
17. The author relied heavily on the data and analysis provided by Keniston (1977) and Lasch (1977).

CHAPTER FOUR
WORKING FOR THE BOSS:
THE HARNESSING OF CONTEMPORARY
LABOR POWER

1. Quoted in *Work in America* (1973).
2. Actually, the argument regarding efficiency is somewhat more complicated than is implied in this passage. What is argued in this chapter is that new techniques (inventions, innovations, machines) are adopted by employers not only to produce more outputs on the basis of less inputs (the classical definition of efficiency) but also to obtain more control over the labor force. If workers are unable to form labor unions or enforce their own work rules, the employer may realize more profits whether or not there is any mechanical superiority to the new techniques. Indeed, the net effect of the routinization and management control of work can be the production of alienation and lowered productivity on the part of the work force. For a more detailed discussion of these issues, see Palmer (1975: 32).
3. The major exception to this pattern was slavery which, although tried initially in the northern colonies as well, proved most profitable in the southern lowlands. Nearly one-fifth of all Americans were slaves originally brought from Africa, according to the first U.S. census in 1790 (Brecher and Costello, 1976: 24).
4. In his historical analysis of this period, Marglin (1974) also emphasized that rather than employing new machinery it was the increased

ability of early factory employers to force workers to labor longer and harder that led to the widespread adoption of this new factory system.

5. Brody (1960) described the results of this new management control over steel production.

6. During this period more militant and radical unions also formed, as symbolized by the International Workers of the World. However noble their purpose, these unions were never able to overcome employer hostility and become a permanent institutionalized part of American society. See discussion by Lens (1973: 151–68).

7. See description by Nelson (1975: 50–51).

8. This account is taken from Callahan (1962).

9. The purpose of Taylor's system was to study and organize work on behalf of management. Taylorism thus was not "scientific" in the sense of attempting to investigate rationally all possible ways of organizing work, as Braverman explained (1974: 86).

10. Biographers such as Kakar (1970) present a picture of Taylor's personality which is generally consistent with these observations by Braverman.

11. Palmer (1975: 32) also emphasized that Taylor intentionally made it difficult for employers to adopt his system piecemeal and thus most of the early adoptions of his system were by smaller firms.

12. The analysis in this section is based on descriptions provided by Greenbaum (1979) and Kraft (1977, 1979).

13. An illustration is provided by Clawson (1980: 195–99) of a situation in which Cyrus McCormick, president of McCormick Harvester Company, introduced machinery to break a strike by skilled workers, even though he knew in advance that these new machines would produce lower quality goods at considerably higher prices than the goods being produced by the workers. In McCormick's view it was important to maintain control over the labor process, and cost considerations were clearly a secondary matter by comparison.

14. Machines also can be used to isolate workers from one another and thus reduce organized labor resistance to management control. Walker and Guest (1952: 72–73), for example, studied an automobile plant employing over one thousand production line workers. They found that in the most typical case a worker had "verbal interaction" with only eight or ten other workers. Each worker had almost no communication (interaction less than three times a day) with workers as close as three work stations away, a distance of no more than about forty feet. Faunce (1958) also found that workers in more highly automated plants became more isolated than comparable workers in less highly mechanized plants.

15. Except as otherwise noted the author has relied heavily in this section on the account by Gartman (1979).

16. It was this record-playback control mechanism that inspired Kurt Vonnegut's book *Player Piano*. Vonnegut was a publicist at General

Electric at the time this machine was being used, and it was at GE that he became acquainted with the record-playback lathe he described in his novel (Noble, 1979: 22–23).

17. Most of the following information on microcomputer production comes from Martinez and Ramo (1980), and Sivanandan (1979).

18. This illustration is taken from *Dollars and Sense* (November 1979).

CHAPTER FIVE
SCHOOLS AND THE IMPERIALISM OF CULTURE

1. The difficulty of learning to talk perhaps can best be comprehended by adults who have themselves attempted to learn to speak a foreign language. Holt (1967: 72–73), for example, portrayed some of the courage needed when one attempts to speak a new language.

2. The character and importance of childhood learning has been exhaustively described by Jean Piaget in his many published works. See, for instance, Gruber and Voneche, eds., 1977. The author has benefited greatly from the excellent discussion of this point by one of Piaget's students and associates, Seymour Papert. See Papert, 1980: 38–39.

3. In 1970 the percentage of adult illiterates in the United States was three times that of the Soviet Union. A summary of research on American adult illiteracy is provided by Kozol (1980: 1–7).

4. Even in the colonial period, however, schooling was often more important in the lives of children from wealthy families, and in many parts of the country they typically had their choice of various private academies and schools that had been developed to serve their special needs. For instance, see the description of American private schools during the colonial period in Cremin, 1970: 517–43. Because of its primary importance in shaping the overall American culture and character, this section will focus on public education.

   The schooling of black Americans is also a separate case study, but it will not be undertaken in this chapter. Colonization of the mind in this instance involved a school system whose primary intent was the perpetuation and maintenance of the American white-dominated racial caste system and the brainwashing of black people to persuade them to accept the logic and/or inevitability of this unjust social arrangement. For a brief study of the history of the role of schooling in the perpetuation of the internal colonization of black Americans, see Carnoy (1974: 270–305).

5. Problems of control were further compounded by the process of urbanization which proceeded at a faster rate between 1820 and 1860 than in any other period in American history. During this forty-year span, for instance, the number of persons living in urban areas increased almost tenfold, from 693,255 to 6,216,518, and the

number of urban areas of more than 5,000 persons in the country increased from 22 to a total of 136 (Tyack, 1974: 31). Behind these statistics also lay massive changes in life-styles and a dramatic decline in the effectiveness of the older system of rural and small-town social controls. Moreover, many of these new urban dwellers were European immigrants who, most believed, would have to be "Americanized" before they could become productive factory workers. Boston, for example, in 1847 alone added more than 37,000 Irish immigrants to its population of 114,000 (Tyack, 1974: 30).

6. The case of the democratic localists, therefore, rested on the importance of communities controlling their own schools. See Katz (1975: 19–20).

7. Schools thus would help stabilize the hierarchical urban social structure and also make orderly and decent people out of the poor. For an explanation, see Bowles (1978: 319).

   During this period, public mass education originated in the rapidly industrializing northeastern states, such as Massachusetts and New York, and this movement spread quickly to all parts of the country except the South. The crumbling of the traditional village society led reformers to create agencies and institutions that would restore order in the lives of urban dwellers: asylums for the insane, almshouses for the poor, and prisons for the criminals. In a similar manner, the young were also taken away from the rest of society for a portion of their lives and separated in schools. Here they were "expected to learn 'order, regularity, industry and temperance,' and 'to obey and respect' their superiors. . . . Schools, like other institutions, were supposed to counteract or compensate for indulgent or neglectful families" (Tyack, 1974: 72).

8. Katz (1975: 3–55) described four major alternative models of school organization which were competing for public acceptance during this period. In the end, however, it was the bureaucratic model that triumphed because of the importance of centralized control and planning to the early industrial leaders.

9. See Bowles and Gintis (1976: 265) for an explanation.

10. This information was disclosed in public hearings before a committee of the U.S. House of Representatives. See description by Karier (1972: 173).

11. Sociologist Michael Young in his satirical novel, *The Rise of the Meritocracy 1870–2033* (1961), coined the term "meritocracy" to describe what he perceived as a probable hierarchy of the future. Projecting himself into the year 2033, Young portrayed how a bureaucratic, expert-dominated society might develop, based on the moral axiom that people are inherently unequal in their talents and abilities and thus should be accorded a station in life corresponding to their various capacities. What would our society be like, he asked, if "IQ + effort = *merit*" were to become our ruling ideology?

   In his novel, Young captured the outlines of the basic process by which society is moving from older forms of domination that relied upon patriarchy and the father's direct control of production and reproduction within the family setting to the more sophisticated types of programmed bureaucratic hierarchy that increasingly characterize the contemporary American scene. "The history of modern society," claimed Lasch (1977: xiv-xv), "is the assertion of social control over activities once left to individuals or their families." As we have seen, the first stage in this process involved removal of production from the household to the factory where it could be supervised more closely by capitalist managers, and the second stage involved the creation of a compulsory, publicly supported school system to homogenize and Americanize the children of working-class families, as portrayed in this chapter. Given the backward nature of the family as an institution, reformers sought to replace the influence of the father by the school, factory, and other modern urban institutions and, consequently, to undermine many of the traditions of American self-reliance.

12. Hoyt (1965) reported that twelve studies examined the performance of teachers, and all except a few found no relationship between college grades and measures of teaching success. The few exceptions reported very low correlations. Seven studies of success in business mostly used income as the measure, and only one found any relationship between it and college grades. Of the five studies of engineers, only one reported a significant positive correlation, and even this was probably due to the use of a seriously flawed measure. The same professors who had graded the engineers when they were students also estimated their professional competence. Eight studies of medical doctors found performance unrelated to undergraduate grade point average. Medical school grades related somewhat to the early success of physicians but only during the first few years of practice. Five studies of scientists showed a low positive correlation between college grades and subsequent research contributions.

13. See, for instance, Eble's discussion of this literature (1976: 113).

14. Described by Robertson and Steele (1971: 32).

15. Available research clearly supports the importance of IQ as a "self-justifying expectation." See, for instance, Rosenthal and Jacobson (1968) and Robertson and Steele (1971: 32–37). "We believe every child is born a potential genius," explained Robertson and Steele (1971: 34). "It is we who erect the low ceilings which keep people from being bright and creative. We know from the start that most of them are average or stupid and we make damn sure it ends up that way."

16. These statistics were presented by Shor (1980: 41).

17. According to a report released in November 1976 at a conference of the National Assessment of Educational Progress, *Michigan State News*, November 12, 1976.

18. The National Center for Educational Statistics has estimated that the total educational expenditures in the United States for 1980–81 were a whopping $181.3 billion (Bacheller, 1981: 737).

19. O'Connor (1973: 23–25) provided an analysis of the effects of the fiscal impact of rising salaries by teachers and other public sector workers as related to the lack of comparable increases in worker productivity.

20. See description of this study by Katz (1975: 78–79).

21. The analysis in this section is based on information presented in Lasch (1978: 127–30).

22. The statistics in this section are taken from Lisman and Ohlinger (1978).

23. See Farson (1974: 98).

24. Many of the ideas in these sections on equivalency examinations, alternative job credentials, and reducing the labeling powers of schools are taken from Holt (1967).

25. See Holt's observation (1976: 194–95).

26. Holt (1976: 197) provides a strong argument, stating that "it should be a punishable offense for a school . . . to make, keep, or circulate such records about children."

27. Many proposals such as these are made by Holt (1972).

28. Fuller is quoted in Gross (1977: 20).

29. These surveys are more fully described in Gross (1977: 49–52).

30. For a detailed description of the theory and practice of free schools, see Graubard (1973).

31. The current economic recession provides teachers with an excellent opportunity to gain more control of their work environments through the collective bargaining process. Given the fact that school boards and administrators are unable, or unwilling, to give teachers increased salaries and fringe benefits, teachers thus can negotiate in a much more serious way for noneconomic job benefits relating to their control of the workplace.

32. Many students experience schools as authoritarian institutions that offer them few rights or options. The legal basis for this argument is provided, for instance, by Harris (1983: 54–58). See also Holt Associates of Boston, Massachusetts, which has compiled a list of lawyers sympathetic to students' rights as well as a history of litigation on this matter (Harris, 1983: 57).

CHAPTER SIX
AUTHORITARIAN DREAMS AND OTHER ASSORTED NUCLEAR NIGHTMARES

1. Although Marxism is irreplaceable as an instrument of analysis, it has, as Gorz (1980: 11) suggested, lost much of its prophetic value. In the grundrisse, Marx discovered the class of "polytechnical

workers" whom he believed would lead the revolution against capitalism. These well-rounded workers, who had both intellectual and manual abilities, would be, Marx thought, the product of late capitalist production. The direction since Taylorism, however, has been toward the development of less skilled and more specialized workers who no longer have the ability (or motivation) to organize the work process themselves. This new labor proletariat thus has no unified conception of the society to come and probably is not the revolutionary class that Marx envisioned. The problem of overcoming bureaucratic domination is more general than that of overcoming capitalist work domination, and the organization of a successful program for transcending this authoritarianism must necessarily be broader than the workers' movement that Marx visualized.

2. These statistics are taken from Weisskopf (1981: 9–10). In November 1981 dollars, the average weekly take-home wages of American workers dropped from $254.79 in 1967 to $226.30 in 1981, a decline of about 11 percent. *Dollars and Sense*, February 1982: 10.

3. See Weisskopf (1981: 11) and Harrington (1980: 40–79). For an analysis of the rapid rise in the costs of basic necessities, see Hayden (1980: 61–69).

4. The official government statistics do not count the increasing number of persons who have given up looking for jobs and part-time workers who are underemployed given their present economic needs. For a discussion of this subject, see Gordon (1977: 70–75).

5. This quotation is from Gorz (1980: 22). For a discussion of this matter, see also Alcaly (1978), Shaikh (1978), and Weisskopf (1978).

6. E. F. Schumacher (as quoted in Barnet, 1980: 262) illustrates this job-displacing trend in developing countries.

7. At least this is the position taken by many economists and informed scholars. See, for example, Heilbroner (1978) and Naisbit (1984).

8. Defenders of military spending also cite the economic benefits of spin-offs from defense to civilian production. However, DeGrasse (1981) and other analysts (for example, see Moberg, 1982) argue that these spin-offs are more than offset by the added taxation and economic burden of this mass diversion of industrial resources.

9. This research is reviewed by Johnson (1978: 110).

10. This analysis by the Club of Rome, a study group from the Massachusetts Institute of Technology, is reported in Meadows et al. (1974).

11. Illich (1976: 3–4) is even more strident in his statement: "The medical establishment has become a major threat to health. . . . Limits to professional health care are a rapidly growing political issue. In whose interest these limits will work will depend to a large extent on who takes the initiative in formulating the need for them: people organized for political action that challenges status-quo professional power, or the health professions intent on expanding their monopoly even further."

12. See Illich (1980: 3).

13. Gorz (1980: 158–60) has summarized this and other studies related to mistakes in medication and various other forms of medical treatment.

14. Many analysts argue that energy growth is crucial for a reduction in unemployment. In reality, however, the purpose of what we commonly call "energy" is to reduce the need for human labor, making it even more difficult to provide jobs for a growing labor force. At the present time, producers take advantage of the abundance of inexpensive energy supplies to introduce highly automated, energy-consuming production techniques, reducing employment per unit of output in both agriculture and manufacturing. For an analysis of how employment would actually be increased by implementing a soft energy future, see Rodberg (1982).

15. The effects of nuclear attacks on the United States have been calculated by Calder (1979), the U.S. Office of Technology Assessment (1982), and others. In the following account the author is not only particularly indebted to the description by Schell (1982) but also benefited from reading Thomas (1981) and the assessment by Ishikawa and Swain (1981) of the damage caused at Hiroshima and Nagasaki.

16. Wolfe (1979) emphasized that the Soviet threat and anti-Soviet war propaganda in the United States "have little to do with national security and much to do with politics." Thus, the Soviet Union is used as an external threat designed to unify Americans who would otherwise disagree with one another and to distract people from the inability of leaders to deal effectively with important economic and domestic problems. Soviet leaders undoubtedly emphasize the "American threat" and engage in anti-American war propaganda for exactly the same reasons.

17. A description of many of the war-winning fantasies is presented by Podhoretz (1980).

18. Many of these problems are dealt with in detail by Fallows (1981).

19. The history of the development of growth politics is analyzed by Wolfe (1982).

CHAPTER SEVEN
GROWING UP HUMAN

1. Numerous case studies and personal accounts of free homes and schools exist in the literature. See, for example, Aldrich (1939), Gordon (1970), Kozol (1972), and Ritter and Ritter (1975).

2. Bernstein (1968) and others (see, Hart, ed., 1970) have raised many legitimate criticisms of Summerhill. It may be the case, for instance, that lack of instructional resources and facilities and difficulties in

hiring effective teachers sometimes handicapped the high-school academic program. The purpose here is not to praise all aspects of the school as it currently exists but rather to use the Summerhill experience as a case study to examine the potential benefits of democratic environments.

3. In this section the author has relied upon the excellent reports by Zwerdling (1977, 1978). All the quoted materials have been taken from these two readings.

4. Workplace democracy sometimes seems to bring about a startling development of persons' capacities and potentials. Consider, for instance, Gordon (1973), who described such growth among a group of older Chinese women.

5. See Gide (1958: 89–90) for a description of the consciousness of externally controlled persons.

6. Summaries of the extensive modeling literature are provided by Aronfreed (1968), Bandura and Walters (1963), and Jones and Gerard (1967: 120–56). Although there are many internal inconsistencies in this research tradition, there is also wide agreement among social scientists about the overall importance of imitation and modeling with regard to the general processes of human development.

7. In support of this proposition could be presented a vast amount of theory and evidence relating to the interpersonal development of the self. See, for instance, the studies summarized by Gergen (1971: 40–64); the concept of leveling was introduced by Satir (1972).

8. For a classic statement in this regard, see Cooley (1956: 168–210).

9. For a summary of the research literature demonstrating the importance of self-disclosure on human development, see Jourard (1971).

Bibliography

Abortion: A Fundamental Right Under Attack. New York: American Civil Liberties Union, 1980.

Achtenberg, Ben. "Working Capital." *Working Papers* 2 (Fall 1974): 5–7.

Adorno, Theodore et al. *The Authoritarian Personality*. New York: Harper and Row, 1950.

Agel, Jerome. *The Radical Therapist*. New York: Ballantine Books, 1971.

Alcaly, Roger. "An Introduction to Marxian Crisis Theory." In *U.S. Capitalism in Crisis*, edited by the Center for the Study of Urban Radical Political Economy. New York: U.R.P.E., 1978.

Aldrich, C. Anderson. *Babies Are Human Beings*. New York: Macmillan Company, 1939.

Alinsky, Saul. *Reveille for Radicals*. New York: Random House, 1946.

———. *Rules for Radicals: A Practical Primer for Realistic Radicals*. New York: Random House, 1971.

Allport, Gordon. *Becoming*. New Haven: Yale University Press, 1955.

Altman, Dennis. Introduction to *The Gay Liberation Book*, edited by Len Richman and Gary Noguera, pp. 14–18. San Francisco: Ramparts Press, 1978.

Anderson, Sandra. "Childbirth as a Pathological Process." *American Journal of Maternal Child Nursing* 2 (1977): 240–44.

Areen, Judith, and Jencks, Christopher. "Educational Vouchers: A Proposal for Diversity and Choice." In *Schooling in a Corporate Society*, edited by Martin Carnoy, pp. 239–49. New York: McKay, 1972.

Aries, Philippe. *Centuries of Childhood*. New York: Vintage Books, 1962.

Aronfreed, Justin. *Conduct and Conscience.* New York: Academic Press, 1968.

Axler, Shelden. "Missile Madness." *People's Voice* (January 1983): 9.

Ayres, Tom. "Lemon Pie in the Sky." *Working Papers* 7 (November–December 1980): 7–8.

Babson, Steve, and Brigham, Nancy. *Why Do We Spend So Much Money?* 3d ed. Somerville, MA: Popular Economics Press, 1977.

Bacheller, Martin, ed. *Hammond Almanac.* Maplewood, NJ: Hammond Almanac, 1981.

Baker, Alan. "Technological Intervention in Obstetrics." *Obstetrics and Gynecology* 51 (1978): 241–44.

Bandura, Albert, and Walters, Richard. *Social Learning and Personality Development.* New York: Holt, Rinehart and Winston, 1963.

Baran, Paul, and Sweezy, Paul. *Monopoly Capital.* New York: Monthly Review Press, 1966.

Barnes, Peter. "Health Care in Seattle." In *Public Policy Reader,* edited by Derek Shearer and Lee Webb, pp. 217–19. Washington, DC: Conference on Alternative State and Local Public Policies, 1976.

———. *The Solar Derby.* Oakland, CA: Community Ownership Project, 1975.

Barnet, Richard. *The Alliance: America, Europe, and Japan.* New York: Simon and Schuster, 1983.

———. *The Lean Years: Politics in the Age of Scarcity.* New York: Simon and Schuster, 1980.

———. *Real Security: Restoring American Power in a Dangerous Decade.* New York: Simon and Schuster, 1981.

Barnet, Richard, and Müller, Ronald. *The Power of the Multinational Corporations.* New York: Simon and Schuster, 1974.

Bay, Christian. *The Structure of Freedom.* Stanford: Stanford University Press, 1958.

Beals, Peggy. *Parents' Guide to the Childbearing Years.* Rochester, NY: International Childbirth Association, 1975.

Beekman, Daniel. *The Mechanical Baby.* Westport, CT: Lawrence Hill and Company, 1977.

Belden, Joe. "Cutting Energy Costs in Nebraska." *Working Papers* 6 (September–October 1978): 12–14.

Benedict, Ruth. *The Chrysanthemum and the Sword.* Boston: Houghton Mifflin Company, 1946.

Bennis, Warren, and Slater, Philip. *The Temporary Society.* New York: Harper and Row, 1968.

Berg, Ivar. *Education and Jobs: The Great Training Robbery.* Boston: Beacon Press, 1971.

Bernard, Jessie. *The Future of Marriage.* New York: Bantam, 1972.

———. "Women, Marriage and the Future." In *Intimate Life Styles*, edited by Joann S. and Jack Delora, pp. 370–75. Pacific Palisades, CA: Goodyear, 1972.

Bernstein, Emmanuel. "What Does a Summerhill Old School Tie Look Like?" *Psychology Today* 2 (October 1968): 37ff.

Blau, Francine, and Hendricks, Wallace. "Occupational Segregation by Sex: Trends and Prospects." *Journal of Human Resources* 14 (Spring 1979): 179–86.

Bluestone, Barry, and Harrison, Bennett. "Why Corporations Close Profitable Plants." *Working Papers* 7 (May–June 1980): 15–23.

Bluestone, Barry; Harrison, Bennett; and Baker, Lawrence. *Corporate Flight: The Causes and Consequences of Economic Dislocation*. Washington, DC: Progressive Alliance Books, 1981.

Blum, Jeffry. *Pseudoscience and Mental Ability*. New York: Monthly Review Press, 1978.

Blumberg, Paul. *Industrial Democracy: The Sociology of Participation*. New York: Schocken Books, 1969.

Boadella, David. *Wilhelm Reich: The Evolution of His Work*. New York: Dell Publishing Company, 1973.

Boggs, Carl, and Plotke, David, eds. *The Politics of Eurocommunism: Socialism in Transition*. Boston: South End Press, 1981.

Bookchin, Murray. *Toward an Ecological Society*. Montreal: Black Rose Books, 1980.

Booth, Heather. "Left with the Ballot Box." *Working Papers* 8 (May–June 1981): 17–20.

Bosker, Gideon. "Death on the Installment Plan." *In These Times* (September 1–8, 1981): 16.

Bouton, Deborah. "In Spring, Some People's Thoughts Turn to Pesticides." *In These Times* (May 27–June 3, 1981): 6–8.

Bowles, Samuel. "The Trilateral Commission: Have Capitalism and Democracy Come to a Parting of the Ways?" *The Progressive* 16 (June 1977): 20–23.

———. "Unequal Education and the Reproduction of the Social Division of Labor." In *The Capitalist System*, 2d ed., edited by Richard Edwards et al., pp. 317–29. Englewood Cliffs, NJ: Prentice-Hall, 1978.

Bowles, Samuel, and Gintis, Herbert. *Schooling in Capitalist America*. New York: Basic Books, 1976.

Bowles, Samuel; Gintis, Herbert; and Meyer, Peter. "The Long Shadow of Work." *Insurgent Sociologist* 8 (Summer 1975): 3–22.

Boyte, Harry. *The Backyard Revolution: Understanding the New Citizen Movement*. Philadelphia: Temple University Press, 1980.

————. "Building the Democratic Movement." *Socialist Review* 8 (October 1978): 17–41.

Brambilla, Roberto, and Longo, Gianni. *Learning from Baltimore.* New York: Environmental Action Institute, 1980.

————. *Learning from Seattle.* New York: Environmental Action Institute, 1980.

Bramhall, David. "Toward a Theory and Practice of the Radical Classroom." *Review of Radical Political Economics* 6 (Winter 1975): 55–65.

Braun, Ernest, and MacDonald, Stuart. *Revolution in Miniature: The History and Impact of Semiconductor Electronics.* Cambridge: Cambridge University Press, 1978.

Braverman, Harry. *Labor and Monopoly Capital.* New York: Monthly Review Press, 1974.

Brecher, Jeremy. "Roots of Power: Employers and Workers in the Electrical Products Industry." *Case Studies on the Labor Process*, edited by Andrew Zimbalist, pp. 206–27. New York: Monthly Review Press, 1979.

————. *Strike!* San Francisco: Straight Arrow Books, 1972.

Brecher, Jeremy, and Costello, Tim. *Common Sense for Hard Times.* New York: Two Continents Publishing Group, 1976.

Brenton, Myron. *The American Male.* Greenwich, CT: Fawcett Premier Books, 1966.

Bridges, Amy, and Hartmann, Heidi. "The Unhappy Marriage of Marxism and Feminism: Towards a More Progressive Union." Mimeographed, University of Massachusetts, 1977.

Brody, David. *Steelworkers in America: The Nonunion Era.* New York: Harper and Row, 1960.

Brown, Michael. "Love Canal and the Poisoning of America." In *Crisis in American Institutions*, 5th ed., edited by Jerome H. Skolnick and Elliott Currie, pp. 297–315. Boston: Little, Brown and Company, 1982.

Brownfield, Charles. *Isolation: Clinical and Experimental Approaches.* New York: Random House, 1966.

Buchsbaum, Andrew. "Pamphleteering is Alive and Well." *Working Papers* 7 (July–August 1980): 63–64.

Bundy, Paul. "Pacific Radio Gets Static from the New Right." *In These Times* (January 14–20, 1981): 13.

Burlage, Robb. "New Health Care Alliance Could Build a New System." *Democratic Left* (June 1979): 9–10.

Burns, Scott. *The Household Economy: Its Shape, Origins and Future.* Boston: Beacon Press, 1975.

Buttrick, John. "The Inside Contract System." *Journal of Economic History* 12 (Summer 1952): 205–21.

Calder, Nigel. *Nuclear Nightmares: An Investigation into Possible Wars.* New York: Viking Press, 1979.

Callahan, Raymond. "Capital Mergers Isolate Unions." *Dollars and Sense* 25 (March 1977): 10–11.

———. *Education and the Cult of Efficiency.* Chicago: University of Chicago Press, 1962.

"Capitalists for a Day." *Dollars and Sense* 15 (February 1983): 19.

Carnoy, Martin. *Education as Cultural Imperialism.* New York: McKay, 1974.

———. "The Role of Education in a Strategy for Social Change." In *The Limits of Educational Reform,* edited by Martin Carnoy and Henry Levin, pp. 269–90. New York: David McKay Company, 1976.

Carnoy, Martin, and Shearer, Derek. *Economic Democracy: The Challenge of the 1980s.* White Plains, NY: M. E. Sharpe, 1980.

Carrillo, Santiago. *Eurocommunism and the State.* New York: Lawrence Hill and Company, 1978.

Case, John, and Taylor, Rosemary, eds. *Co-ops, Communes and Collectives.* New York: Pantheon Books, 1979.

Chernow, Ron. "Grey Flannel Goons: The Latest in Union Busting." *Working Papers* 8 (January–February 1981): 19–25.

Clawson, Dan. *Bureaucracy and the Labor Process: The Transformation of U.S. Industry, 1860–1920.* New York: Monthly Review Press, 1980.

Clement, Norris. "Radical Pedagogy in the University?" *Review of Radical Political Economics* 6 (Winter 1975): 42–47.

Cloward, Richard, and Piven, Francis. *Radical Social Work.* New York: Pantheon Books, 1975.

Cluster, Dick, and Rutter, Nancy. *Shrinking Dollars, Vanishing Jobs.* Boston: Beacon Press, 1980.

Cohen, David, and Lazerson, Marvin. "Education and the Corporate Order." *Socialist Revolution* 2 (March 1972): 3–42.

Commoner, Barry. *The Closing Circle: Nature, Man and Technology.* New York: Alfred A. Knopf, 1971.

———. *The Politics of Energy.* New York: Alfred A. Knopf, 1979.

"Computers Chip Away at New Markets." *Dollars and Sense* 51 (November 1979): 12–13.

Cooley, Charles H. *Human Nature and the Social Order.* Glencoe, IL: Free Press, 1956.

Cooley, Mike. *Architect or Bee?* Boston: South End Press, 1982.

Cooper, David. *The Death of the Family.* New York: Vintage Books, 1970.

Crawford, Alan. *Thunder on the Right.* New York: Pantheon Books, 1980.

Cremin, Lawrence. *American Education: The Colonial Experience, 1607–1783.* New York: Harper and Row, 1970.

————. *The Transformation of the School: Progressivism in American Education,*
    1876–1957. New York: Alfred A. Knopf, 1964.
Cunningham, Ann. "Preventive Medicine." *Working Papers* 9 (January–
    February 1983): 28–36.
Datesman, Susan, and Scarpitti, Frank, eds. *Women, Crime, and Justice.*
    New York: Oxford University Press, 1980.
David, Deborah. *The Forty-Nine Percent Majority: The Male Sex Role.*
    Reading, MA: Addison-Wesley, 1976.
Davis, Angela. *Women, Race, and Class.* New York: Random House, 1983.
Davis, Kingsley. "Final Note on a Case of Extreme Isolation." *American
    Journal of Sociology* 52 (March 1947): 432–37.
DeGrasse, Robert, Jr. *The Costs and Consequences of Reagan's Military
    Buildup.*Washington, DC: Council on Economic Priorities, 1981.
Dewey, John. *Democracy and Education.* New York: Macmillan, 1916.
Dickson, David. *The Politics of Alternative Energy.* New York: Universe
    Books, 1974.
Dowd, Douglas. "The Centralization of Capital." In *The Capitalist System,*
    2d ed., edited by Richard Edwards et al., pp. 126–33. Englewood
    Cliffs, NJ: Prentice-Hall, 1978.
Doyal, Leslie. *The Political Economy of Health.* Boston: South End Press,
    1979.
Dreier, Peter. "The Politics of Rent Control." *Working Papers* 6 (March–
    April 1979): 55–63.
DuBois, Ellen. "The Nineteenth-Century Women's Suffrage Move-
    ment and the Analysis of Women's Oppression." In *Capitalist
    Patriarchy and the Case for Socialist Feminism,* edited by Zillah Eisen-
    stein, pp. 137–50. New York: Monthly Review Press, 1979.
Dunlap, Ralph, and Dills, Ralph. "Redlining." In *Public Policy Reader,*
    edited by Derek Shearer and Lee Webb, pp. 400–16. Washington,
    DC: Conference on Alternative State and Local Public Policies,
    1976.
Dworkin, Andrea. *Our Blood: Prophecies and Discourses on Sexual Politics.*
    New York: Perigee Books, 1976.
————. *Right-wing Women.* New York: Perigee Books, 1978.
Easton, Barbara. "Feminism and the Contemporary Family." *Socialist
    Review* 8 (May–June 1978): 11–36.
Eble, Kenneth. *The Craft of Teaching.* San Francisco: Jossey-Bass, 1976.
Edwards, John. "The Future of the Family Revisited." In *Intimate Life
    Styles,* edited by Joann S. and Jack Delora, pp. 348–57. Pacific
    Palisades, CA: Goodyear, 1972.
Edwards, Richard. *The Capitalist System.* 2d ed. Edited by Michael Reich
    and Thomas Weisskopf. Englewood Cliffs, NJ: Prentice-Hall, 1972.

————. *Contested Terrain: The Transformation of the Workplace in the Twentieth Century.* New York: Basic Books, 1979.

Ehrensaft, Diane. "When Women and Men Mother." *Socialist Review* 10 (January–February 1980): 37–73.

Eisenstein, Zillah. *Capitalist Patriarchy and the Case for Socialist Feminism.* New York: Monthly Review Press, 1979.

Ellul, Jacques. *The Technological Society.* New York: Vintage Books, 1964.

English, Deirdre. "The Politics of Porn." *Mother Jones* 9 (April 1980): 20–23.

Erickson, Erik. *Childhood and Society.* 2d ed. New York: W. W. Norton and Company, 1963.

Estellachild, Vivian. "Hippie Communes." In *Intimate Life Styles,* edited by Joann S. and Jack Delora, pp. 332–37. Pacific Palisades, CA: Goodyear, 1972.

Evans, Ann. "Cooperatives." In *America's Cities and Counties,* edited by Lee Webb. Washington, DC: Conference on State and Local Policies, 1983.

Evans, Christopher. *The Micro Millennium.* New York: Pocket Books, 1979.

Evans, Sara. *Personal Politics: The Roots of Women's Liberation in the Civil Rights Movement and the New Left.* New York: Alfred A. Knopf, 1979.

Eyster, Richard. "Seymour Papert and the Logo Universe." *Creative Computing* 7 (December 1981): 70–74.

Fager, Chuck. "The Anti-Abortion Movement Can't Make Its Own Choice." *In These Times* (January 13–19, 1982): 6.

Fallows, James. *National Defense.* New York: Random House, 1981.

Fanon, Frantz. *Black Skin, White Masks.* New York: Grove Press, 1967.

Farber, Jerry. "Why People Love Capitalism." *The University of Tomorrowland.* New York: Pocket Books, 1972.

Farley, Lin. *Sexual Shakedown: The Sexual Harassment of Women on the Job.* New York: Warner Books, 1978.

Farson, Richard. *Birthrights.* New York: Penguin Books, 1974.

Faunce, William. "Automation in the Automobile Industry." *American Sociological Review* 23 (August 1958): 401–07.

Featherstone, Joseph and Helen. "The Cult of Measurement." *Working Papers* 6 (March–April 1978): 10–11.

————. "Teachers: Helping Themselves." *Working Papers* 7 (May–June 1979): 2–3.

Festinger, Leon. "Informal Social Communications." In *Current Perspectives in Social Psychology,* edited by E. P. Hollander and R. G. Hunt, pp. 409–20. New York: Oxford University Press, 1963.

Fisher, Steve. "Teaching Pride and Power." *In These Times* (April 25–May 1, 1979): 19.

Flacks, Richard. *Conformity, Resistance, and Self-Determination.* Boston: Little, Brown and Company, 1973.

Flexner, Eleanor. *Centuries of Struggle.* New York: Atheneum, 1974.

Fonda, Jane. *Jane Fonda's Workout Book.* New York: Simon and Schuster, 1981.

Freeman, Richard. *The Over-Educated American.* New York: Academic Press, 1976.

Freire, Paulo. *Pedagogy of the Oppressed.* New York: Seabury Press, 1970.

Freud, Sigmund. *Civilization and Its Discontents.* New York: W. W. Norton and Company, 1961.

————. *A General Selection from the Works of Sigmund Freud,* edited by John Richman. Garden City, NY: Doubleday Anchor Books, 1957.

————. *Introductory Lectures on Psychoanalysis.* New York: W. W. Norton and Company, 1966.

Friedan, Betty. *It Changed My Life: Writings on the Women's Movement.* New York: Random House, 1977.

————. *The Second Stage.* New York: Summit Books, 1981.

Friedman, Milton. *Free to Choose: A Personal Statement.* New York: Harcourt Brace Jovanovich, 1980.

Fromm, Erich. *The Art of Loving.* New York: Bantam Books, 1956.

————. *Escape from Freedom.* New York: Holt, Rinehart and Winston, 1947.

————. Foreword to *Summerhill: A Radical Approach to Child Rearing,* by A. S. Neill. New York: Hart Publishing Company, 1960.

————. *Man for Himself.* New York: Holt, Rinehart and Winston, 1947.

Gallup, George. *The George Gallup Poll: 1935–1971.* Vol. 2. New York: Random House, 1972.

Garson, Barbara. *All the Livelong Day: The Meaning and Demeaning of Routine Work.* Garden City, NY: Doubleday and Company, 1975.

Gartman, David. "Origins of the Assembly Line and Capitalist Control of Work at Ford." In *Case Studies on the Labor Process,* edited by Andrew Zimbalist, pp. 193–205. New York: Monthly Review Press, 1979.

Geller, Ruth. *Seed of a Woman.* New York: Imp Press, 1979.

Gergen, Kenneth. *The Concept of Self.* New York: Holt, Rinehart and Winston, 1971.

Germond, Jack, and Witcover, Jules. "Teachers Major in Practical Politics." *Detroit Free Press* (April 19, 1982): 12.

Gide, André. *The Immoralist.* New York: Vintage Books, 1958.

Gitlin, Todd. *The Whole World is Watching: Mass Media in the Making and Unmaking of the New Left.* Berkeley: University of California Press, 1980.

Glenn, Evelyn, and Feldberg, Roslyn. "Proletarianization Clerical Work: Technology and Organizational Control in the Office." In *Case*

Studies on the Labor Process, edited by Andrew Zimbalist, pp. 51–72. New York: Monthly Review Press, 1979.

Goldhaber, Michael. "Politics and Technology: Microprocessors and the Prospect of a New Industrial Revolution." *Socialist Review* 10 (July–August 1980): 9–32.

Goodfield, June. *Playing God: Genetic Engineering and the Manipulation of Life*. New York: Random House, 1977.

Goodman, Paul. *Compulsory Mis-Education and the Community of Scholars*. New York: Vintage Books, 1962.

———. "Memoirs of an Ancient Activist." In *The Gay Liberation Book*, edited by Len Richman and Gary Noguera, 23–29. San Francisco: Rampart Press, 1978.

Gordon, David, ed. *Problems in Political Economy: An Urban Perspective*. 2d ed. Lexington, MA: D. C. Heath, 1977.

Gordon, Linda. *The Fourth Mountain: Women in China*. Somerville, MA: New England Free Press, 1973.

Gordon, Linda, and Hunter, Allen. "Sex, Family and the New Right: Anti-Feminism as a Political Force." *Radical America* 11 (November 1977): 9–25.

Gordon, Suzanne. "Half-Time Blues." *Working Papers* 8 (May–June 1981): 36–41.

———. "The Ultimate Single Issue." *Working Papers* 9 (May–June 1982): 21–25.

Gordon, Thomas. *Parent Effectiveness Training Notebook*. Pasadena, CA: Effectiveness Training Associates, 1972.

———. *P.E.T.: Parent Effectiveness Training*. New York: Peter H. Wyden, 1972.

Gorz, André. *Ecology as Politics*. Boston: South End Press, 1980.

———. *Strategy for Labor*. Boston: Beacon Press, 1968.

Gouldner, Alvin. *Patterns of Industrial Bureaucracy*. Glencoe, IL: Free Press, 1954.

Graubard, Allen. *Free the Children: Radical Reform and the Free School Movement*. New York: Pantheon Books, 1973.

———. "From Free Schools to Educational Alternatives." In *Co-ops, Communes and Collectives*, edited by John Case and Rosemary Taylor, pp. 49–65. New York: Pantheon Books, 1979.

Greenbaum, Joan. *In the Name of Efficiency: Management Theory and Shop-floor Practice in Data-Processing Work*. Philadelphia: Temple University Press, 1979.

Greenstein, Fred. "Personality and Political Socialization: The Theories of Authoritarian and Democratic Character." In *Conformity, Resistance, and Self-Determination*, edited by Richard Flacks, pp. 61–72. Boston: Little, Brown and Company, 1973.

Greer, Colin. *The Great School Legend: A Revisionist Interpretation of American Public Education.* New York: Basic Books, 1972.

Greven, Philip. "Family Structure in Seventeenth-Century Andover, Massachusetts." In *The American Family in Social-Historical Perspective*, 2d ed., edited by Michael Gordon, pp. 20–37. New York: St. Martin's Press, 1978.

Griffin, Susan. "Rape: The All-American Crime." *Ramparts* 10 (September 1971): 26–36.

Gross, Bertram. *Friendly Fascism: The New Face of Power in America.* New York: M. Evans and Company, 1980.

Gross, Edward. "Plus Ça Change? . . . The Sexual Structure of Occupations over Time." *Social Problems* 16 (Fall 1968): 202.

Gross, Ronald. *The Lifelong Learner.* New York: Simon and Schuster, 1977.

Grossman, Rachael. "Growers Prefer Machines to UFW Members." *Dollars and Sense* 35 (March 1978): 14–16.

———. "Women's Place in the Integrated Circuit." *Southeast Asia Chronicle* 66 (January–February 1979).

"The Growing Disaffection with 'Workaholism.'" *Business Week* (February 27, 1978): 97–98.

Gruber, Howard, and Voneche, J. Jacques, eds. *The Essential Piaget.* New York: Basic Books, 1977.

Gunn, Christopher. "A New Model of Self-Management." *Working Papers* 8 (March–April 1981): 17–21.

———. "Toward Workers' Control." *Working Papers* 7 (May–June 1980): 4–7.

Gutman, Herbert. *Work, Culture and Society in Industrializing America.* New York: Alfred A. Knopf, 1966.

Hagstrom, Jerry. "Whose Co-op Bank?" *Working Papers* 7 (September–October 1980): 24–31.

Hamblin, Robert et al. "Changing the Game from 'Get the Teacher' to 'Learn.'" *Transaction* (January 1969): 20–31.

Harcatz, Kate. "The Education of Kate Harcatz: The Education of an Undergraduate." *Change Magazine* 2 (May–June 1970): 12–26.

Harlow, Harry, and Harlow, Margaret. "Social Deprivation in Monkeys." *Scientific American Reprints* (November 1962).

Harrington, Michael. *Decade of Decision: The Crisis of the American System.* New York: Simon and Schuster, 1980.

Harris, Michael. "No More Teachers' Dirty Looks: Is Compulsory Education an Idea Whose Time Has Gone?" In *Education 83/84*, edited by Fred Schultz, pp. 54–58. Guilford, CT: Dustin Publishing Group, 1983.

Hart, Harold, ed. *Summerhill: For and Against*. New York: Hart Publishing Company, 1970.

Hartmann, Heidi. "Capitalism, Patriarchy, and Job Segregation by Sex." In *Capitalist Patriarchy and the Case for Socialist Feminism*, edited by Zillah Eisenstein, pp. 137–50. New York: Monthly Review Press, 1978.

Haughey, John. "The Commune—Child of the Seventies." In *Intimate Life Styles*, edited by Joann S. and Jack Delora, pp. 328–32. Pacific Palisades, CA: Goodyear, 1972.

Hayden, Tom. *The American Future: New Visions Beyond Old Frontiers*. Boston: South End Press, 1980.

Heilbroner, Robert. *Beyond Boom and Crash*. New York: W. W. Norton, 1978.

Henderson, Hazel. *Creating Alternative Futures: The End of Economics*. Boston: South End Press, 1978.

Henley, Nancy M. *Body Politics: Power, Sex, and Nonverbal Communication*. Englewood Cliffs, NJ: Prentice-Hall, 1977.

Henry, J. S. "From Soap to Soapbox: The Corporate Merchandising of Ideas." *Working Papers* 7 (May–June 1981): 55–57.

Hentoff, Nat. *The First Freedom*. New York: Dell Publishing Company, 1981.

Herndon, James. *How to Survive in Your Native Land*. New York: Simon and Schuster, 1977.

Hess, Karl. *Community Technology*. New York: Harper and Row, 1979.

HEW Task Force Report. *Work in America*. Cambridge, MA: M.I.T. Press, 1973.

Hite, Shere. *The Hite Report*. New York: Dell Publishing Company, 1976.

Hoffman, Nancy. "Teaching Change: Education to Reform the Cities." *Working Papers* 3 (Spring 1975): 37–43.

Holt, John. *Freedom and Beyond*. New York: Delta Books, 1972.

————. *How Children Learn*. New York: Pitman Publishing, 1967.

————. *Instead of Education: Ways to Help People Do Things Better*. New York: E. P. Dutton, 1976.

Horney, Karen. *Feminine Psychology*. New York: W. W. Norton and Company, 1967.

————. *Neurosis and Human Growth*. New York: W. W. Norton and Company, 1950.

————. *Our Inner Conflicts*. New York: W. W. Norton and Company, 1945.

Howard, Robert. "Brave New Workplace." *Working Papers* 7 (November–December 1980): 21–31.

Howard, Ted, and Rifkin, Jeremy. *Who Should Play God?* New York: Delacarte Press, 1977.

Howe, Florence, and Lauter, Paul. "How the School System Is Rigged for Failure." In *The Capitalist System*, edited by Richard Edwards et al., pp. 229–35. Englewood Cliffs, NJ: Prentice-Hall, 1972.

Howe, Louise. *Pink Collar Workers*. New York: Avon Books, 1977.

Hoyt, Donald. "The Relationship Between College Grades and Adult Achievement: A Review of the Literature." *ACT Research Report*, no. 7 (September 1965): 1–12.

Hunnius, Gerry; Garson, David; and Case, John, eds. *Workers' Control*. New York: Vintage Books, 1973.

Hunt, Morton. "The Future of Marriage." In *Intimate Life Styles*, edited by Joann S. and Jack Delora, pp. 399–411. Pacific Palisades, CA: Goodyear, 1972.

Illich, Ivan. *Celebration of Awareness*. Garden City, NY: Doubleday and Company, 1971.

———. "Infant's Mind in a Teen's Body." *Detroit Free Press* (November 18, 1970): 6A.

———. *Medical Nemesis: The Expropriation of Health*. New York: Pantheon Books, 1976.

"The Impact of the Hyde Amendment on Medically Necessary Abortions." *ACLU Reports*. New York: American Civil Liberties Union, 1982.

"Is Business Improving the Quality of Work?" *Dollars and Sense* 14 (August 1982): 6–8.

Ishikawa, Eisei, and Swain, David. *Hiroshima and Nagasaki: The Physical, Medical and Social Effects of the Atomic Bombings*. New York: Basic Books, 1981.

Jacoby, Henry. *The Bureaucratization of the World*. Berkeley: University of California Press, 1973.

Jencks, Christopher. *Inequality: A Reassessment of the Effect of Family and Schooling in America*. New York: Harper and Row, 1972.

———. "Should the News Be Sold for Profit?" *Working Papers* 7 (July–August 1979): 12–13.

———. "What's Behind the Drop in Test Scores?" *Working Papers* 6 (July–August 1978): 29–41.

Jenkins, David. "Beyond Job Enrichment: Workplace Democracy in Europe." *Working Papers* 2 (Winter 1975): 51–57.

Johnson, Christopher. "Our Investment in Public Education." In *Education 83/84*, edited by Fred Schultz, pp. 163–65. Guilford, CT: Dustin Publishing Group, 1983.

Johnson, Phillip. "A Brave New Workplace." *In These Times* (November 14, 1982): 15.

Johnson, Warren. *Muddling Toward Frugality: A Blueprint for Survival in the 1980s*. Boulder, CO: Shambhala Publications, 1978.

Jones, Edward, and Gerard, Harold. *Foundations of Social Psychology.* New York: John Wiley and Sons, 1967.

Jourard, Sidney M. *Self-Disclosure: An Experimental Analysis of the Transparent Self.* New York: John Wiley and Sons, 1971.

———. *The Transparent Self: Self-Disclosure and Well-Being.* Princeton, NJ: D. Van Nostrand Company, 1964.

Kahn, Si. *How People Get Power.* New York: McGraw-Hill Book Company, 1970.

Kakar, Sughir. *Frederick Taylor: A Study in Personality and Innovation.* Cambridge, MA: M.I.T. Press, 1970.

Kanter, Rosabeth. "A Good Job Is Hard To Find." *Working Papers* 7 (May–June 1979).

———. *Men and Women of the Corporation.* New York: Basic Books, 1977.

———. "Work in America." *Daedalus* 107 (Winter 1978): 47–48.

Karier, Clarence. "Testing for Order and Control in the Corporate Liberal State." *Educational Theory* 22 (Spring 1972): 154–80.

Katz, Michael. *Class, Bureaucracy, and Schools.* New York: Praeger Publishers, 1975.

———. *The Irony of Early School Reform.* Boston: Beacon Press, 1968.

Kay, Alan C. "Microelectronics and the Personal Computer." *Scientific American* 237 (September 1977): 231–44.

Kehberg, Kent, and Pollack, Richard. "Videodisks in the Classroom: An Interactive Economics Course." *Creative Computing* 8 (January 1982): 98–102.

Keniston, Kenneth. *All Our Children.* New York: Harcourt Brace Jovanovich, 1977.

Kirschner, Edward, and Bach, Eve. "The Potential of Cooperative Housing." Oakland, CA: Regional Housing Newsletter, 1974.

Kirschner, Edward, and Morey, James. "Controlling a City's Wealth: The Lessons of New Town Development." *Working Papers* 2 (Spring 1973): 9–19.

Kolko, Gabriel. *The Triumph of Conservatism.* Chicago: Quadrangle Books, 1963.

Koppelman, Charles. "An Island Takes on the Phone Company." *Mother Jones* 2 (June 1977): 13–18.

Kotler, Milton. *Neighborhood Government.* Indianapolis: Bobbs-Merrill, 1969.

Kozol, Jonathan. *Free Schools.* New York: Bantam Books, 1972.

———. *Prisoners of Silence.* New York: Continuum, 1980.

Kraft, Philip. "The Industrialization of Computer Programming: From Programming to 'Software Production.'" In *Case Studies on the Labor Process*, edited by Andrew Zimbalist, pp. 1–17. New York: Monthly Review Press, 1979.

———. *Programmers and Managers: The Routinization of Computer Programming in the United States*. New York: Springer-Verlag, 1977.

Kuttner, Bob. "Stone Soup: Why Neighborhood Housing Services Work." *Working Papers* 7 (September–October 1980): 32–41.

Laing, R. D. *The Divided Self*. New York: Penguin Books, 1960.

Lappe, Frances, and Collins, Joseph. *Food First: Beyond the Myth of Scarcity*. Boston: Houghton Mifflin Company, 1977.

Lasch, Christopher. *Haven in a Heartless World*. New York: Basic Books, 1977.

Lasswell, Harold. "Democratic Character," *Political Writings*. Glencoe, IL: Free Press, 1951.

Lazerson, Marvin. *Origins of the Urban School: Public Education in Massachusetts, 1877–1915*. Cambridge, MA: Harvard University Press, 1971.

LeBarre, Weston. *The Human Animal*. Chicago: University of Chicago Press, 1954.

Lee, Dorothy. *Freedom and Culture*. New York: Capricorn Books, 1939.

Lens, Sidney. *The Labor Wars*. Garden City, NY: Doubleday and Company, 1973.

Lerner, Michael. *The New Socialist Revolution*. New York: Delta Books, 1973.

Lerza, Catherine. "McHale's Pennsylvania Plan." In *Public Policy Reader*, edited by Derek Shearer and Lee Webb, p. 144. Washington, DC: Conference on Alternative State and Local Public Policies, 1976.

Lerza, Catherine, and Jacobson, Michael, eds. *Food for People, Not for Profits*. New York: Ballantine Books, 1975.

Levin, Henry. "The Case for Community Control of Schools." In *Schooling in a Corporate Society*, edited by Martin Carnoy, pp. 193–210. New York: David McKay Company, 1972.

Levine, Judith. "Do-It-Yourself in the Bronx." *Working Papers* 6 (March–April 1979): 20–23.

Levine, Stanley. "Stimulation in Infancy." *Scientific American* 202 (May 1960): 80–86.

Lindesmith, Alfred; Strauss, Anselm; and Denzin, Norman. *Social Psychology*. 4th ed. Hinsdale, IL: Dryden Press.

Lindsey, Robert. "Horse Trading is Making a Comeback." *Detroit Free Press* (November 21, 1976): 5–6.

Lisman, David, and Ohlinger, John. "Must We All Go Back to School?" *The Progressive* 42 (October 1978): 35–37.

Livingston, James. "Democracy Interferes with Free Enterprise." *In These Times* (January 28–February 3, 1981): 11.

Lodwick, Dora, and Morrison, Denton. "Appropriate Technology." In *Rural Society in the U.S.*, edited by Don Dillman and Daryl Hobbs, pp. 44–53. Boulder, CO: Westview Press, 1982.

Lotspeich, Margaret, and Kleymeyer, John. *How to Gather Data About Your Neighborhood*. Chicago: American Society of Planning Officials, 1978.

Lovins, Amory. *Soft Energy Paths*. New York: Harper and Row, 1977.

Lowen, Alexander. *Love and Orgasm*. New York: Macmillan Company, 1965.

Lublin, Joann. "Farmers' Markets Sprout Inside the Cities." In *Public Policy Reader*, edited by Derek Shearer and Lee Webb, p. 145. Washington, DC: Conference on Alternative State and Local Public Policies, 1976.

Luria, Dan, and Russell, Jack. *Rational Reindustrialization: An Economic Development Agenda for Detroit*. Detroit: Widgetripper Press, 1981.

MacKinnon, Catharine. *Sexual Harassment of Working Women*. New Haven, CT: Yale University Press, 1979.

MacLean, Judy. "Roots of the Women's Movement." *Socialist Review* 10 (March–June 1980): 233–43.

Magnacca, Sandy, and Murphy, Gail. *Handbook in Prepared Childhood*. Wayne, NJ: Avery Publishing Group, 1976.

Magney, John. "New Wave Co-ops Prosper." *In These Times* (November 5–11, 1980): 24.

———. "The Co-op Movement Is Still Small, But Growing Rapidly." *In These Times* (October 22–28, 1980): 16.

Malinowski, Bronislaw. *The Sexual Life of Savages*. New York: Harcourt, Brace and World, 1929.

Malson, Lucien. *Wolf Children and the Problem of Human Nature*. New York: Monthly Review Press, 1972.

Marcuse, Herbert. *Reason and Revolution*. New York: Humanities Press, 1955.

Marcuse, Peter. "Redlining: Banks." *Working Papers* 7 (July–August 1979): 3–4.

Marglin, Stephen. "What Do Bosses Do? The Origins of Functions of Hierarchy in Capitalist Production." *Review of Radical Political Economics* 6 (Summer 1974): 33–60.

Markoff, John, and Stewart, Jon. "The Microprocessor Revolution: An Office on the Head of a Pin." *In These Times* (March 7–13, 1979): 12–14.

Martin, Josh. "Plugging in Public Power." *In These Times* (May 16–22, 1979): 12–13.

Martinez, Sue, and Ramo, Alan. "In the Valley of the Shadow of Death." *In These Times* (October 8–14, 1980): 12–13.

Marx, Karl. *Capital*. Vol. 1. New York: International Publishers, 1967.
————. *Economic and Philosophical Manuscripts of 1844*. New York: International Publishers, 1964.
Marzani, Carl. *The Promise of Eurocommunism*. New York: Lawrence Hill, 1981.
Maslow, Abraham. *Motivation and Personality*. 2d ed. New York: Harper and Row, 1970.
Mayo, John. "The Role of Microelectronics in Communication." *Scientific American* 237 (September 1977): 192–209.
McCarthy, Coleman. "A Fishing Cooperative Survives." In *Public Policy Reader*, edited by Derek Shearer and Lee Webb, p. 364. Washington, DC: Conference on Alternative State and Local Public Policies, 1976.
McCartney, Robert. "A Minor Renaissance in Turning City Halls into Centers of Culture." In *Public Policy Reader*, edited by Derek Shearer and Lee Webb, p. 107. Washington, DC: Conference of Alternative State and Local Public Policies, 1976.
McCloskey, Michael. "Environmental Tenants Have Become Values, Not Issues." *Kansas City Star*, December 29, 1982.
McCuen, Laura. "Computer Growth Lauded." *State News*, January 11, 1983.
McDermott, John. *The Crisis in the Working Class: Some Arguments for a New Labor Movement*. Boston: South End Press, 1980.
————. "Technology: The Opiate of the Intellectuals." *New York Review of Books* (July 31, 1969): 25–35.
Mead, Margaret. *Culture and Commitment*. Garden City, NY: Doubleday and Company, 1970.
Meadows, Donella H. et al. *The Limits to Growth*. 2d ed. New York: Universe Books, 1974.
————. "Microcomputers: Big Profits from Tiny Chips." *Dollars and Sense* 34 (February 1978): 3–5.
Michaels, Dia. "Community TV Hope Flickers." *In These Times* (November 12–18, 1980): 8.
Milkman, Ruth. "Organizing and Sexual Division of Labor." *Socialist Review* 10 (January–February 1980): 95–150.
Miller, S. M. "The Making of a Confused, Middle-Aged Husband." In *Men and Masculinity*, edited by Joseph Pleck and Jack Sawyer, pp. 44–52. Englewood Cliffs, NJ: Prentice-Hall, 1974.
Mills, C. Wright. *The Sociological Imagination*. New York: Oxford University Press, 1959.
Milner, Murray, Jr. *The Illusion of Equality*. San Francisco: Jossey-Bass, 1972.

Mitscherlich, Alexander. *Society Without the Father*. London: Tavistock Publications, 1969.

Moberg, David. "The Car Crash: Detroit's Greed and Stupidity Collide with the Changing Market." *In These Times* (May 28–June 3, 1980): 7–10.

—. "Cracking Campus Cynicism." *In These Times* (September 24–30, 1980): 11–14.

—. "Experimenting with the Future." In *Co-ops, Communes and Collectives*, edited by John Case and Rosemary Taylor, pp. 274–311. New York: Pantheon Books, 1979.

—. "From Rent Control to Municipal Power." *In These Times* (January 12–18, 1983): 11–13.

—. "Politics of Growth Won't Work in an Era of Hard Choices." *In These Times* (May 5–11, 1982): 2.

—. "Retooling the Industrial Debate." *Working Papers* 8 (November–December 1980): 32–39.

Montagu, Ashley. *On Being Human*. New York: Hawthorn Books, 1950.

Montgomery, David. *Workers' Control in America: Studies in the History of Work, Technology, and Labor Struggles*. Cambridge: Cambridge University Press, 1979.

Morgan, Robin. *Going Too Far: The Personal Chronicle of a Feminist*. New York: Vintage Books, 1978.

Morris, David. "Energy, Democracy and the Carter Energy Plan." In *The Federal Budget and Social Reconstruction*, edited by Marcus Raskin, pp. 265–86. Washington, DC: Institute for Policy Studies, 1978.

Morrison, Denton. "Equity Impacts of Some Major Energy Alternatives." In *Energy Policy in the United States*, edited by Seymour Warkov. New York: Praeger Publishers, 1978.

—. "Soft Tech/Hard Tech, Hi/Tech/Lo Tech: A Social Movement Analysis of Appropriate Technology." Paper presented at the Institute for Environmental Studies (Urbana-Champaign, IL), October 1, 1982.

Moustakas, Clark. *Creativity and Conformity*. Princeton, NJ: D. Van Nostrand Company, 1967.

Müller, Ronald. *Revitalizing America: Politics for Prosperity*. New York: Simon and Schuster, 1980.

Mussachia, Mark. "Three Views on Reich's Concept of Sexual Repression." *Monthly Review* 26 (November 1974): 49–55.

Nader, Ralph, and Ross, Donald. *Action for a Change*. New York: Grossman Publishers, 1971.

Nader, Ralph; Green, Mark; and Seligman, Joel. *Taming the Giant Corporation*. New York: W. W. Norton and Company, 1976.

Naisbit, John. *Megatrends: Ten New Directions Transforming Our Lives*. New York: Warner Books, 1984.

Neill, A. S. *The Free Child*. London: Herbert Jankins, 1953.

———. *Freedom–Not License!* New York: Hart Publishing Company, 1966.

———. *Summerhill*. New York: Hart Publishing Company, 1960.

Nelson, Daniel. *Managers and Workers: Origins of the New Factory System in the United States, 1880–1920*. Madison: University of Wisconsin Press, 1975.

Nesbit, Jeff. "Security Is Not a Nuclear Blanket." *In These Times* (February 2–8, 1983): 2.

Neumann, A. Lin. "Hospitality Girls in the Philippines." *Southeast Asia Chronicle* 66 (January–February 1979).

"The New Industrial Relations." *Business Week* (May 11, 1981): 84–98.

Newt Davidson Collective. *Crisis at C.U.N.Y.* New York: Newt Davidson Collective, 1974.

Nichols, Jack. *Men's Liberation*. New York: Penguin Books, 1975.

Noble, David. *America by Design: Science, Technology, and the Rise of Corporate Capitalism*. New York: Basic Books, 1977.

———. "Social Choice in Machine Design: The Case of Automatically Controlled Machine Tools." In *Case Studies on the Labor Process*, edited by Andrew Zimbalist, pp. 18–50. New York: Monthly Review Press, 1979.

Noyce, Robert. "Microelectronics." *Scientific American* 237 (September 1977): 62–69.

O'Connor, James. *The Fiscal Crisis of the State*. New York: St. Martin's Press, 1973.

Ollman, Bertell. *Alienation*. 2d ed. Cambridge: Cambridge University Press, 1976.

———. "Is There a Marxian Ethic?" *Science and Society* 35 (Summer 1971): 56–68.

———. "Social Revolution and Sexual Revolution." *Monthly Review* 25 (September 1973): 37–52.

Olsen, David. "Labor's Stake in a Democratic Workplace." *Working Papers* 8 (March–April 1981): 12–17.

Olsen, David, and Parker, Richard. "Lessons of a Dog Food Democracy." *Mother Jones* 2 (June 1977): 19–20.

O. M. Collective. *The Organizer's Manual*. New York: Bantam Books, 1971.

Onosko, Tom. "Vision of the Future." *Creative Computing* 8 (January 1982): 84–94.

Oppenheimer, Martin. *The Urban Guerrilla*. Chicago: Quadrangle Books, 1969.

Oppenheimer, Martin, and Lakey, George. *A Manual for Direct Action.* Chicago: Quadrangle Books, 1964.

Palmer, Bryan. "Class Conception and Conflict: The Thrust for Efficiency, Managerial Views of Labor, and the Working Class Rebellion." *Review of Radical Political Economics* 7 (Summer 1975): 31–49.

Papert, Seymour. *Mindstorms: Children, Computers, and Powerful Ideas.* New York: Basic Books, 1980.

Pateman, Carole. *Participation and Democratic Theory.* Cambridge: Cambridge University Press, 1970.

Patton, R., and Gardner, L. *Growth Failure and Maternal Deprivation.* Springfield, IL: Charles C. Thomas Publishers, 1963.

Paxton, Tom. *What Did You Learn in School Today?* New York: Harmony Music, 1965.

Perls, Frederick. *Gestalt Therapy Verbatim.* Lafayette, CA: Real People Press, 1969.

"Pesticides Create a 'Circle of Poison.'" *Dollars and Sense* 67 (May–June 1981): 6–19.

Pinchbeck, Ivy. *Women Workers and the Industrial Revolution 1750–1850.* New York: F. S. Crofts and Company, 1930.

Platt, John. "Beyond Freedom and Dignity: A Revolutionary Manifesto." *Center Magazine* 5 (March–April 1972): 34–52.

Pleck, Joseph. *Men's New Roles in the Family: Housework and Child Care.* Ann Arbor, MI: Institute for Social Research, 1976.

Pleck, Joseph, and Sawyer, Jack. *Men and Masculinity.* Englewood Cliffs, NJ: Prentice-Hall, 1974.

Podhoretz, Norman. *The Present Danger.* New York: Simon and Schuster, 1980.

Powell, Walter. "The Blockbuster Decade: The Media as Big Business." *Working Papers* 7 (July–August 1979): 50–54.

Primack, Phil. "Soft Energy and Hard Times." *Working Papers* 7 (September–October 1980): 15–23.

"Prof: Women Affected More by Technological Revolution." *MSU News Bulletin* (September 26, 1982): 12.

Purrington, Beverly. "Effects of Children on Their Parents: Parents' Perceptions." Ph.D. dissertation, Michigan State University, 1980.

Raskin, Marcus. *Being and Doing.* New York: Random House, 1971.

————. *The Federal Budget and Social Reconstruction.* Washington, DC: Institute for Policy Studies, 1978.

Rasmus, Jack. "Why Management Is Pushing 'Job Enrichment.'" *International Socialist Review* 2 (December 1974): 23–46.

Ravitch, Diane. *The Great School Wars: A History of the Public Schools as Battlefield of Social Change.* New York: Basic Books, 1974.

Rawlins, V. Lane, and Ulman, Lloyd. "The Utilization of College Trained Manpower in the United States." In *The Federal Budget and Social Reconstruction*, edited by Marcus Raskin, pp. 343–48. Washington, DC: Institute for Policy Studies, 1978.

Reece, Ray. *The Sun Betrayed*. Boston: South End Press, 1979.

Reich, Michael. "The Development of the Wage-Labor Force." In *The Capitalist System*, 2d ed., edited by Richard Edwards et al., pp. 179–85. Englewood Cliffs, NJ: Prentice-Hall, 1978.

Reich, Wilhelm. *Character Analysis*. 3d ed. New York: Simon and Schuster, 1972.

———. *The Function of the Orgasm*. New York: Simon and Schuster, 1973.

———. *The Mass Psychology of Fascism*. New York: Simon and Schuster, 1970.

———. *Sex-Poll Essays, 1921–1934*. Edited by Lee Baxandall. New York: Vintage Books, 1972.

"The Reindustrialization of America." *Business Week* (June 30, 1980): 55–142.

Ridgeway, James, and Conner, Bettina. "Public Energy: Notes Toward a New System." *Working Papers* 2 (Winter 1975): 45–48.

Rifkin, Jeremy. *Own Your Own Job*. New York: Bantam Books, 1977.

The Rights of Children. Berkeley: Berkeley Conference on Children's Rights, 1970.

Ritter, Paul, and Ritter, Jean. *Free Family and Feedback, 1949–1974*. London: Victor Gollancz, 1975.

Robertson, Don, and Steele, Marion. *The Halls of Yearning*. New York: Harper and Row, 1971.

"Rock and Recession." *Dollars and Sense* 15 (February 1983): 10.

Rodberg, Leonard. "Employment Impact of the Solar Transition." In *Crisis in American Institutions*, 5th ed., edited by Jerome H. Skolnick and Elliott Currie, pp. 541–62. Boston: Little, Brown and Company, 1982.

Rogers, Carl. *Freedom to Learn*. Columbus: Charles E. Merrill, 1969.

———. *On Becoming a Person*. Boston: Houghton Mifflin Company, 1961.

Rogers, Carl, and Dymond, Rosalind, eds. *Psychotherapy and Personality Change*. Chicago: University of Chicago Press, 1954.

Rohatyn, Felix. "Article on Planning." *New York Review of Books*, 1980.

———. "The Coming Emergency and What Can Be Done About It." *New York Review of Books* (December 4, 1980): 20–22.

———. "Felix Rohatyn's Biggest Deal." *Working Papers* 8 (September–October 1981).

――――. "New York and the Nation." *New York Review of Books* (January 21, 1982): 26–28.

――――. "Reconstructing America." *New York Review of Books* (March 5, 1981): 35–40.

Rokeach, Milton. *The Open and Closed Mind.* New York: Basic Books, 1960.

Roose, Paul. "The New Technology Will Only Ring Once." *In These Times* (July 15–28, 1981): 5–9.

Rosenthal, Robert, and Jacobson, Lenore. "Teacher Expectations for the Disadvantaged." *Scientific American* 218 (April 1968): 19–23.

Rothchild-Whitt, Joyce. "Private Ownership and Worker Control in Holland." *Working Papers* 8 (March–April 1981): 22–25.

Rowbotham, Sheila. *Women, Resistance and Revolution.* New York: Vintage Books, 1974.

Rubin, Gayle. "The Traffic in Women: Notes on the 'Political Enemy' of Sex." In *Toward an Anthropology of Women*, edited by Rayna Reiter, pp. 157–210. New York: Monthly Review Press, 1975.

――――. *Worlds of Pain.* New York: Basic Books, 1976.

Russell, Bertrand. *Roads to Freedom.* New York: Barnes and Noble, 1965.

Russell, Raymond; Hochner, Art; and Perry, Stewart. "San Francisco's 'Scavengers' Run Their Own Firm." *Working Papers* 5 (Summer 1977): 30–36.

Ryan, Mary. "Femininity and Capitalism in Antebellum America." In *Capitalist Patriarchy and the Case for Socialist Feminism*, edited by Zillah Eisenstein, pp. 151–72. New York: Monthly Review Press, 1979.

Ryan, William. *Blaming the Victim.* New York: Vintage Books, 1971.

Satir, Virginia. *Peoplemaking.* Palo Alto, CA: Science and Behavior Books, 1972.

Schaef, Anne. *Women's Reality: An Emerging Female System in the White Male Society.* Minneapolis: Winston Press, 1981.

Scharfenberg, Kirk. "The Community as Bank Examiner." *Working Papers* 7 (September–October 1980): 30–35.

Schell, Jonathan. "The Fate of the Earth, Part I." *The New Yorker* (February 1, 1982): 47–112.

Schneider, Stephen. "Less Is More: Conservation and Renewable Energy." *Working Papers* 6 (March–April 1978): 49–58.

――――. "Where Has All the Oil Gone?" *Working Papers* 6 (January–February 1978): 31–42.

Schoonmaker, Mary Ellen. "Special Deliveries." *In These Times* (December 8–14, 1982): 12–13.

Schumacher, E. F. *Small is Beautiful: Economics as if People Mattered.* New York: Harper Torchbooks, 1973.

Schur, Robert. "Growing Lemons in the Bronx." *Working Papers* 7 (September–October 1980): 42–51.

Semas, Philip. "'Free' Universities: Many Still Thriving." *Chronicle of Higher Education* (November 22, 1976): 4.

Shaiken, Harley. "Numerical Control of Work: Workers and Automation in the Computer Age." *Radical America* 13 (November–December 1979): 25–38.

Shaikh, Anwar. "An Introduction to the History of Crisis Theories." In *U.S. Capitalism in Crisis*, edited by Center for the Study of Urban Radical Political Economy, pp. 219–40. New York: U.R.P.E., 1978.

Sharp, Gene. *Exploring Nonviolent Activities*. Boston: Porter Sargent Publishers, 1970.

Shearer, Derek. "State Needs a Public Energy Corporation." In *Public Policy Reader*, edited by Derek Shearer and Lee Webb, p. 303. Washington, DC: Conference on Alternative State and Local Public Policies, 1976.

Shearer, Derek, and Webb, Lee. "Billions of Dollars and No Sense." In *Public Policy Reader*, edited by Derek Shearer and Lee Webb, pp. 367–68. Washington, DC: Conference on Alternative State and Local Public Policies, 1976.

Sheehy, Gail. *Passages: Predictable Crises in Adult Life*. New York: Bantam Books, 1976.

Shor, Ira. *Critical Teaching and Everyday Life*. Boston: South End Press, 1980.

Shostrom, Everett. *Man, the Manipulator*. New York: Bantam Books, 1968.

Silberman, Charles. *Crisis in the Classroom: The Remaking of American Education*. New York: Vintage Books, 1971.

Sivanandan, A. "Imperialism and Disorganic Development in the Silicon Age." *Race and Class* 21 (Autumn 1979): 111–26.

Skinner, B. F. *Science and Human Behavior*. New York: Free Press, 1953.

Sklar, Holly. "Trilateralism: Managing, Dependency and Democracy." In *Trilateralism: The Trilateral Commission and Elite Planning for World Management*, edited by Holly Sklar, pp. 1–57. Boston: South End Press, 1980.

Smith, Clive. "The Business Press Comes of Age." *Working Papers* 7 (November–December 1980): 70–72.

Smith, Ralph E. *The Subtle Revolution: Women at Work*. Washington, DC: Urban Institute Press, 1979.

Smuts, Robert. *Women and Work in America*. New York: Schocken Books, 1971.

"Socialism: Trials and Errors." *Time* (March 13, 1978): 24–44.

Spitz, Robert. "Hospitalism: Genesis of Psychiatric Conditions in Early Childhood." *Psychoanalytic Study of the Child* 1 (1945): 53–74.

Spring, Joel. *Education and the Corporate State.* Boston: Beacon Press, 1972.

———. *The Sorting Machine: National Educational Policy Since 1945.* New York: David McKay Company, 1976.

Squires, Gregory. *Education and Jobs.* Rutgers: Transaction Books, 1979.

———. *The Learning Exchange: An Alternative in Adult Education.* Michigan State University: Institute for Community Development, 1975.

Squires, Gregory, and DeWolfe, Ruthanne. "Redlining: Insurance Companies." *Working Papers* 7 (July–August 1979): 5–6.

Starr, Paul. "Controlling Medical Costs Through Countervailing Power." *Working Papers* 5 (Summer 1977): 10–11.

Steinem, Gloria; Edgar, Joanne; and Thom, Mary. "Post-ERA Politics: Losing a Battle but Winning the War?" *Ms Magazine* (January 1983): 35–36.

Stephenson, Hugh. *The Coming Clash: The Impact of Multinational Corporations on National States.* New York: Saturday Review Press, 1972.

Stewart, Charles. "Allocation of Resources to Health." *Journal of Human Resources* 6 (October 1971): 15–22.

Stillman, Don. "The Devastating Impact of Plant Relocations." *Working Papers* 6 (July–August 1978): 42–53.

Stone, Katherine. "The Origins of Job Structures in the Steel Industry." *Review of Radical Political Economics* 6 (Summer 1974): 61–97.

Stone, Peter. "Joe Kennedy vs. the Gang of Seven." *Working Papers* 8 (January–February 1981): 12–14.

Sward, Keith. *The Legend of Henry Ford.* New York: Rinehart, 1948.

Taylor, Frederick W. *The Principles of Scientific Management.* New York: Harper and Brothers, 1911.

———. *Shop Management.* New York: Harper and Brothers, 1903.

———. "Testimony Before the Special House Committee to Investigate the Taylor and Other Systems of Management." Reprinted in *Scientific Management.* New York: Harper and Row, 1947.

Tepperman, Jean. *Not Servants, Not Machines: Office Workers Speak Out!* Boston: Beacon Press, 1976.

———. *60 Words a Minute and What Do You Get?* Somerville, MA: New England Free Press, n.d.

Terkel, Studs. *Working.* New York: Avon Books, 1972.

Thomas, Lewis. "Unacceptable Damage." *New York Review of Books* (September 24, 1981): 3–8.

Thompson, Edward P. *The Making of the English Working Class.* New York: Pantheon, 1963.

Thorne, Barrie, and Yalom, Marilyn, eds. *Rethinking the Family: Some Feminist Questions.* New York: Longman, 1981.

Thorow, Lester. *The Zero-Sum Society.* New York: Basic Books, 1980.

Toffler, Alvin. "The Fractured Family." In *Intimate Life Styles*, edited by Joann S. and Jack Delora, pp. 375–86. Pacific Palisades, CA: Goodyear, 1972.

———. *The Third Wave.* New York: Bantam Books, 1980.

Trilateral Task Force on the Governability of Democracies. *The Crisis of Democracy.* New York: New York University Press, 1975.

Tyack, David. *The One Best System.* Cambridge, MA: Harvard University Press, 1974.

U.S. Bureau of the Census. *Historical Statistics of the U.S.—Colonial Times to 1857.* Washington, DC: Government Printing Office, 1960.

U.S. Office of Technology Assessment. "The Effects of Nuclear War." In *Crisis in American Institutions*, 5th ed., edited by Jerome H. Skolnick and Elliott Currie, pp. 514–30. Boston: Little, Brown and Company, 1982.

Vernon, Raymond. *Sovereignty at Bay.* New York: Basic Books, 1971.

Waldron, Tammy Travis. "Sexual Harassment." *Michigan State University Woman* (May 16, 1980): 1–2.

Walker, Charles, and Guest, Robert. *The Man on the Assembly Line.* Cambridge, MA: Harvard University Press, 1952.

Walker, Kathryn, and Woods, Margaret. *Time Use: A Measure of Household Family Goods and Services.* Washington, DC: American Home Economics Association, 1976.

"Wall Street Catches Gene-Slicing Bug." *Dollars and Sense* 63 (January 1981): 15–17.

Washburn, Sherwood. "Tools and Human Evolution." *Scientific American Reprints* (September 1960).

Watson, Bill. "Counter-Planning on the Shop Floor." *Radical America* 5 (May–June 1971): 77–85.

Watson, John. *Behaviorism.* Chicago: University of Chicago Press, 1974.

Weber, Max. "Bureaucracy." In *From Max Weber*, edited by Hans Gerth and C. Wright Mills, pp. 196–244. New York: Oxford University Press, 1958.

Weinstein, James. *The Corporate Ideal in the Liberal State 1900–1918.* Boston: Beacon Press, 1968.

Weir, David, and Schapiro, Mark. *Circle of Poison.* San Francisco: Institute for Food and Development Policy, 1981.

Weisberg, Barry. *Beyond Repair: The Ecology of Capitalism.* Boston: Beacon Press, 1971.

Weisskopf, Thomas. "The Current Economic Crisis in Historical Perspective." *Socialist Review* 57 (May–June 1981): 9–53.

———. "Marxist Perspectives on Cyclical Crisis." In *U.S. Capitalism in Crisis*, edited by Center for the Study of Urban Radical Political Economy, pp. 241–60. New York: U.R.P.E., 1978.

Wessendorf, James. "The Sexualization of Male Crime." *In These Times* 7 (January 9–16, 1983): 5–10.

Whiting, J. W., and Child, I. L. *Child Training and Personality: A Cross-Cultural Study.* New Haven: Yale University Press, 1953.

Winnick, Andrew. "The Time Has Come for Socialized Energy." *In These Times* (June 6–12, 1979): 17.

Witte, John. *Democracy, Authority, and Alienation at Work.* Chicago: University of Chicago Press, 1980.

Wolfe, Alan. *America's Impasse: The Rise and Fall of the Politics of Growth.* New York: Pantheon, 1981.

———. "Capitalism Shows Its Face: Giving Up on Democracy." In *Trilateralism: The Trilateral Commission and Elite Planning for World Management*, edited by Holly Sklar, pp. 295–307. Boston: South End Press, 1980.

———. *The Rise and Fall of the 'Soviet Threat': Domestic Sources of the Cold War Consensus.* Washington, DC: Institute for Policy Studies, 1979.

Work Relations Group. "Uncovering the Hidden History of the American Workplace." *Review of Radical Political Economics* 10 (Winter 1978): 1–23.

Yankelovich, Daniel. *New Rules: Searching for Self-Fulfillment in a World Turned Upside Down.* New York: Random House, 1981.

Young, Michael. *The Rise of the Meritocracy, 1870–2033.* Baltimore: Penguin, 1961.

Young, Theodore. Personal communication to the author, November 1975.

Zaretsky, Eli. *Capitalism, the Family, and Personal Life.* New York: Harper and Row, 1973.

Zimbalist, Andrew. "The Limits of Work Humanization." *Review of Radical Political Economics* 7 (Summer 1975): 50–59.

———. "Technology and the Labor Process in the Printing Industry." In *Case Studies on the Labor Process*, edited by Andrew Zimbalist, pp. 103–26. New York: Monthly Review Press, 1979.

Zwerdling, Daniel. "At IGP, It's Not Business as Usual." *Working Papers* 5 (Spring 1977): 68–81.

———. *Democracy at Work.* Washington, DC: Association for Self-Management, 1978.

———. "Employee Ownership: How Well Is It Working?" *Working Papers* 7 (May–June 1979): 15–27.

Index